The Criminalization of
Black Children

The Criminalization of Black Children

Race, Gender, and Delinquency in Chicago's Juvenile Justice System, 1899–1945

Tera Eva Agyepong

The University of North Carolina Press CHAPEL HILL

*This book was published with the assistance of the Authors Fund
of the University of North Carolina Press.*

© 2018 The University of North Carolina Press
All rights reserved
Set in Espinosa Nova by Westchester Publishing Services

The University of North Carolina Press has been a member of the
Green Press Initiative since 2003.

Library of Congress Cataloging-in-Publication Data
Names: Agyepong, Tera Eva, author.
Title: The criminalization of black children : race, gender, and delinquency in
  Chicago's juvenile justice system, 1899–1945 / Tera Eva Agyepong.
Other titles: Justice, power, and politics.
Description: Chapel Hill : University of North Carolina Press, [2018] |
  Series: Justice, power, and politics | Includes bibliographical references
  and index.
Identifiers: LCCN 2017033417| ISBN 9781469638652 (cloth : alk. paper) |
  ISBN 9781469636443 (pbk : alk. paper) | ISBN 9781469638669 (ebook)
Subjects: LCSH: Juvenile justice, Administration of—Illinois—Chicago. |
  African Americans—Illinois—Social conditions—20th century. |
  African American juvenile delinquents—Illinois.
Classification: LCC HV9105.I3 A79 2018 | DDC 364.36089/96073077311—dc23
  LC record available at https://lccn.loc.gov/2017033417

Cover photographs of children, ca. 1941, by Edwin Rosskam, courtesy of the
Library of Congress Prints and Photographs Division. Front: *Children Playing
on the Street, Black Belt, Chicago, Illinois* (LC-USF33-005190-M4); back:
Untitled (LC-USF33-005126-M3).

Portions of chapter 3 have been previously published in a different form as
"Aberrant Sexualities and Racialised Masculinization: Race, Gender and the
Criminalisation of African American Girls at the Illinois Training School for
Girls at Geneva, 1893–1945," *Gender and History* 25:2 (August 2013): 270–93.
Used here with permission.

To my parents, Akosua Anima and Kwasi Ntra,
for all that you are, all that you have been,
and all that you have given me.

Contents

Illustrations and Tables

Acknowledgments

I could never have enough words to express my deep gratitude to and appreciation of all who have nurtured the research and writing of *The Criminalization of Black Children*. I am nevertheless happy for the opportunity to do so within these few pages. Generous financial support in the form of grants and fellowships has allowed me to focus primarily on research or writing at key moments of this project's development: the Woodrow Wilson Women's Studies Dissertation Fellowship, Northwestern University's Archival Research Grant through the Department of African American Studies, and the Sexuality and Health Fellowship through Northwestern University's Department of Gender Studies provided me with critical support during the project's early stages. The Lee and Mary Clare McHugh Sanders Endowed Professorship in History at my home institution, DePaul University, supported the completion of this book by allowing me to take a one-year leave from teaching. DePaul University also supported my research and writing through summer faculty research grants and an undergraduate research assistant grant.

The assistance of the numerous librarians, archivists, and curators I have met has been indispensable. The archivists and curators at the Illinois State Archives at Springfield, the Vivian Harsh Collection at the Carter G. Woodson Library, the Black Metropolis Research Consortium Survey, Geneva Historical Society, Chicago Historical Society, Special Collections Research Center at the University of Chicago, Hull House Museum, University of Illinois Special Collections Library, and Cook County Clerk's office deserve my sincere thanks. I will always also remember the patience and expertise of the librarians at the Northwestern University Interlibrary Loan Department, Northwestern University Government Data Library, Abraham Lincoln Library, Municipal Reference Collection at the Harold Washington Library, and DePaul University Richardson Library.

My professional and scholarly life has been blessed by gifted and generous colleagues and mentors. Martha Biondi and Dorothy Roberts have been instrumental in their mentorship, support, feedback, encouragement, and constructive criticism of this book. They have had faith in this project, even in moments when my own faith faltered, and were committed to helping me see it through from the time it was just a seedling of an idea during my graduate student days at Northwestern University. Emerging scholars are lucky if they find one such mentor; I have been privileged enough to have two. Many others I was privileged to meet during my time at Northwestern University have also lent their advice and support to the research and writing of this book: Celeste Watkins-Hayes, Dylan Penningroth, Darlene Clark Hine, Sandra Richards, Mary Patillo, Michelle Wright, Richard Iton, Barnor Hesse, Sylvester Johnson, Ji-Yeon Yuh, Steven Epstein, and Hector Carillo all deserve my thanks.

I will never forget how Simmie Baer fought tirelessly with me and used her networks to help me gain access to the critical Cook County Juvenile Court archival records. They have been closed by law since 1987 and can be accessed only by researchers who obtain a court order from the presiding juvenile court judge. Simmie Baer, Bernardine Dohrn, and Julie Biehl, all of whom I met at the Children and Family Justice Center at Northwestern Law, deserve my special thanks for enhancing my scholarly interest in race and juvenile justice by introducing me to the practice of juvenile justice law.

Scholars at the 2016 two-day-long Law and Humanities Junior Scholars Workshop at the University of California, Los Angeles, provided me with some of the most formative feedback I have ever received on this project. Martha S. Jones was one of the first scholars outside of my committee to give me rigorous feedback about my work after I had the privilege of meeting her in 2011 at "We Must First Take Account," the University of Michigan's first Law and History Conference. She and Norm Spaulding of Stanford Law were the commentators for a draft chapter I presented from my book. Both of them did a close reading of that chapter ahead of time. Their feedback reshaped how I thought not only about that particular chapter but about the project as a whole.

My colleagues at the Chicago American Bar Foundation and DePaul University's Departments of History and African and Black Diaspora Studies have also invested time and energy in this project. The camaraderie and intelligent feedback they have given me through workshops, faculty research seminars, and impromptu conversations have all made this work better. My undergraduate research assistant Ashley Johnson, whom I have had the privilege of working with for the past two years, has also lent her support in so many ways.

My family and close friends have also intellectually supported this project. More important, however, they have sustained my heart and spirit along this almost decade-long journey. Were it not for them, I would not have been able to weather the sometimes stormy seasons of life. By buttressing me, they ultimately buttressed this project. To my mother, who was not alive to see the genesis or completion of this project, thank you for loving me and showing me what it means to live a life of conviction, courage, strength, and grace through your example. Thank you for teaching me to fervently pursue what I want, believing in me, and inspiring me to be the best I can be. To my father, thank you for always being my spiritual and emotional rock. It was you who kindled my love of learning and introduced me to the world of reading and books. Randy and Eli, thank you for your love, protection, support, and constant comic relief. Your support has meant more to me than you will ever know. Daniel, thank you for inspiring in me a deep love, strength, and ability to persevere beyond what I ever thought was humanely possible. And my sister-friend Margaret Nkechi, thank you for nurturing my soul, being a listening ear, and always supporting me.

The Criminalization of
Black Children

Introduction

Contingent Childhood: Black Children and the Making of Juvenile Justice

On June 1, 1922, Ronald Bird, a thirteen-year-old from Kentucky, was pronounced "delinquent" in Chicago's juvenile court. Ronald was but one among a large stream of southern black children who migrated to Chicago with their parents and found themselves greeted by a new juvenile justice system. The juvenile court labeled Ronald a "delinquent," a legal term intended to be applied to children who broke the law, even though he had not committed any crimes. Like many similarly situated black children who appeared in juvenile court between 1899 and 1945, Ronald encountered a community so circumscribed by race and divested of resources that his childhood vulnerability was eclipsed by a racialized process for criminalization in the state's juvenile justice system. The combination of his blackness, extreme poverty, lack of adequate parental care, and youth primed him for being labeled "delinquent" before he even set foot inside the juvenile court.

Abby E. Lane, the principal of the Carter School who submitted the initial petition that led to Ronald being hauled into juvenile court, explained in a letter that although she was alleging the "offense" of "habitual truancy," he had actually not violated any of Illinois's compulsory education laws. The laws made habitual non–school attendance punishable by commitment to the Chicago Parental School, a boarding home for children. Lane asserted that Ronald "was perfect in attendance" at school, and her real reason for submitting the petition was because Ronald did not have anyone to take care of him. His parents were unable or unwilling to care for him, and he "left home frequently returning neither for food nor sleep." And "although [his] attendance had not been such as to warrant making out a Parental School application," Lane felt, "something should be done to keep him off the streets and away from bad company." She asked the juvenile court to send him to the "Parental School because [she] knew of no better place for him."[1] Widespread discrimination against black children in charity homes for children in Chicago and the lack of community resources for children in black neighborhoods meant there were few other alternatives where Ronald could receive care.[2]

Cook County Juvenile Court complied with Lane's request and placed Ronald in the Parental School. Ronald's entanglement with the juvenile justice system did not end there, however. For reasons his case record does not make apparent, in June 1925 he was eventually transferred to Chicago and Cook County School for Boys, an institution for delinquents, on the grounds that he "was and is incorrigible." His relationship with the juvenile justice system did not end until he was finally released from the School for Boys at age sixteen.[3]

To centralize the experiences of children like Ronald in this narration of the nation's first juvenile justice system, *The Criminalization of Black Children* embarks on its journey in early twentieth-century Chicago. A city in the midst of rapid, often turbulent change, Chicago was the epicenter of the Progressive child-saving movement and the home of the nation's very first juvenile court. Progressives' successful advocacy for a nonpunitive juvenile justice system was undergirded by the rehabilitative ideal—the notion that children were inherently innocent and entitled to a justice system separate from adults. The emergence of Cook County Juvenile Court in 1899 signaled the success of this new ideological movement and the emergence of a juvenile justice system.[4] This new form of state intervention into children's lives, which relied on institutional interventions to care for poor and disabled children and reform children who committed crimes, was distinct from nineteenth-century houses of refuge and reformatories because it was fueled by a distinct Progressive ideological movement and intricately intertwined with juvenile courts.[5] The early twentieth century also marked a time when the city found itself reconfiguring and rearticulating notions of "whiteness" and "blackness" as immigrants from southern and eastern Europe as well as southern black migrants entered the city.

Scholars have contributed to our understanding of the rich and nuanced historiography of the juvenile justice system by examining the complex ways in which class, European immigration, and gender structured the application of the rehabilitative ideal. Nevertheless, there is a virtual absence of information about African American children's experiences and the way in which intersecting notions of race, gender, and sexuality simultaneously structured the practice of juvenile justice before 1950. Because historical narratives have focused almost exclusively on the experiences of poor and immigrant white children, however, information about the ways in which race circumscribed beliefs about childhood innocence and rehabilitation is limited.[6] The privileging of white children's experiences in juvenile justice histories has occluded the way in which early twentieth-century notions of race, new constructions of childhood innocence, and the migration of African Americans to urban centers in the North influenced juvenile justice discourse and practice. The majority of juvenile delinquents were male, and the few scholars that have explored girls' experiences in the juvenile justice system have not made the experiences of girls of color the focal point of their studies.[7] As a result, there is a particular lack of information about African American girls' experiences in the early juvenile justice system.

According to the predominant narrative, Progressive reformers' promulgation of the rehabilitative ideal was grounded in a universal belief in childhood innocence and led to the emergence of county- and state-level juvenile justice systems across the country. In the latter half of the century, more aggressive policing, longer prison sentences, the "War on Drugs," the ascendancy of the conservative movement, and negative depictions of African American children in the media collectively displaced the rehabilitative ideal. Consequently, most histories of racialized criminalization have focused on the post–Civil Rights era in the urban North or the Jim Crow era in the South.[8] When the history of juvenile justice in Illinois is recounted with African American children at the forefront of the story, it is not accurate to speak of the rise and fall of a rehabilitative ideal. Black Chicagoans' experiences suggest that urban black communities in the North were forced to contend with the race-based criminalization and confinement of a significant number of their children long before the modern era of hyperincarceration.

This case study of African American children suggests that the discourse of rehabilitation and the institutional apparatus of the juvenile justice system were key components in facilitating a process of racialized criminalization, instituting a punitive turn long before the backlash against the Civil Rights movement and War on Drugs. Over the course of the juvenile justice system's evolution through World War II, juvenile justice practitioners and Chicagoans from a variety of backgrounds debated and redefined the very meaning of childhood delinquency. Although whether the juvenile justice system was ever actually "rehabilitative" in practice is debatable, what is clear is that the rehabilitative intentions and discourse surrounding juvenile justice did not emerge with black children in mind. Poor native white and European immigrant children were its intended beneficiaries. This reality not only fundamentally shaped the practice of juvenile justice and the ways in which juvenile justice practitioners articulated racialized notions of childhood innocence and delinquency; it also facilitated the state of Illinois's transition to a more punitive form of juvenile justice. The infection of racial prejudice not only circumscribed the juvenile justice system's handling of black children but also led to a demise of the rehabilitative ideal that ultimately changed the administration of justice for all children.

Chicago—the heart of the Reform movement and the site of the nation's first juvenile court—provided a plethora of resources for this study. *The Criminalization of Black Children* draws on a wide array of sources from the Vivian Harsh Collection at the Carter G. Woodson Library and the Black Metropolis Research Consortium Survey. Because African Americans in Chicago have a rich history of organizing and creating self-help institutions, early twentieth-century black women's clubs, religious organizations, and civil rights groups left an abundance of information about the ways in which they proactively sought to mitigate the effects of black children's exclusion from the rehabilitative project. Manuscript collections at the Chicago Historical Society and the University of Illinois at Chicago Special Collections Library also contain vital information about community organizations' attempts to build institutions for black children and counteract negative portrayals of black children in popular media.

Manuscript collections, government documents, and case files at Cook County Juvenile Court, the Chicago Historical Society, the University of Illinois at Chicago Special Collections Library, the Illinois State Archives at Springfield, the Abraham Lincoln Library, the Hull House Museum, and the Northwestern University Government Data Library also contained sources that were vital to reconstructing black children's encounters with juvenile justice. The large bodies of scholarship that social scientists, psychiatrists, and medical practitioners generated about black children and delinquency during this period were also critically important sources. In addition, newspaper articles, judicial opinions, and state laws helped elucidate the story of the convergence between the evolution of juvenile justice policies and the racialized constructions of delinquency.

A crucial import of these sources is the way in which they reveal the gendered and racialized milieu under which rehabilitative programs were worked out in Chicago and juvenile justice institutions. Although the existence of these sources allowed the uncovering of African American children's experiences, and the ways contestations over rehabilitation were negotiated on the ground, there are some inherent methodological challenges in their use. The children's own words, as well as their families', are missing in many of these sources. Even when they do appear, court workers', staff members', or interviewers' own thoughts and voices filter them. Nevertheless, the information was used to glean, as much as was possible, the children's own thoughts and feelings about their encounters with juvenile justice.

CHAPTER 1 ELUCIDATES the community milieu in which the nascent juvenile justice system operated. Racialized notions of childhood, Progressive uplift, and the politics of child welfare primed African American children to be marked as delinquents before they even formally entered the juvenile justice system. The vast majority of public and private agencies for poor, abused, neglected, or abandoned children excluded African American children because of their race even as they readily accepted white and European immigrant children. This dearth of institutional resources for black children only became exacerbated as an increasing number of African Americans entered the city as a result of the Great Migration. Chicago's growing black community adapted to this milieu by doing their own "child-saving" and immediately inserting themselves into a juvenile justice system that played a defining role in shaping the trajectory of many black children's lives.

The juvenile court became an institution that mediated the tensions between black migration, transitioning notions of race, and the dearth of community resources for black children in Chicago. Black migrant children who were newcomers from the South were particularly vulnerable to being caught up in the web of Cook County Juvenile Court and its ancillary institutions. Chapter 2 documents the way the juvenile court and these ancillary institutions—the Juvenile Detention Center, Chicago Parental School, and Institute for Juvenile Research—handled black children's cases. It also delineates the impact the disproportionate number of black children in juvenile court and an artificial inflation of the number of delinquent black children had on the evolution of juvenile justice law. The sympathetic public sentiment that had made the Progressive juvenile justice movement viable had begun to wane by the 1930s. As a result, juvenile justice laws began to be more punitive, and the rehabilitative ideal began to be dismantled.

Chapter 3 examines the state's flagship institution for delinquent girls. It reveals the way intersecting notions of race, gender, and sexuality shaped reformers' and practitioners' implementation of juvenile justice. African American girls at the Illinois Training School were blamed for the interracial sexual relationships staff members and professionals abhorred and were considered the most violent girls in the institution. More important, they became subject to a race-specific and gendered construction of female delinquency in the institution. Unlike the image of a fixable, inherently innocent delinquent that spurred the child-saving movement, black girls were cast as inherently deviant, unfixable, and dangerous delinquents whose negative influences could contaminate other children in the institution.

Chapter 4 examines how demographic changes at the Illinois Training School for Boys at St. Charles were linked to a punitive turn in institutional policies and state juvenile confinement laws. When the number of African American boys at St. Charles increased over time as a result of migration and discrimination in charity institutions for children in Chicago, the institution's staff members, state legislators, and residents in surrounding cities refined their notion in discourse and in practice of what kind of boy St. Charles was intended to house. This hysteria eventually led the Illinois state legislature to mandate that the first maximum-security prison for children in the history of the state be built for the "dangerous type of boy" whom the larger public believed was no longer suited for St. Charles.

THE CRIMINALIZATION OF BLACK CHILDREN renders visible the ways in which racialized notions of childhood innocence and delinquency shaped the evolution of juvenile justice in Illinois. Black children occupied an ideological and lived space of contingent childhood. Childhood has never been simply a biological category that intersects with chronological age. It has always been a socially and legally constructed category that intersects with other constructed identities like race, gender, and class. Black children's status as "child" was contingent in that it could be highlighted or erased in different contexts. At the level of the state, black children's childhood was recognized to the extent that their legal status as a "person under the age of eighteen" made them candidates for entry into the juvenile—as opposed to the adult criminal—justice system.

The constructions of childhood innocence, vulnerability, and rehabilitation that triggered the emergence of juvenile justice and protective investments in Chicago did not apply to black children, however. In juvenile justice discourse and practice, black youths were included as children for some purposes and excluded for others. This account of the ways in which the very presence of black children in the urban North shaped the evolution of the nation's very first juvenile justice system reveals that the criminalization of black bodies was not geographically limited to the Jim Crow South or temporally limited to the late twentieth century. Rather, it was a key component of urban black life in Chicago long before the end of World War II and the advent of the Civil Rights movement. This story of the racialized criminalization of black children is ultimately a story of the making of race in modern America.

CHAPTER ONE

Race-ing Innocence

The Emergence of Juvenile Justice
and the Making of Black Delinquency

> **Delinquent Girl Petition:** In the matter of Mary Tripplet
> **Date:** August 7, 1899
> **Age:** 11
> **History of the Case:** Mary is a dependent. This girl's father has left
> the state and her mother is dead.
> **Circuit Court of Cook County Warrant:** You are hereby authorized
> to take forthwith into your charge and care Mary Tripplet . . . and
> convey her to the Illinois Industrial School for Girls.

In 1899, an eleven-year-old orphan named Mary Triplett was labeled "de-linquent" in Chicago's juvenile court. Even though Mary, described in court records as a "colored Baptist" from Memphis, Tennessee, had not committed any crimes, juvenile court workers—perhaps due to clerical error—filed Mary Tripplet's case on a "Delinquent Girl Petition" form. Mary was brought into court by "colored missionary" Elizabeth McDonald, the sole black probation worker, because she needed help. The clerk noted on Mary's petition, "This girl is charged by Mrs. McDonald of being a dependent child [and] has no person to take care of her. Her father has left this state and her mother is recently dead. She is therefore a dependent girl."[1]

As an orphan, Mary fit the definition of a dependent child under the 1899 Juvenile Court Act because she did not have "proper parental care or guardianship." Under the act, a child became "dependent" if he or she were orphaned or did not have safe or appropriate parental care due to abuse, neglect, abandonment, or extreme poverty. Mary's experience of being labeled a "delinquent"—a child who committed a crime—even though she was actually dependent, was an administrative move that foreshadowed the categorization of numbers of dependent black children who found themselves in juvenile court between 1899 and 1945. This erasure of black children's dependency in juvenile court ultimately racialized the categories of "dependency" and "delinquency."

Progressive reformers who toured the city's jails as part of their charity work in the late nineteenth century asserted their disapproval and shock at seeing "quite small boys confined in the same quarters with murderers, anarchists, and hardened criminals." As a result, they began to advocate for a separate criminal justice system for children. The Juvenile Court Act of 1899, which the state legislature passed as a result of the reformers' successful promulgation of notions of childhood innocence, vulnerability, and rehabilitation, marked the birth of the juvenile justice system. The act mandated that a "court for children" be established in the city of Chicago. This new state apparatus was intended to gently guide and protect all dependent and delinquent children within its jurisdiction. This Progressive "child-saving" movement was premised on the rehabilitative ideal—the belief that children were inherently innocent, entitled to protection from the state, and should not be punished but reformed when they committed crimes.[2]

Racialized notions of childhood, Progressive uplift, and the politics of child welfare primed African American children to be marked as delinquents before they even set foot inside the juvenile court. Chicago's growing African American community adapted to this milieu by doing their own "child saving" and inserting themselves into a juvenile justice system that began to play a defining role in the trajectory of many black children's lives in the city. The constructions of childhood innocence, "dependency," and "delinquency" were contested racial projects in discourse and practice. In Chicago, although native white and European immigrant children's vulnerability struck a chord and registered in the city's social consciousness, black children's vulnerability did not.

The majority of homes for dependent children in early twentieth-century Chicago were private and religious institutions that excluded black children. The few black-owned and -operated homes for dependent children that existed were often filled to capacity and underfunded because of institutional racism. The problematic dearth of institutional resources was only exacerbated as an increasing number of southern black migrants poured into the city. The citywide discrimination against dependent African American children had reverberations in all corners of the juvenile justice system, as the juvenile court and public institutions for delinquent children had to accommodate an increasingly disproportionate number of black children. Institutions intended for children who had committed crimes quickly became the primary mode of "care" for dependent black children in Chicago, as juvenile court judges found themselves processing the cases of dependent black children as if they were delinquents. This led to a process of racialization in which black children were increasingly and artificially associated with "delinquency" while the term "dependent" was artificially whitened.

The racialized limits of the child-saving movement, as well as the disinvestment in resources for black children at the community level, shaped the evolution of juvenile justice and the image of a dependent and delinquent child. The dearth of community resources for black children in general, and dependent black children in particular, was also linked to Progressive reformers' discursive differentiation between native white, European immigrant, and black communities, the amount of resources they poured into these communities, and their efforts to divest money and power from black-controlled institutions for dependent and delinquent children. Reformers' conclusion that black people, unlike European immigrants, lacked "civilization" and "morality" in their communities, placed African Americans beyond the scope of any meaningful reform—and by extension, child saving.[3] Processes of institutional exclusion and inclusion reinscribed and created racialized conceptions of childhood vulnerability and affected the likelihood of whether children would be treated as a "dependent" or "delinquent" in the juvenile justice system.

THE FIRST PART of this chapter will situate Progressive reformers' impetus to promulgate a rehabilitative ideal and advocate for the establishment of a juvenile justice system amidst transitioning notions of race, European immigration, black migration, and the city's evolving child welfare system. The latter part of the chapter will situate the African American community's efforts to care for black children in light of the racial limits of child saving, the state's disinvestment in black-owned institutions for dependent children, and the consequent racialization of childhood dependency and delinquency in the juvenile justice system.

The Racial Limits of Progressive Child Saving

Progressive reformers spearheaded efforts to establish a juvenile justice system in Chicago. The most ardent supporters of the 1890s juvenile court movement were members of the Chicago Woman's Club and reformers like Jane Addams, Lucy Flowers, and Julia Lathrop. They envisioned a "parental court" where "a child should be treated as a child" and the "parental authority of the State should be exercised instead of the criminal power." Their advocacy was rooted in the belief that children are the most vulnerable members of society, and they should not be prosecuted and incarcerated alongside adults when they commit crimes. Rather, they should be rehabilitated, since as a class, children are inherently innocent.[4] As black migrants and immigrants from southern and eastern Europe poured into Chicago, new challenges produced by urbanization and industrial expansion created demands for new services and regulations. Much of Progressive reformers' activism, which flourished between 1890 and 1920, was intended to address these perceived problems. Progressive activism expanded the role of the government in private life.[5] Reformers were particularly concerned with the impact urbanization and industrial expansion had on children—particularly immigrant youths. Their advocacy resulted in the Illinois legislature passing the 1899 Act to Regulate the Treatment and Control of Dependent, Neglected, and Delinquent Children and the establishment of Cook County Juvenile Court. The Juvenile Court Act was the culmination of nearly thirty years of reform efforts and brought together a network of private and state-run institutions that handled the cases of children who were processed in the new juvenile court. This constellation of institutions resulted in a juvenile justice system.[6] The act was also accompanied by a variety of other child-centered reforms, including the provision of financial support for new playgrounds, day nurseries, preschools, and compulsory education laws. Other cities followed Chicago's example, and juvenile courts proliferated around the nation.[7]

The crystallization of institutional practices and juvenile justice laws through the First and Second World Wars coincided with the Great Migration and dramatic shifts in the racial composition of the city. The mass movement of African Americans from the rural South to cities like Chicago, New York, and Philadelphia commenced in earnest during World War I and ignited racial tensions across the North. Chicago offered black migrants new industrial employment opportunities and freedom from legally sanctioned racial discrimination.

The *Chicago Defender*, the most widely read black newspaper in the South, promised high-paying jobs and painted the city as a land of opportunity. Although the *Chicago Defender* functioned as a national forum where African Americans advocated for civil rights and voiced their discontent against lynching, rape, mob violence, disfranchisement, and other racialized violence, the newspaper was also steeped in local city affairs. Many southerners imagined a northern "promised land" based on images rooted in the *Defender*'s descriptions of black life in Chicago. Even for southerners who eventually chose other northern destinations, the city was a powerful symbol of migration, agency, and hope.[8]

The surge in Chicago's black population dramatically changed the nature of the city's social, political, economic, and housing landscape.[9] The

Dependent boy in Chicago, circa 1891. Courtesy of Library of Congress Prints and Photographs Division, Washington, D.C.

first wave of migrants, who came between 1910 and 1940, entered Chicago during the First World War and the Great Depression. The second wave, which lasted from 1940 to 1970, coincided with World War II and the Civil Rights movement. In 1890, African Americans made up 1.3 percent of the city's population. The percentage jumped to 4 percent in 1920 and again to 7.3 percent in 1934. The first wave of migration alone increased the population of African Americans from 44,000 to 234,000. This meant that the black population increased tenfold between 1900 and 1940, when African Americans made up 8 percent of the city's population.[10] The visibility of growing numbers of black people in Chicago was heightened because black neighborhoods, which initially encompassed a thin corridor in neighborhoods that extended south from downtown in 1910, became a thirty-five-block-long geographical area called the "Black Belt."[11] Black neighborhoods were more isolated than European immigrant neighborhoods, as by 1930 two-thirds of African Americans lived where 90 percent or more of the residents were black, and another 20 percent lived in a neighborhood where the concentration was more than 50 percent.[12]

Racial hostility in Chicago escalated right alongside black migration and reached a crescendo with the infamous race riot of 1919. The competition for economic resources during the Great Depression also aggravated racial animosity. Chicago's major white newspapers reflected and shaped public opinion by featuring stories portraying black southerners with pessimism and fear. Newspapers such as the *Chicago Tribune*, the *Daily News*, and the *Herald Examiner* published articles that not only overstated the volume of migration but evoked images of hordes of African Americans inundating the city along with disease, vice, and low standards of living. In 1916 and 1917, these three major city newspapers published forty-five articles on black migration from the South. Most of the articles dramatically overstated the volume of migration. The Chicago Commission on Race Relations found that half of all newspaper articles about African Americans ridiculed black people or focused on violence and criminality. With headlines such as "Negroes Arrive by Thousands—Peril to Health" and "Half a Million Darkies from Dixie Swarm to the North to Better Themselves," alongside descriptions of "Queer scenes" at train stations and references to "pickaninnies," newspapers connoted images of a dangerously different set of new arrivals.[13]

The anti-immigrant sentiment that instigated the Johnson Reed Act of 1924, which capped the number of southern and eastern Europeans allowed to enter the United States, also ran high in Chicago. Black newcomers, however, caught the bulk of racial hostility. Chicago experienced what white American journalist Ray Stannard Baker called a rapid rise in "race feeling and discrimination." In 1922, the Chicago Commission on Race Relations, an investigative committee appointed by Governor Frank Lowden to investigate the causes of a 1919 race riot, found widespread beliefs among white Chicagoans that "the Negro is more prone than the white to commit sex crimes[,] particularly rape . . . [and] that he commits a disproportionate number of crimes involving felonious cuttings and slashings." The perceived influx of a criminal southern black population into the city caused white residents particular angst, as many believed "the recent migrant from the south [was] more likely to offend than the Negro who resided longer in the North."[14]

This juvenile justice system—the focal point of Chicago's Progressive child-saving movement—marked an acceleration of government interventions into children's lives.[15] Reformers envisioned a court staffed by judges that embodied the role of a "kind and just parent," as opposed to an impartial arbitrator. Cook County Juvenile Court and public and private institutions that cared for dependent and delinquent children made up this new system of justice.[16] The "rehabilitative ideal" undergirded the juvenile justice. The ideal presupposed that crime was a symptom of pathology most often brought on by the environment.[17] One of the juvenile court's first judges, Judge Julian Mack, echoed this sentiment when he asked, "Why is it not . . . instead of asking merely whether a boy or girl has committed a specific offense . . . right to take him in charge, not so much to punish as to reform, not to degrade but to uplift, not to crush, but to develop, not make him a criminal but a worthy citizen?[18] The emergence of juvenile justice and the successful promulgation of a rehabilitative ideal was predicated on a shift away from conceptualizations of children as mini-adults toward a relatively new notion of children as precious, vulnerable innocent beings entitled to protection from the state.

During the colonial era, children were seen as adults in training, and religious and secular authorities alike viewed childhood as a period of human depravity.[19] Rather than being perceived as delicate, awe-inspiring individuals who inhabited a period of life that should be cherished, children in colonial America were seen as unformed, animalistic beings because of their inability to care for themselves and behave as adults. Rather than relishing in their children's youth and prolonging it, parents hurried their children into adulthood so that they could take on more responsibilities.[20] In the nineteenth century, this cultural conception of childhood shifted, and the image of children as inherently depraved beings who needed to be rushed into adulthood melted away. Childhood began to be viewed as a very special period of plasticity where people could be shaped and molded in the best way possible to fit into the norms and expectations of society. Now an object of Victorian-era fascination and care, childhood became the quintessential representation of innocence, purity, and malleability.[21] This cultural shift in notions of childhood was accompanied by changes in laws, policies, and institutions. The number of orphanages, houses of refuge, reform schools, and special children's hospitals proliferated. The notion that children were the embodiment of innocence and malleability provided the ideological building blocks of the juvenile justice system.[22]

Whiteness, however, was a key component of access to the rehabilitative ideal. Negative constructions of black children in advertisements, literature, stage plays, films, and social science racially circumscribed notions of childhood innocence and vulnerability. African American children had been routinely portrayed as comical, insensate, inferior nonpersons in popular culture. Images of black children circulated around the singular trope of the pickaninny—a wild, savage-like, barely clothed being who was not susceptible to the same kind of physical pain as other humans, let alone vulnerable children—began to appear in popular culture in the nineteenth century.[23] These images continued to circulate through the Civil Rights movement. "Pickaninny" originated from the Spanish world *pequenino*, which means "small child." In the United States, "pickaninny" became a pejorative world used exclusively for black children.[24]

Pickaninnies were often portrayed with dark or jet-black skin, large eyes, an exaggerated mouth, and dirty or scant clothing. Insensateness—the inability to feel pain—was the foremost and most enduring characteristic of pickaninnies. The insensate pickaninny connoted an animal-like being lacking innocence and impervious to physical and emotional harm even in the most dangerous situations. Pickaninnies were the objects of unrestrained violence in popular images. They were shown being beaten, scalded, attacked by animals, neglected, and dismembered. Tigers, dogs, geese, and, more often than not, alligators were usually the source of these attacks. In these images, pickaninnies were depicted as being either fearlessly oblivious to danger or comically shaking with fear. Their responses to physical attacks included laughing or yelping—reactions that never revealed or expressed the realistic amount of pain that would accompany such an injury.[25]

This cultural trope functioned as a racist discourse that purged black children of innocence and put them outside the logic of child saving and protection. In popular culture, white children were constructed as embodiments of innocence while black children deflected it.[26] This cultural history of black children's routine construction as subhuman beings who could not feel pain existed alongside the emergence of a redefinition of childhood that made the conception of juvenile justice and a rehabilitative ideal possible. The ubiquity of images of insensate pickaninnies occluded African American children's association with vulnerability and malleability—quintessential characteristics of new notions of innocent childhood. If black children, because of their insensateness, were not actually children—or, at best, a different kind of child—their particular vulnerabilities and suffering could not register in the same way. Cultural conceptions of white childhood, however, had become synonymous with innocence and malleability. It was powerful enough to inspire child protection and Progressive child saving.

Although the popular figure of the pickaninny operated as a means through which black dehumanization was reinforced and rationalized in the cultural arena, academic literature in the fields of social science and medicine claimed to provide a new body of proof that was used as evidence of African American children's racial inferiority. In the early twentieth century, medical and social scientific literature essentially translated negative constructions of black children in popular culture into a purportedly scientific form by continuing the practice of constructing African American children as fundamentally and intrinsically different from white children.

Through the first half of the twentieth century, medical researchers set out to discover whether morphological differences or health disparities between blacks and whites resulted from a "peculiarity of the [black] race." Researchers conducted a spate of studies regarding differential sex ratios among black and white infants, nose structures, sensory differences, response rates, and the relative activity of black and white infants. These studies setting out to find racial differences among children—particularly in infancy, the stage of life people were imagined to be at their most vulnerable and malleable—reinforced a notion not only of black children's intrinsic difference but of their un-reformability. It also constructed black children as physiologically different and inferior to white children.[27]

Social scientists used mental tests to confirm presupposed differences between white and black children. An 1890 study, for example, used a variety of measures, including the length and width of the children's heads and their skin's sensitivity to heat, to make conclusions about racial differences in sensory discrimination. The authors of the study concluded that "colored children are much more sensitive to heat" and that "the cause of this difference in the colored children is racial."[28] In a series of studies conducted between 1915 and 1917, influential psychologist William Pyle concluded that "negro children have three fifths to three fourths the learning capacity of white children." He argued that these studies, which utilized "a special apparatus calling for motor coordination and association," conclusively proved intrinsic differences between the races even though he eliminated variables of experience and environment that may have shaped the results.[29] Studies like this operated as objective "data" that proved racial differences among children's basic intellectual function.

Outcomes of studies where black children were shown to be more intelligent or "quicker" than young white children were often explained away. Some psychologists argued that black children's superior performance was, in fact, evidence of mental inferiority. Higher scores among black children were viewed as evidence of black people reaching their maximum—but ultimately lower—intellectual capacity at younger ages. Researchers hypothesized that over time, these advanced abilities would disappear. In 1897, for example, G. R. Stetson conducted a study of five hundred black and five hundred white fourth-grade students in Washington, D.C. Stetson found that African American students had a higher average score than white students, as they excelled in three out of the four given tests. Stetson concluded, however, that their higher average scores were evidence of "inferior reasoning power."[30]

This purportedly objective proof of black inferiority and physical difference re-energized and created a new form of racist assumptions that further dehumanized black children. At the very moment that the importance of nurture—as opposed to nature—became a critical component of the new conceptions of childhood innocence and plasticity that undergirded the emergence of juvenile justice, experts in the fields of medicine, psychology, and anthropology were marshaling a barrage of evidence about black children's presumed biological and mental inferiority to native white and European immigrant children. Because science, the only reliable source of knowledge for many, by means of experimentation and testing increasingly pointed to the inferiority of black children, it set them beyond the purview of protection and rehabilitation. It facilitated their relegation to an intrinsically criminal element in juvenile justice institutions that needed to be separated from other children and forcefully punished.

Progressive reformers made distinctions between African Americans and European immigrants and poured the bulk of their resources into addressing white immigrants' needs while ignoring African Americans, even though both groups shared similar challenges. This discrepancy was mirrored in juvenile justice and child welfare institutions.[31] It was also accompanied by a discursive casting of African Americans as culturally inferior to the European immigrants these institutions largely concerned themselves with. In *In Freedom's Birthplace*, Progressive reformer John Daniels attributed the poverty in Boston's black communities to African Americans being "the farthest in the rear" of any race "in the inculcation among its members of any positive code of morality and any general ethical standards." For Daniels, culture was race and blacks were on the lowest rungs of civilization.[32]

The distinctions Progressive reformers made between African Americans and white immigrants were often rooted in intersecting notions of race, gender, and sexuality. For reformers, black women's perceived immorality was one of the foremost signifiers of African Americans' cultural inferior-

ity. In her book about African American life in New York, Mary Ovington, a philanthropist and Progressive reformer, noted the ostensible "very
large percentage of crime among colored women" and the "unduly large percentage of disorderly depraved girls." She concluded that the primary explanation for the disproportionate number of black prostitutes in the city
was rooted not so much in poverty but in an allegedly deficient culture. She
rooted this deficit in history, by arguing that slavery so severely handicapped
the black family that it was "inevitable that numbers of their women should
be slow to recognize the sanctity of home and the importance of feminine
virtue."[33] Progressive activist Louise de Koven Bowen's *Colored People of Chicago* similarly argued that the problems of slavery, migration, urbanization,
infant mortality, and industrialization—coupled with discrimination in
housing, employment, and education—had compromised black women's morality.[34] Reformer Frances Kellor also argued that prostitution among native white and immigrant communities occurred because vulnerable women
became victims of industrialization, while prostitution among African
American women occurred because of their own moral weakness.[35]

In "Social Control," a 1911 article written for the *Crisis*, Jane Addams—
Chicago's leading reformer and founder of the Hull House—came to a similar
conclusion about prostitution in Chicago's African American community.
She stated that the "very large number of colored girls entering a disreputable life" was not surprising, because blacks had "the shortest history of
social restraint." Her distinction between African Americans and white
immigrants—particularly Italians—is striking, as she believed that "One
could easily illustrate this lack of social control by comparing the experiences of a group of colored girls with those of a group representing the
daughters of Italian immigrants, or of any other Southern European peoples."
She supported her claim by arguing that Italian girls were less vulnerable
to prostitution because they had a longer history of social restraint than African Americans: "The Italian parents represent the social traditions which
have been worked out during centuries of civilization. . . . [I]t is largely
through these customs and manners that the new groups are assimilated into
civilization."[36] Italian immigrants' whiteness—or European-ness—which had
been "worked out during centuries of civilization," was thus a measure of
their superior fitness and assimilability. Historian Thomas Gugliemo's study
of Italian immigrants in Chicago, *White on Arrival: Italians, Race, Color, and
Power in Chicago*, delineated an example of this by showing that despite native white Chicagoans' belief that Italians were culturally inferior, "they were
still largely accepted as white" by people and institutions as variant as

"naturalization laws and courts, the U.S. Census, unions, employers, neighbors, realtors, settlement houses, and political parties."[37]

The Hull House put these beliefs into practice. Jane Addams critiqued the "rising tide" of racial discrimination and animosity against black migrants in Chicago and was a founding member of the National Association for the Advancement of Colored People (NAACP). Nevertheless, African Americans were largely excluded from Hull House programming—much of which was aimed at improving the lives of children—even though the second largest black community in the city enveloped the settlement. The Hull House summer camp and Cooperative Jane Club, a boarding house for working girls, were both open only to white girls until the 1940s. On the few occasions when African Americans were included in Hull House programming, it was in a segregated setting. When Jane Addams founded a black mothers' club in 1928, members and their babies, unlike members of the white mothers' club, were not invited to any community activities or put on mailing lists.[38] Louise de Koven Bowen noted that the few blacks who occasionally attended a club meeting or class "were not always welcomed warmly."[39] Like other white settlements, Chicago's Hull House movement largely excluded African Americans from the purview of their social welfare programs during the first half of the twentieth century. Settlements across the urban North either established separate branches and segregated activities for blacks or shut down and followed their white immigrant neighbors to different parts of the city when blacks became a majority of the neighborhood population.[40]

Few Progressive reformers in Chicago were moved enough to ameliorate the world black children and adults encountered—a world where African Americans fared worse in finding jobs and housing than immigrants and where rampant poverty made it difficult for African Americans to adequately fund their independent social service institutions. Poverty and criminal behavior in white immigrant communities led social scientists and Progressive reformers to pool their resources and demand citywide help in their attempt to ameliorate economic, social, and political inequalities in European immigrant communities. Reformers' antiprostitution campaigns, improvements in housing sanitation, and community beautification programs all occurred outside black neighborhoods.[41] In a speech before Chicago's exclusive white City Club, W. E. B. Du Bois said this of Progressive reformers' relative lack of compassion and interest in the issues plaguing the African American community: "There is always that feeling of remoteness, the feeling that it is not their problem." As Du Bois noted, compassion, a crucial component of reform, did not motivate white Progressive

reformers to embrace the "Negro in their midst" or inspire the chil
movement that brought about the advent of juvenile justice.[42]

As opposed to protecting black children from the "social ills" acc
ing urbanization, some Progressive reforms actually made African American
children more vulnerable to them and primed them for being marked as delinquents in juvenile court. Reformers worked hand in hand with politicians
and police officers to clean up Chicago's vice districts—areas where prostitution and gambling were common. This advocacy resulted in the relocation—
and subsequent concentration of—vice districts in black neighborhoods. The
popular report *A Social Evil in Chicago*, a 1911 study of prostitution and vice in
the city, noted that "The history of the social evil in Chicago is intimately
connected with the colored population. . . . Whenever prostitutes, cadets and
thugs were located among white people and had to be moved for commer-
cial or other reasons, they were driven to undesirable parts of the city. . . .
This part of the city is the largest residence section of colored families."

African American children were thus not only forced to live in the most
vice-ridden parts of the city but were more likely to be lured by it as they
went about their everyday lives. Progressive reformers and child welfare
organizations were aware of this, and the Juvenile Protective Association, a
Progressive child welfare club, noted in its 1913 study *The Colored People
of Chicago* that African American girls were more likely to be lured into
prostitution as a result of the city's vice relocation policies and the concentration of prostitution rings in black neighborhoods. The study's authors
reported that employment agencies "routinely" sent black girls to "work as
maids in houses of prostitution." However, these same agencies hesitated
to send white girls there because they feared reprisal.[43]

Notions of race, which made criminality and cultural deficiency synonymous with blackness, and the lack of investment in black children ham-
pered child saving and shaped dependent black children's experiences in the
juvenile justice system. African American children bore the brunt of state
administrators' and Progressive reformers' disinvestment in black communities, as virtually none of the community-based child-centered reforms like
playgrounds, day nurseries, clinics, public baths, and relief stations were located in black neighborhoods. Black children were not welcome in the city's
playgrounds or the public waters of Lake Michigan, as white adults and
children alike protested at their very presence. A 1914 study of recreational
options in Chicago showed that black children regularly used only two of
the fifteen public parks and playgrounds in the city.[44] When a fifteen-year-
old African American boy enjoying Lake Michigan floated his raft over to

Children playing "Ring around the Rosie" on the South Side of Chicago, circa 1941. Courtesy of Library of Congress Prints and Photographs Division, Washington, D.C.

a portion of the lake designated as the "white" side, he drowned to death after a white man threw a stone at him for reaching this imaginary racial line. This murder of a black child whose only desire was to access public recreation the same way other children did instigated the city's infamous 1919 race riot.[45] This lack of recreational spaces in black neighborhoods and racist policing of playgrounds and public beaches in other parts of the city were symptoms of growing hostility against black migrants and a citywide disinvestment of black children.[46]

"A Most Unjust Condition of Public Affairs": Care for Dependent Black Children in Chicago

Black children occupied a space of contingent childhood, as their age-based differentiation did not serve to protect them or cast them as innocent beings. Rather, their vulnerability was rendered invisible even as they became hypervisible for the purposes of punitive state intervention. Few white public and private charities in Chicago cared for black children before 1916.

Louise de Koven Bowen noted that day nurseries and orphanages in Chicago "refused to receive colored children on the ground that 'other people objected to them.'" "It is becoming a custom," she explained further, "on the part of many places to refuse colored children with the cryptic utterance 'We have no room.'" Among the religious charities, Catholic orphanages admitted a few black children. Because most African Americans were Protestant and the orphanages gave priority to children of the Catholic faith, the impact of these institutions was limited. White Protestant organizations, however, were more racially exclusive than Catholic ones and consistently refused to provide care for black children until 1953.[47]

As black migration increased and racial hostility rose during the First World War, the few nonreligious charities that did provide care for dependent black children, particularly those serving large numbers of newly arrived European immigrants, also began to exclude black children. This was also true of homes for dependent children in cities such as Cleveland, New York, and Philadelphia. As a result, black children in the North, who often had the highest poverty rates, had virtually no access to social services for children. The Soldiers' and Sailors' Home for Children and the Chicago Home for Girls, both public institutions, were two of the few institutions for dependents that accepted black children before the Great Migration. As migration brought more African Americans into the city, the Soldiers' and Sailors' Home eventually refused to admit any black children. The Chicago Home for Girls, an institution for pregnant, dependent, and delinquent girls, also capped the number of African Americans it would admit to a level that was lower than it was before black migration. This is particularly notable because the Chicago Home for Girls was located in a district that eventually became almost entirely black.[48]

The Chicago Orphan Asylum was the only long-term private home for dependent children that accepted African Americans. The number of black children in the home steadily decreased, however, as black migration into the city increased.[49] Two other private temporary institutions for dependent children, the Chicago Home for the Friendless, which was founded by a white women's club and directed by both Protestant and Jewish directors, and the Chicago Foundling Home, also accepted African American children. Children were admitted to the Chicago Home for the Friendless in the case of parental illness and housing emergencies like evictions and fires. It placed a quota on black admissions by capping it at 25 percent. The population of African American children rarely approached the quota, however, even as the number of black children in the city increased. The

Chicago Foundling Home, which served young expectant mothers and their babies, similarly admitted native white and European immigrant girls over African Americans.

The Illinois Technical School for Colored Girls, a Catholic institution founded by of the Sisters of the Good Shepherd, was the only white charity that bucked this trend, although it admitted African Americans on a segregated basis. It was incorporated in 1911 by state law and received public funds. Although it was originally founded for the "care and education of dependent colored girls between the ages of six and sixteen," it eventually shifted its attention away from dependent girls and became a boarding home and resource for working- and middle-class African American girls.[50]

The Chicago Urban League (CUL), a civil rights organization whose primary goal was to help African American migrants transition to life in the city, identified the challenges facing black children, particularly dependent migrant children. The eradication—or, at least, amelioration of these challenges—had become a focal point of the CUL's advocacy by 1919. Between 1918 and 1930, the CUL held several conferences to figure out the best way to help dependent African American children. The conferences included brainstorming sessions about how to best help homeless black children and their mothers. They also discussed research by social scientists such as black sociologist Earl Moses, who studied the experiences of dependent and delinquent black children in the juvenile justice system.[51] As late as 1945, a CUL study found that private institutions for dependent children that were supported by public funds still regularly excluded African American children or imposed quotas on the number of black children they would allow in their homes. The study described one case involving five African American siblings as "typical": "There were five of the children. Their mother, having gone to Mississippi to the funeral of a relative, had evidently chosen not to come back. . . . The worker at the juvenile court to whom the bewildered father had brought the children spent from 12:15 to 3:30 at the telephone trying to find a place that would take them. At the end of the three hours, she had not been able to find an institutional home in Chicago that would take any of the five Negro youngsters."[52]

Black Clubwomen and the Care of "Poor Unfortunate" Children

Black people spearheaded a number of institutions for poor, dependent, and delinquent black children in early twentieth-century Chicago, both as a response to discrimination against African American children in child welfare institutions and as part of a continuation of the racial uplift programs created by the black middle class.[53] By relying on extended kin networks, creating informal foster families, establishing community-funded homes, training schools, and youth clubs, and organizing recreational activities, African Americans created a child-saving movement in their own right. Black clubwomen were often at the forefront of these efforts.[54] Black clubwomen had a long history of recognizing black children's vulnerability and creating institutions to care for them. The exploitation of African American children in convict lease gangs—a vulnerability specific to black children that remained a threat through the first half of the twentieth century—spurred black clubwomen to action. At the very first national meeting of the National Association of Colored Women's Clubs (NACWC) in 1896, clubwomen mobilized support for black children being exploited in the southern criminal justice system.[55] Their advocacy on behalf of children moved north along with migration, and clubwomen established organizations across the urban North. Clubwomen advocated for protection and support of "poor and wayward" black children by using various means.[56]

Clubwomen in Chicago established private day nurseries, kindergartens, orphanages, industrial schools, reformatories, and other institutions for dependent and delinquent black children. Clubwomen including Joanna Snowden, Ida Lewis, and Irene McCoy Gaines volunteered their time to advocate for black children appearing before the juvenile court and worked as probation officers. In addition to working as a court probation officer, clubwoman and antilynching activist Ida B. Wells founded the Negro Fellowship League in 1910 to provide recreational outlets and employment services for young black men and boys. Chicago clubwomen also donated funds and volunteered at the Amanda Smith Home, the first black-owned institution to receive public funds from the state, and founded the Phyllis Wheatley Home for working young women and girl migrants.[57]

Members of the Phyllis Wheatley Club, one of the oldest black women's clubs in Chicago, founded the Phyllis Wheatley Home for Girls in 1907. Club members embodied the NACWC motto of "lifting as we climb" and dedicated themselves to providing social welfare, charity, education, and employment services to poor and working-class African Americans in the city. They provided accommodations, social outlets, and employment services for young African American women and girls so that they would not go "astray by being led unaware into disreputable homes, entertainment and employment." Although it became a vital resource for girls and families of the Great Migration, it alone could not cure the needs of an increasing number of dependent girls in Chicago.[58] The Wheatley Club also organized a Sunshine Club for girls ages nine to eighteen to provide care, social camaraderie, and distractions from the potential lure of the vice districts that city officials and Progressive reformers constantly relocated into black neighborhoods.[59]

The City Federation of Colored Women's Clubs, an offshoot of the NACWC, founded the Federated Home for Dependent Negro Children in 1927 to provide care for "the children of the community" who did not have "adequate homes." The City Federation of Colored Women's Clubs regularly organized clubs, dances, picnics, and social events for black youths.[60] Because the Federated Home was founded during the Great Depression and was primarily supported by the NACWC Chicago branch's dues and donations from African Americans, proper financial and organizational maintenance of the home was difficult. It housed only an average of twenty-two children a year until it closed down in 1939.[61]

Black clubwomen's particular interest in the protection of dependent African American girls explains their keen support of Mator McFerrin, a fifteen-year-old dependent girl who became a ward of the juvenile court. McFerrin was raped and impregnated by a thirty-three-year-old white male, Frank Chaplin. Black clubwomen showed up in juvenile court en masse the day McFerrin was scheduled to have her case heard. Prominent member of the City Federation of Colored Women's Clubs and probation officer Joanna Snowden played a central role in her case.[62] McFerrin had been declared a dependent in juvenile court because she did not have parents who could give her proper care. The *Chicago Defender* closely followed clubwomen's support of this "poor unfortunate child" who was "made an object of a white brute's lust." According to the *Defender*, Snowden held baby Clarence, McFerrin's son, as the fifteen-year-old told her story in court. Clubwomen showed up en masse because they wanted to highlight not only the seriousness and injustice of McFerrin's case but the long history of white men's sexual exploitation of black women and girls in light of Progressive reformers' hysteria over white slavery. Chaplin was ultimately found guilty in the Court of Domestic Relations and ordered to pay child support to McFerrin on baby Clarence's behalf.[63]

Chicago's black clubwomen paired their child saving with a vicious antivice campaign during the Progressive era. Clubwomen sought to ameliorate, as best they could, the environments black children lived in. By doing so, they fought against the very social conditions that made black children vulnerable to being labeled delinquent in juvenile court. In 1914, the *Chicago Defender* featured a story about clubwomen Alberta Moore Smith and Jessie Thomas, who shut down a vice den that recruited African American girls and made sure the vice den's owner was prosecuted in court. The article lauded "the splendid work done by her [Alberta Smith] and Mrs. Jessie Thomas in ferreting out and bringing to justice Reverend Theodore Thomas whose children's school for crime was aired in the Juvenile Court."[64] A 1918 article, "Roots out Nests of Iniquity," again gave Jessie Thomas, who was also a probation officer, "unbounded praise" for contributing to the protection of African American boys and girls from vice. Thomas notified the court that two women were renting rooms "to contribute to the delinquency" of minors for "immoral purposes." As a result, Judge Wells M. Cook of the Morals Court fined the women $100.[65]

Clubwomen's care for dependent black children also took the form of holding benefits and soliciting monetary contributions and toys for dependent children. In 1912, Alberta Moore Smith organized a social event for juvenile court wards. Smith, and the ten other clubwomen she invited to help her host the benefit, held a fund-raising event located in a clubroom at Ida B. Wells-Barnett's Negro Fellowship League. Smith also asked other black juvenile court probation officers, county probation officers, a Juvenile Protective Association officer, a police probation officer, and black teachers to send her the names of other poor, orphaned, or neglected children they knew who were in need of some "Christmas cheer." The event was a success, as a number of black Chicagoans participated and the 210 children in attendance were "laden with toys, candies, new stockings, shoes, underwear, gloves ... [and] bountifully supplied with fruits, ice cream and cakes."[66]

Many clubwomen followed in the footsteps of Elizabeth McDonald, the "colored missionary" who accompanied Mary Tripplet to juvenile court in 1899, by working as juvenile court probation officers. Gertrude Smith, one of the juvenile court's earliest black probation workers, was particularly notable for her care and protection of black children. After probation work became professionalized in 1903, juvenile court probation workers were required to pass a civil service exam. Smith, who became the first black member of the Cook County Probation Officers' Association, was among the first twenty-six civil service workers to be appointed. She remained a probation worker until her death in 1914.[67] Clubwomen's direct work with the juvenile court continued through the 1930s, with women such as Ina Abernathy, a probation officer; Charlotte Jackson, who became the head clerk of the juvenile court; Clotee Scott, who worked in the mothers' pension division; and Edith Smith, who was elected to the juvenile court bench in the 1940s.

Other Black Organizational Care for Dependent Children

Publicly funded institutions for black children that were founded by African Americans, churches, and the CUL also cared for dependent children. The first publicly funded black home for dependent children was founded in Harvey, about twenty miles south of Chicago, in 1899 by Amanda Berry Smith. Born in Maryland to enslaved parents, Smith was an evangelist who was well known for her religious devotion and gift for public speaking. Before starting her home for dependent girls, Smith served as a missionary in Asia and Africa under the auspices of the English Missionary and Temperance Society. Smith decided to devote her final years to the care of dependent children, and at age sixty, she spent her life savings—$1,000—establishing the home.[68] As W. E. B. Du Bois noted in his 1909 study of African American self-help organizations, the Amanda Smith Home was the "object to which she" devoted "the closing years of her unselfish life."

Black Chicago celebrated the Amanda Smith Home for Girls, which provided care to "colored children who, by death of parents, or otherwise, have been left without homes or natural protectors."[69] A 1913 *Chicago Defender* article echoed much of the community's sentiments when it said of the home, "For years our citizens have needed such work. . . . Both Protestant and Catholic institutions draw the color line against our girls, and having no suitable place to send our orphan and dependent girls, it became necessary at times to send dependent girls to the State School for Delinquent Girls. That is a most unjust condition of public affairs which gives to a white orphan girl care . . . and then instead of caring for an orphaned [black] girl either farms her out in private homes or sends her to prison. If our girls are to be 'Jim Crowed' at all we prefer to have them sent to an institution organized, maintained and controlled by our people."[70]

Seven years later, Elizabeth McDonald established the Louise Home, the second institution for dependent black children in Chicago. McDonald was also an evangelist and was one of the first probation officers who worked for the juvenile court when it opened in 1899. Although some white probation officers worked with black children, the evidence indicates that the bulk of McDonald's cases were African American children. She did excellent work, according to juvenile court judges who spoke publicly of her work "in terms of the highest praise." Probation officers did not earn incomes until

1904, and after this date, the evidence indicates that McDonald was paid less than her white counterparts. As late as 1909, when McDonald was the last remaining member of the court's original group of probation workers, she continued to work on a largely voluntary basis even though probation officers began to be salaried in 1904.[71]

It is not clear why McDonald's salary was smaller than that of other probation workers. Probation workers were paid through public and private funds from organizations such as the Juvenile Court Committee—later known as the Juvenile Protective Association—and it is probable that racial discrimination prevented her from garnering private support for her efforts. Juvenile Court Committee records show that in 1904, they approved a salary of $100 a month for all the probation officers except McDonald and a newcomer, who were each offered $30 a month. Prominent black city residents including Ferdinand Barnett, attorney and husband of Ida B. Wells, Assistant County Attorney L. B. Anderson, and two newspaper editors wrote a letter to the Juvenile Court Committee protesting the meager salary that McDonald was offered. It is not clear if and how the Juvenile Court Committee increased her salary, but McDonald elected to continue to work for the juvenile court.[72]

McDonald's work as a probation officer made her keenly aware of the problem of the lack of proper care for dependent black children. Her primary concern was that dependent black children were treated in juvenile court as if they had committed crimes and were sent fifty miles away to state institutions for delinquent children in Geneva and St. Charles. McDonald founded the Louise Home for dependent children. Eventually, the home also began to admit some delinquent children. In 1913, the Louise Home became a single-sex institution and was renamed the Louise Training School for Boys. Subsequently, it was incorporated under the state of Illinois's Industrial Schools Act and became eligible to receive state funds.[73]

The Amanda Smith and Louise institutions were the only black-owned and -operated institutions to receive public money under the Industrial Schools Act. White child welfare workers opposed the Amanda Smith School's housing of dependent children, and the school eventually had its license revoked as the result of a mysterious 1919 fire that led to the death of two children and caused significant damage to the building.[74] The Louise School also received staunch opposition from white child welfare workers and was shut down as a result of financial constraints and McDonald's deteriorating health. McDonald tried unsuccessfully to save the Louise School by relocating it and having it become a part of the campus of the

Glenwood Manual Training School in 1913, a public home for delinquent and dependent boys. Philanthropist Julius Rosenwald agreed to financially support the home on the condition that the Glenwood School agree to the relocation. However, the director of the school rejected this move "primarily because the boys of the Louise Manual Training School are uniformly younger than the boys for whose care Glenwood is now organized."[75] After the Louise Home officially shut down in 1920, the only formal state-supported institution dedicated to the care of dependent African American children was the Catholic-run Illinois Technical School for Colored Girls.[76]

African American churches in Chicago also provided care for poor, orphaned, and abandoned children. The city's black community had a rich and diverse religious life. "Old line" churches such as African Methodist Episcopal and Olivet Baptist often offered spiritual counsel alongside social service programs for southern migrants. Their programs for children included youth clubs, athletic leagues, and other recreational activities.[77] Other religious organizations created boarding homes for dependent children, although many of these were fleeting, existed on an ad hoc basis, and did not have official names. In 1907, a minister started a general trade school where students between the ages of five and fifteen ate meals, sang hymns each morning, learned trades, and had a Bible lesson every day. Unlike many other church-based homes for children, it experienced longevity, and by 1926, the home had grown to include six buildings and enrolled an average of fifty children every year. Financial support for the home came largely from church contributions.[78] In 1913, a home was founded by the Jerusalem Church, a store-front worship group, and maintained by its prophet "for the purpose of aiding the poor and needy and to safeguard the moral and religious uplift of dependents." By 1919, the home had all but shut down because of the prophet's poor health and insufficient financial contributions, and it cared for only one nine-year old boy. Other church-run institutions for dependent black children included the White Cross Midnight Missionary Association's Home for Colored Girls, which was established in 1912, and the Church of God and Saints of Christ Orphanage and Home for Colored Children, which was founded in 1914.[79]

Chicago Urban League and the Care of Black Children

The local branch of the Urban League, which was founded in 1916, also supported dependent black children by donating funds, conducting studies, mediating black children's and families' relationships with the juvenile court, and advocating in front of city and state officials on their behalf. A 1917 pamphlet summarized the Chicago Urban League's work for the year by focusing on the assistance it gave the juvenile court "regarding families with whom children might be boarded" because of the dearth of institutional resources for dependent black children.[80] The same year, the CUL lent organizational support and provided helpful information to the Juvenile Protective Association, the Infant Welfare Association, and the Amanda Smith Home.[81]

The CUL also held several conferences to figure out the best way to help dependent black children. These conferences, which began in 1918, lasted through 1950. The CUL's 1933 conference, entitled "A Century of Progress in Race Relations," was one of the most notable and included presentations on "The Care of Dependent Children," "The Function of Private Agencies," "Work of the Protective Agencies for Juveniles," "The Underprivileged Boy," "Reclaiming the So-Called Bad Boy," "The Use of Playgrounds, Parks and Beaches," and "Recreation and Neighborhood Activities."[82] The CUL also criticized institutions that discriminated against black children and urged the juvenile court to hire more probation officers as well as "a special worker to give full time to discovery of foster homes in the State of Illinois." The CUL stressed that both public and private institutions should be included.[83]

The CUL also attempted to ameliorate the dearth of institutional resources for black children by organizing several programs to prevent African American children from winding up in juvenile court in the first place. The CUL targeted specific problems such as double-shift schools, inferior educational buildings, inadequate housing, residential overcrowding, and the lack of recreational facilities and playgrounds for black children. It also urged churches to cater to African American children so that their faith could act as a buttress against the vice and temptations for delinquent behavior that the disinvestment in black communities aggravated.[84] The CUL's Youth Department, Better Conduct Program, and Department of Industrial Relations gave black children advice about avoiding delinquency, provided them with job training, and taught them about national and international politics.[85] The CUL also founded the Douglass School—a public school that fell under the management of the Board of Education—for African American girls who were pregnant or already young mothers. The goal of the Douglass School was to allow the girls to complete their education as "much of the stigma which might have attached to them was removed."[86] By producing research and engaging in advocacy on behalf of dependent black children, the CUL became a vital resource for black children, black parents, juvenile court officers, and charity workers.[87]

The CUL played a vital role in mediating the relationship between the juvenile court and the black community. Child advocates and juvenile court employees including Judge Julian Mack, clubwoman Joanna Snowden, and Hull House founder Jane Addams were among its earliest members. As a result, the CUL monitored black children's experiences in court and did what it could to help juvenile court workers secure foster families for dependent African American children.[88]

The CUL pushed juvenile court workers to try harder to find placements for dependent black children. A mother of three from Clarksdale, Mississippi, who had been living in Chicago for six years sought the CUL's assistance in locating her kidnapped children. The mother and her children had rented a room in Harvey, Illinois, after being evicted from their Chicago residence because of her husband's disruptive behavior. Her husband eventually deserted the family. Upon returning home one day, a friend informed her that her children "had been taken by a man in a car." The CUL helped the mother find her children. When the mother contacted the CUL again because she got evicted and was having trouble providing for them, they urged her to contact the juvenile court so that it could help her locate a home for her children until she could find a place to live. It also advised her to go to the Court of Domestic Relations to secure a warrant for her husband on the grounds of desertion. Initially, the juvenile court said it would be unable to find a place for the children. After some "considerable discussion" with a juvenile court worker, however, the CUL eventually convinced the worker to try harder. The juvenile court worker eventually found shelter for the two older children. The youngest child—an infant—stayed with her mother.[89]

The CUL served as an important referral service for black children in juvenile court through World War II. In 1948, the juvenile court referred two daughters of a young mother from Alabama to the CUL because their father had abandoned them. The CUL proceeded to locate a boarding home for the children and their mother.[90] In another case, the juvenile court referred a pregnant teenager from Lawrence County, Mississippi, who was living with her friends in a kitchenette. As a result, the CUL successfully located better accommodation for the teenager.[91]

Some African American parents also sought the Chicago Urban League's assistance in fighting the juvenile court's commitment of their children to state institutions for delinquent children. A mother from Arkansas who worked in Chicago as a notary public asked the League to help her get her daughter released from the Illinois Training School for Girls at Geneva. It is unclear why her daughter had been committed to Geneva in the first place, although the mother mentioned there had been a "school problem." The CUL wrote to Elizabeth Lewis, the superintendent of the Training School, to request the daughter's release. Although the records do not indicate whether the CUL's petition was successful, they do suggest that some African American families viewed the CUL as an important advocate when they encountered the juvenile justice system.[92]

Part of the CUL's work on behalf of black children included attempts to prevent black children from ending up in juvenile court in the first place, so much of its work targeted delinquent black children as well. Its very first annual report of 1918 stated that one of its priorities was "looking into delinquency among colored children appearing before the juvenile court, with the view of getting some prevention work established." Its 1932 annual report still reflected this priority, as the CUL's Department of Research described its "compilation of data regarding social and economic problems among Negroes" as a "fundamental feature" of its activities.[93] Among the studies supported by the CUL's Research Division were sociologist Earl Moses's *Juvenile Delinquency among Negroes in Chicago* and *Community Factors in Negro Delinquency* and E. Franklin Frazier's *The Negro Family in Chicago*.[94] Moses and Frazier made their findings available to social service organizations— including the juvenile court—working with African American children.

The CUL began holding conferences solely on the topic of delinquent black children in juvenile court in 1925. A conference entitled "The Problems and Needs of Negro Youth as Revealed by Delinquency and Crime Statistics" featured the CUL's preliminary data on children labeled delinquent in juvenile court.[95] Upon completion of Moses's study on black delinquency in Chicago, the CUL organized another conference in 1932 entitled "Juvenile Delinquency in the Negro Community" for scholars, concerned citizens, juvenile court employees, and other social service workers. Among the attendees was the director of the Institute for Juvenile Research, the state criminologist, and the assistant superintendent of public schools.[96]

The Forcible Transfer of the Care of Black Children from the Amanda Smith and Louise Homes to the State

With the exception of the Amanda Smith and Louise homes, which received public funding, the network of black women's clubs and churches that founded institutions for black children was almost exclusively funded by African Americans. Black Chicagoans, unlike other communities that were primarily constituted by newcomers to the city, were left to provide care for their vulnerable children alone. The collection of privately and publically funded black-managed homes for dependent children could not accommodate the increasing numbers of dependent children in the community. Moreover, black-owned homes such as the Amanda Smith and Louise homes that did, in fact, received funding from the state were eventually wrested from the black community's hands.

The process of transferring institutional care for African American children at the Amanda Smith and Louise homes to the state was a long and deliberate process on the part of white social workers and reformers. Child welfare workers and city officials believed that these homes—and other black-owned and -operated institutions for dependent and delinquent children that emerged in early twentieth-century Chicago—could not "properly care" for black children. More specifically, they believed that African Americans did not have the appropriate skills to manage such institutions or the ability to manage money. State investigators initially commended the quality of care they provided for children and cleared them for access to public funds.[97] Nevertheless, the state never provided them with a sufficient amount of funding in spite of their incorporation under the Industrial Schools Act. The lack of state support, the black community's poverty and inability to raise sufficient funds, and private organizations' failure to donate funds to these institutions posed serious problems for the Louise and Smith homes. As time went by, city inspectors overlooked the institutions' funding challenges, and commissioners who visited the homes complained about mismanagement.[98] One city inspector who visited the Amanda Smith and Louise homes strongly encouraged them to recruit white board members because of his belief that black people were incapable of sufficiently managing institutions and therefore needed white leadership.[99]

White reformers and child welfare workers were also motivated to close black-owned and -operated institutions because, unlike African American child advocates, they believed African American children were better served in home-based programs. White child welfare reformers increasingly embraced "home finding" and deinstitutionalization as a method of care for dependent children of all races. They believed that black child welfare was out of step with modern policy visions, which had come to favor home-based care for dependent children. Black activists and reformers were less enthusiastic than white reformers about home-based care for a few important reasons. In light of extended kin networks and the long history of "taking in" dependent children in the African American community, a home-finding (now known as foster care) program for dependent black children in Chicago may have seemed superfluous.[100] Another factor may have been the reality that the number of people willing to meet licensing standards so that they could house dependent children was so low that it could not sufficiently address the need for care of dependent children.[101] This difference in vision, relative lack of state support, and reformers' beliefs about African Americans' inability to manage their own institutions led child welfare reformers to transfer complete control over publicly funded institutional care of dependent children from black people.

Both Edith Wyatt, a Hull House activist, and Amelia Sears, a renowned social welfare reform leader, actively worked to shut down the Louise School and Amanda Smith Home in order to transfer the care of children to a state home-finding agency. They conferred with Juvenile Court judge Arnold about shutting down the Louise School so that the boys could be placed in family homes. Judge Arnold "approve[d] heartily" and stated that if they "could show him any plan for placing boys now in the Louise Manual Training School in family homes he would immediately remove them" from the Louise School. Amelia Sears noted in a letter to State Board of Charities secretary William C. Graves in 1919 that she had successfully "gotten the license of the Amanda Smith [Home] revoked at considerable effort" and was negotiating with the attorney general's office to go even further by completely dissolving the charter. She noted with frustration that although the effort was "fraught with great difficulty," she was nevertheless committed to eliminating "undesirable provisions for the colored children"—namely, the Amanda Smith and Louise homes—"and substituting satisfactory provision."[102] Amelia Sears and William Graves formally convened a committee at the Women's City Club to consider what kind of provisions could be made for dependent black children. Miss Amelia Sears, Mr. T. Arnold, and Mr. W. S. Reynolds then recommended a home-placing plan that took the formal care of dependent black children out of the black community and placed it in a new division of the Illinois Children's Home and Aid Society (ICHA).[103]

The ICHA was a home-finding agency and, at the time, the only agency that found homes for dependent black children in Chicago. A committee made up of the city's eminent child welfare workers convened to discuss how to properly care for children left homeless as a result of the fire at the Amanda Smith Home. At a 1920 meeting, the committee decided to establish the Bureau for Dependent Colored Children of ICHA, a racially segregated program with its own advisory committee, staff, boarding homes, and fund-raising. The fund-raising arm of the Bureau for Dependent Colored Children, called the Colored Children's Auxiliary, was responsible for raising funds from the black community. The advisory committee included only one African American—Dr. George Cleveland Hall, director of Provident Hospital—within its ranks. Jewish philanthropist Julius Rosenwald, as well as the Chicago Community Trust, supplemented the funds African Americans donated to the Colored Children's Auxiliary during its first year. The funds provided the bureau with its first $12,000, which paid the director and two African American social workers a salary.[104]

Ironically, the bureau began to suffer from the same kind of financial struggles as the black institutions from which it had wrested the care of dependent African American children. Like these black institutions, it partially relied on funds solicited from the city's impoverished African American community for its budget. Beginning in the ICHA's first year of operation, the *Chicago Defender* featured several articles about "homeless children" and solicited donations for ICHA with "costs about $5 a week."[105] ICHA's internal documents show that African Americans gave generously in the opening years of the Colored Children's Auxiliary even though "unemployment and poverty [had] pressed more severely on the colored people than on any other group in the community." A 1927 tabulation of donations by African Americans added up to $13,885. African Americans supplemented this financial contribution through the number of dependent African American children they took in free of charge and without boarding payments from the state. That year, African Americans also held a charity ball and fund-raised.[106]

By 1928, however, the bureau's financial support by white philanthropists had waned, and the juvenile court and other public institutions no longer freely gave the ICHA a vote of confidence. The bureau, which served as many as three hundred black children, could not meet the demand for home-finding services for black children as the migration of poor African Americans into the city skyrocketed.[107] Dependent black children continued to languish in the juvenile court's detention home indefinitely and were committed to public institutions for delinquent children at St. Charles and Geneva in spite of the bureau's efforts.[108] The situation became so desperate that juvenile court workers began to lodge complaints at the ICHA because of its inability to meet the growing needs of dependent black children. As a result, in 1928 the bureau's work was eventually transferred to the Joint Service Bureau, a clearinghouse for applications to Protestant institutions in Cook County. This transfer, which resulted in the creation of the Department of Child Placing for Negro Children, was also strictly segregated and under white leadership. The department became an entirely publicly funded program in 1931, when it merged with the Children and Minors Service.[109]

The Racialization of Delinquency

The city's refusal to provide sufficient funds to black-owned homes for dependent children, in addition to the strict quotas and outright exclusion of black children in white institutions for dependents, was a key ingredient in the construction of racialized delinquency.[110] The Children and Minors Service, like the ICHA Colored Children's Auxiliary, could not meet the growing need of dependent care for African American children. This transfer of care only complicated the problem. It primed the category "dependent" to become associated with whiteness because dependent white children had more access to resources and were less likely to be committed to institutions for children who committed crimes. Conversely, black children were set up to be "delinquents" before they even entered the juvenile justice system.

Racial discrimination against black children at the community level had an impact on Cook County Juvenile Court's disposition of dependent black children's cases from its inception. Black children found themselves in juvenile court as dependents for a variety of reasons, including the death of a parent, parental divorce or separation, abuse, neglect, or the desertion of the father. African American children were consistently and disproportionately represented among the ranks of dependent children through World War II. African Americans made up less than 3 percent of Chicago's child population by 1920 but were 7 percent of dependent children processed in Cook County Juvenile Court.[111] Nevertheless, judges and probation officers in juvenile court processed the cases of dependent black children, like that of Mary Tripplet, as if they were delinquents by marking their forms "delinquent" instead of "dependent" and committing black children to public institutions for delinquent children.[112]

The Training School for Boys at St. Charles and the Training School for Girls at Geneva, and, to a lesser extent, the Chicago Parental School for truant children, became the primary mode of state "support" for dependent black children. Unlike private and religious homes for dependent children, public institutions for children who committed crimes did not exclude children on the basis of their race. A memo from the Joint Service Bureau Department of Child Placing of Negro Children—a referral agency that opened in the 1930s to help manage the large number of underresourced black migrant children during the Depression—noted with consternation that "reformatories are housing unusually large percentages of Negro children where they had to be sent for lack of different facilities." Juvenile court probation and parole officers similarly noted during an interview with black sociologist Earl Moses that "The difficulty of providing adequate care for the dependent and neglected colored children constitutes one of the greatest problems with which the court has to deal."[113]

Juvenile court workers also concluded that black children's cases were complicated by a lack of resources in Chicago that were comparable to those available to native and immigrant white children in the same circumstances, as "practically no institutions are to be found in the community to which this group of colored children may be admitted." They argued that the juvenile court's commitment of black children to institutions for delinquent children was unique when compared with the court's treatment of other new city residents. They explained the commitment of dependent African American boys to St. Charles this way: "Jewish, Italian, Polish and other groups have coordinating agencies which work with boys of those groups, making a St. Charles Commitment the last resort. Even with the coordinating efforts of some agencies Negroes lack many facilities which make an institutional commitment necessary earlier that would probably otherwise be made."[114]

Older dependent black children had a much harder time than younger children. African American boys were very difficult to place.[115] However, probation and parole officers complained that the lack of facilities for dependent African American girls was especially challenging: "Facilities for non-institutional and institutional care of Negro delinquent girls are even more lacking than for Negro boys. . . . The situation with reference to the delinquent colored girl is even more desperate. The State Training School for Girls at Geneva is the only institution to which they are admitted."[116]

African American children went on to make up a disproportionate number of children at institutions for delinquents, not because they committed more crimes than any other group of children, but because of racial discrimination at the community level and the juvenile court's limited institutional options for the care of dependent black children. This overrepresentation of black children at state institutions for delinquent children reveals the way black children's lives were profoundly affected by their exclusion from homes for dependent children and a lack of community resources before they even encountered the juvenile justice system. By the time they reached their first point of contact with juvenile justice—through the juvenile court, a police station, or referral agency for dependent children—they were primed to be labeled and treated like children who had committed crimes.

Racist stereotypes about African Americans' lack of civilization and proclivity for criminal behavior shaped the very meaning and practice of juvenile justice. White and soon-to-be white children from eastern and southern Europe benefited from the child-saving movement and child welfare institutions by receiving care after being processed in juvenile court as dependents. Dependent black children, in contrast, were subject to the more punitive arm of the system after being processed in juvenile court. Ultimately, the dearth of child welfare resources for dependent African American children was linked to the racial limits of Progressive reform and notions of childhood innocence and rehabilitation. As they did in the city of Chicago, black children and adults were forced to contend with the disinvestment in black childhood and the racialization of delinquency within the walls of the state's new juvenile justice institutions. This first level of engagement began inside Cook County Juvenile Court.

CHAPTER TWO

Boundaries of Innocence

Race, the Emergence of Cook County
Juvenile Court, and Punitive Transitions

JUDGE BARTELME: Have you told your mother Hilda, about your
    father coming to your room?
HILDA SANDERS: Yes, both of us told her, and she says it is a story.
JUDGE BARTELME: Then she did tell you some time ago about it?
    Ever speak to him about it?
MRS. SANDERS (MOTHER): Yes Ma'am, and he denied it, says there
    ain't no such thing . . .
DORIS SANDERS: If I tell the truth about the man, will you not send
    me to the Detention Home? I was only trying to save him . . .
JUDGE BARTELME: What is the truth? . . .
DORIS SANDERS: This is the truth: [H]e told me if I would tell on
    him he would knock the hell out of me the first time he did it. . . .
    He threw me on the bed. I was just twelve years old.[1]

Doris, a sixteen-year-old African American girl, her fourteen-year-old sister
Hilda, and their mother, Mrs. Sanders, stood before Judge Mary Bartelme,
Cook County's first female juvenile court judge, on September 6, 1922. Alberta Moore Smith, the girls' probation officer and one of Cook County
Juvenile Court's few African American workers, was also present as they
laid bare their family secrets and conflicts in court. Doris and Hilda were
recent migrants to Chicago, having moved from Kentucky with their mother
and stepfather only a few years earlier.

The Sanders family came under the juvenile court's radar as a result of
Hilda's truancy from school and commitment to the Chicago Parental School,
a boarding home for truants and children who had behavioral problems in
school, one year earlier. When Judge Bartelme asked Hilda, who was in sixth
grade, why she did not go to school, she said, "I wasn't fixed to go, didn't
have my hair fixed to go and didn't have a dress ready to go." Doris told
Judge Bartelme she had to work as a domestic instead of going to school.
She said that she "didn't remain in school" because she had to work to support the family and "didn't have proper clothing." The girls' stepfather, who

worked at a steel mill and made thirty cents per hour, paid only half the rent and refused to help Mrs. Sanders financially support Doris and Hilda.

Smith, the probation officer, stated that she had been "trying to adjust matters in the [Sanders'] home since June." Before details about her husband's sexual abuse of Doris and Hilda were revealed in court, Mrs. Sanders complained about them to Judge Bartelme: "They do not act like they ought to, they are ruining themselves, and they think I am against them but I am fighting for them . . . this thing staying out until 1 and 2 o'clock at night, that don't do no good." Mrs. Smith reported the family and told them to appear in juvenile court once she realized "there is something a little deeper than we have been able to fathom" and that the disagreeable family dynamic was not simply a result of the girls' truancy and late nights on the town. Smith asked that the girls be removed from their home so that Doris could be placed in a boarding home for young working women and Hilda be placed in a "family school home." In Smith's opinion, this was the best way for the girls to be protected and properly cared for: "I feel the girls need protection, I know the mother is a good woman, hard-working and honest, but I am really convinced that the girls must have told her something about these constant visits of that stepfather and I know they are unhappy."[2]

The significance of Doris and Hilda's encounter with juvenile justice, and their exchange with their mother and Judge Bartelme in court, is that it typifies the experience of thousands of African American children who found themselves in Cook County Juvenile Court during the first half of the twentieth century. Many of the city's young black residents came under the jurisdiction of the juvenile court because of problems in school and truancy. For students like Doris, who worked as a domestic instead of going to school, their truancy was a function of poverty and efforts to financially support their families. Like the Sanders, black children also often found themselves in the juvenile justice system at the same time as their siblings. In juvenile court, children found the public—and sometimes private power of home— and state converging upon them. In spite of this, many children—like Hilda, who disagreed with her mother in open court, and Doris, who asked Judge Bartelme if she could avoid the Juvenile Detention Home if she told the truth about her stepfather—used the courtroom as a forum to negotiate and exercise agency over their own lives whenever they could.

Black migrant children who were newcomers from the South were particularly vulnerable to being caught up in the web of Cook County Juvenile Court and its ancillary institutions. These ancillary institutions—which included the Juvenile Detention Home, Chicago Parental School, and

Institute for Juvenile Research—played critical roles in the juvenile court's apprehension, treatment, and disposition of cases. This meant that for many black children who found themselves in court, this initial encounter was followed by multiple other contacts with state juvenile justice institutions. As the city experienced dramatic demographic shifts because of the mass migration of southern African Americans into its core, the proportion of black children winding up in juvenile court increased and Cook County Juvenile Court played an increasingly important, though often overlooked, role in shaping black life in Chicago.

The juvenile court became an institution that mediated the tensions between black migration, widespread beliefs about inherent black criminality, and the dearth of community resources for black children in Chicago. The vast majority of public and private agencies for poor, abused, neglected, or abandoned children excluded African American children because of their race. Because for many children the juvenile court was simply an initial stopping point before being sent to an institution for children who committed crimes, discrimination against black children at the community level shaped the disposition of cases in juvenile court.

The juvenile court consequently played an active role in constructing the image of a "delinquent" child by disproportionately applying the label to black children and inflating the actual number of black children who committed crimes. Over time, this led to a racialized process of criminalization as the image of a delinquent child became conflated with the image of a black child. As the images of the perceived type of children in juvenile court changed, the popular and political sentiments that made the juvenile court movement viable during the Progressive era waned.

The juvenile court always had opponents who believed that the justice system should not mitigate punishment based on the age of the offender. As the demographics of children appearing before the juvenile court changed alongside an increasingly threatening and racialized construction of the type of delinquent child in the system, however, racism became a powerful currency juvenile court opponents used to convert their ideology into public policy. By the 1930s, a full-fledged political assault on the rehabilitative ideal resulted in the juvenile court being divested of its primary jurisdiction over children who committed crimes. The 1935 case of Susie Lattimore, a fifteen-year-old African American girl convicted of murder, was a critical tool in dismantling the rehabilitative ideal that ultimately changed the nature of juvenile justice.

The Emergence of Cook County Juvenile Court

The General Assembly's passage of the Juvenile Court Act of 1899 marked the political ascension of the notion that children—because of their vulnerability, inherent innocence, and potential to be rehabilitated—needed their own separate nonadversarial court. Cook County Juvenile Court's early annual reports reveal the centrality of this understanding of child protection and rehabilitation. For example, the court's 1906 report announced: "The theory of the juvenile court law is based upon equity, upon the idea that when the State lays its hand upon a dependent or delinquent child, that that child is to have done for him what he needs to have done to make him a safe and effective citizen."[3]

The law, known formally as an "Act to regulate the treatment and control of dependent, neglected and delinquent children," merged reformers' concerns about child welfare with crime control and gave the juvenile court original jurisdiction over children's cases. The juvenile court labeled a person under the age of eighteen who broke the law a "delinquent." The court applied the term "dependent" to an abused, neglected, or abandoned person under the age of eighteen who did "not have proper parental care or guidance." Three dispositions of cases were possible under the Juvenile Court Act: probation in the child's home or the home of a relative, the appointment of a guardian with the right to place the child in another home, and commitment to an institution.[4] Cook County Juvenile Court committed delinquent children to institutions established under the state's Industrial and Training Schools Act.[5] These institutions for delinquent children included the John Worthy School for Boys, Illinois Industrial School for Girls at Geneva, Training School for Boys at St. Charles, Glenwood Manual Training School, Park Ridge School, the Chicago Home for Girls, and the Chicago Home for Boys. Delinquent and dependent children stayed in the Juvenile Detention Home until their court dates or institutional commitments. The juvenile court committed dependent children, along with children who were labeled as physically or psychologically handicapped, to a variety of public and private homes in Chicago.

Five years after the General Assembly passed the act, the same group of Progressive reformers who advocated the establishment of the juvenile court collaborated to form the Juvenile Protective Association (JPA). The JPA raised funds to pay probation officers and established the Juvenile Detention Home so that children awaiting processing in court would not be imprisoned alongside adults.[6] The goals of the Juvenile Detention Home, which was established in 1901, paralleled those prescribed in the 1899 act. Its purpose was to protect children from the influences of hardened criminals and provide children awaiting juvenile court hearings with a suitable and safe facility. Initially a separate structure, the juvenile court and detention home were eventually incorporated into the same building in 1906.[7] This group of activists also founded the Institute for Juvenile Research (IJR), a therapeutic institution, to work in concert with the juvenile court.[8] IJR facilitated one of the most crucial aspects of the "rehabilitation" of children who were processed in juvenile court. IJR was a child-study clinic that employed psychiatrists, psychologists, and physicians who studied the causes of the "behavioral disturbances" of children assigned to it by the juvenile court. Charitable institutions for dependent and delinquent children eventually began to refer children to IJR as well.[9]

Volunteers from the Hull House, Catholic Visitation and Aid Society, and other private associations provided the juvenile court with the majority of its first probation officers. Elizabeth McDonald, an evangelist who founded the Louise Home for black children who found themselves in juvenile court, was the first and only African American in the group of women probation officers that served the court when it opened in 1899. Probation officers were responsible for helping the children and families under their care resolve the very problems that landed them in court. Probation officers also often worked with teachers, employers, religious leaders, and children's friends to get more information about an issue or help resolve behaviors the juvenile court deemed problematic.[10]

In addition to arbitrating the cases of dependent and delinquent children, the juvenile court also administered pensions to widowed or abandoned mothers and enforced Illinois's compulsory education laws. The state's Compulsory School Attendance Law, which the General Assembly passed in 1883, required children between the ages of eight and fourteen to attend a public or private school. The state legislature passed the Parental School Law—which was a product of the advocacy of members of the Hull House and Chicago Woman's Club—alongside the Juvenile Court Act in 1899. The Parental School Law mandated that boards of education in cities with populations over 100,000 establish boarding schools for children who did not attend school or comply with school rules.[11] The Chicago Parental School, which was initially a male-only institution, was intended to be a place of "last resort" for truant children. As the superintendent of the school explained in the institution's seventh annual report, "No child should ever be taken from his home and sent to a truant school until after some preliminary steps have been taken." The juvenile court's arbitration of compulsory school attendance laws and commitment of children to the Chicago Parental School had become an entrenched part of the court's work by 1910. Every Friday morning, juvenile court judges heard the cases of children who had been arrested for skipping school or accused by their principals of breaking school rules. By 1913, up to three-quarters of children who were brought into juvenile court on truancy cases were committed to the Chicago Parental School.[12]

Black Children in Juvenile Court

Black children were overrepresented in Cook County Juvenile Court from its inception. Although they made up only 1 percent of the city's child population in 1900, 5 percent of children appearing in juvenile court were African American. This percentage slowly increased, and by 1912, the proportion of African Americans among all children appearing in juvenile court had reached 14 percent. This was over twice their proportion in the general population. For African American girls, this was three and a half times their proportion of the population.[13] Between 1913 and 1919, when African Americans still made up 3 percent of the city's population, the proportion of African American boys in juvenile court was roughly 7 percent, though the proportion of black girls had increased to 15 percent of all the children appearing in juvenile court.[14]

This disproportion increased as black migration into the city accelerated. By 1930, 21 percent of the children who found themselves in juvenile court were black, even though less than 7 percent of the city's population was black (see table 1).[15]

The number of African American children who were labeled delinquent in juvenile court increased steadily throughout the first wave of migration.[16] Black sociologist Earl Moses noted in his 1935 study for the Chicago Urban League that the rate of black juvenile delinquency in Chicago was "increasing in startling proportions" and "growing much faster than the growth in the Negro population."[17] Using data from the Census Bureau, Moses noted that the proportion of delinquent African American children in the city increased from 3.5 percent in 1900 to 21 percent in 1930. This sevenfold increase was in stark contrast to the threefold increase in the city's black

TABLE 1 Proportion of delinquent and dependent black children appearing in Cook County Juvenile Court between 1920 and 1925[1]

	1920	1921	1922	1923	1925
% of dependent black children	7%	4%	4%	5%	6%
No. of dependent black girls	40	26	37	60	50
No. of dependent black boys	45	30	26	51	75
Total no. of dependents of all races	1,262	1,292	1,422	1,535	2,013
% of delinquent black children	12%	11%	15%	15%	17%
No. of delinquent black girls	128	100	116	108	98
No. of delinquent black boys	182	194	177	161	326
Total no. of delinquents of all races	2,550	2,786	1,906	1,770	2,513

Source: See statistical tables and appendices in Cook County Juvenile Court, *Juvenile Court and Juvenile Detention Home of Cook County Annual Report of 1921*, Municipal Reference Collection, Harold Washington Library, Chicago Public Libraries.

[1] The year 1924 was not included because of incomplete data.

population. Over the same period, the proportion of African American city residents had increased from 1.8 percent to 6.9 percent.[18] A state parole officer cited in Moses's study also picked up on this trend: "The sensational increase in juvenile Negro delinquency gives the greatest concern to all good citizenship. . . . The number of white boys has remained practically at a standstill, if not at a decrease, while that of Negro boys shows an increase far out of proportion to race statistics."[19] Moses attributed this increase to the lack of community-based institutional resources for African American children in Chicago, the stresses of migration from the South, and stereotypes about African American criminality.

Children generally found themselves in Cook County Juvenile Court for a variety of reasons. Police officers, probation workers, and truant officers apprehended children who were runaways, homeless, orphaned, abused or neglected by their parents, found playing hooky from school, wandering the streets late at night, or breaking the law. William, a Mississippi migrant whose father deserted him when he was only three days old, is a good example of this. He came under the juvenile court's jurisdiction after police officers picked him up in 1922 because he was walking around alone at night. His mother, who gave birth to him at age sixteen, told court officers she was having trouble properly caring for him. His first contact with the juvenile court began at age six when he was placed in the Juvenile Detention Home because he ran away from home and was "beyond the control of his mother." When he was eight, his mother referred him to the juvenile court because he was "incorrigible" and "constantly truanted from home and school," and she could no longer care for him. William had repeated contacts with the juvenile court and detention home through his teenage years, and his relationship with his mother remained tense. The juvenile court eventually committed him to the Chicago Parental School because he was a "truant."[20]

Parent–child conflicts, which could be exacerbated because of the transition from a rural to urban environment, led some parents to refer their own children to the juvenile court.[21] Older siblings, neighbors, and teachers also referred children to Chicago's juvenile court. It was not unusual for black children—particularly those who had traveled with their parent from the South—to have their siblings, mothers, and fathers also embroiled in other branches of the city or state justice system. These branches include the Morals Court, Criminal Court, city jails, and prisons.[22]

Perceptions of crime were gendered, and many girls were arrested or committed to the juvenile court by family members for engaging in premarital sex, going to dance halls, or getting rides from strange men or for a host of other behaviors that violated Victorian norms of appropriate female behavior.[23] Girls who were sexually assaulted could be blamed for the crimes perpetrated against them and labeled a "sex delinquent" in juvenile court.[24] Pearl, a fourteen-year-old African American girl who "was brought to Chicago" at age seven by a great aunt and uncle, ended up in juvenile court after an adult man raped and impregnated her. Her aunt took her to the juvenile court in 1930 when she was seven months pregnant in order to secure care for Pearl and the baby because she did not have enough resources to support both of them. The juvenile court judge, however, labeled her a "sex delinquent" and referred her to Provident Hospital to treat the gonorrheal infection her assailant gave her. The judge mandated that she remain in the hospital until she had her baby, then be transferred to an institution for delinquents called the Chicago Home for Girls. Upon release from the hospital, Pearl and her baby stayed at the Chicago Home for Girls for fourteen months. Her rapist, who pled guilty, was sentenced to the House of Corrections for six months for his "inability to pay a fine." Isabel, a fourteen-year-old orphaned black girl who lived with an aunt, was similarly sentenced to the Chicago Home for Girls in 1930. She was labeled a "sex delinquent" in court after she was sexually assaulted by her father and older cousin. Unlike

Pearl, however, the Chicago Home for Girls refused to keep her "because of her youth," and she ended up in foster care.[25]

Police Surveillance in Black Neighborhoods and Arrest Rates

Police surveillance in black neighborhoods and the disproportionate arrest rates of African American children also primed black children to be over-represented in juvenile court. Sociologist E. Franklin Frazier's analysis of arrest rates in 1926 revealed that police surveillance in Chicago's black neighborhoods led to extremely high arrest rates for African American children. Police arrested an astonishing 43 percent of all black boys in neighborhoods for delinquency. The highest rates of arrest were in the poorest black neighborhoods closest to downtown Chicago (see table 2). Frazier noted that the surge in black arrests was linked to the dramatic increase in the city's black population after World War I. Further, African Americans' settlement in some of the poorest and most deteriorated parts of the city was linked to high arrest rates for juvenile delinquency.[26]

These arrest rates should not be conflated with African American boys' actual rates of delinquency. As the Chicago Crime Commission noted in the Commission on Race Relations' report, arrest rates in Chicago during the 1920s were not good indicators of actual crime because "(1) a large number of persons may be arrested for complicity in a single crime; (2) many innocent persons are arrested through misapprehension and later discharged; and (3) the vast majority of arrests are for petty offenses that are not serious enough to be called 'crimes' at all." The commission highlighted the racialized disposition of cases by police and courts: "The Negro will be debited with all the crimes he commits," it found, "while figures for other groups will probably not indicate the full extent of their criminality." It also noted that law enforcement officials had a disposition, "conscious or unconscious, to arrest Negroes more freely than whites, to book them on more serious charges, to convict them more readily, and to give them longer sentences."[27]

Black sociologist Monroe Work reached a similar conclusion after his study of black crime rates in Chicago revealed that the "ratio of arrests for the foreign population and the ratio of arrests for the total white population [was] about the same," while the "proportion of arrest among the negroes [was] about six times as great as the proportion of arrest among the total foreign population."[28] Although the relatively high arrest rates of black

TABLE 2 Arrest rates for delinquency in seven zones of black South Side neighborhoods in 1926

	Zone 1	Zone 2	Zone 3	Zone 4	Zone 5	Zone 6	Zone 7
Rate	42.8	31.4	30	28.8	15.7	9.6	1.4

Source: Data in table from E. Franklin Frazier's study of arrest rates in Chicago. Study data appear in E. Franklin Frazier, *The Negro Family in Chicago*, 371–73.

youths should not be considered a barometer of actual delinquency, they do shed light on why the number of African American children appearing in juvenile court was so high.

Benign Neglect and the Overrepresentation of Black Children in Juvenile Court

At the community level, the overrepresentation of black children in juvenile court was also linked to stereotypes about black criminality, the geographical distribution of community resources, policing patterns, educational and employment discrimination against black youths, the lack of recreation options in black neighborhoods, and the exclusion of African Americans by homes for dependent children.

Employment discrimination against African Americans of all ages increased the likelihood that black children would end up in juvenile court and labeled delinquent. Most labor unions excluded blacks and effectively put skilled jobs out of their reach even when they were qualified to perform the work. When African Americans did find jobs, they received less income than white workers for performing the same type of work.[29] This employment discrimination put black children in a very precarious position by not only reinforcing and aggravating their relative poverty but also increasing their incentive to engage in crimes of poverty.

Prostitution was directly correlated to poverty, employment discrimination, and the city's relocation of vice districts to black neighborhoods.[30] Beginning in 1910, law enforcement officials and Progressive reformers collaborated to "clean up" the city's vice district. Instead of eliminating vice districts, most of these "cleanup" efforts simply relocated them to African American neighborhoods. Not only were African American children forced to live in the most vice-ridden parts of the city, but girls in particular were more likely to be lured into prostitution.[31]

The *Chicago Defender* made note of the relationship between poverty and the number of black children in juvenile court in several articles. A 1921 article, "Cornering the Corner Gang," noted, "66 percent of our boy population comes under the head of the underprivileged class." It explained that poverty and southern origin made African American children—particularly boys—vulnerable to being charged with larceny in juvenile court. "[T]he boy from some rural Southern district, poorly clad, illiterate and unaccustomed to the city way," the article explained, "is best known by the police records and the records to be found in the juvenile court.... He [has] two things open to him—the streets and the poolrooms.... Multiply this boy several thousand, then add the untractable home product, and you have a boy problem on your hands."[32]

A 1928 *Defender* article similarly highlighted the association between black delinquency in the city, poverty, and economic discrimination: "The big city boy with an appetite for apples, but without the pennies to purchase them is hauled into the juvenile court for petty larceny and on the first or second offense is committed to a reformatory.... Our present youth is just as good and generous as the young people of the past." The *Defender* put the bulk of responsibility for black children being treated as delinquents on the juvenile courts: "[I]t is solely the method of handling the present situation that is at fault. Thousands of our Chicago boys are being incarcerated each year for little acts of petty stealing.... Juvenile courts should exercise the means of leading our boys and girls into the right direction and not into resentment and forced association with seasoned criminals.[33]

African American boys who were interviewed in city jails for a 1910 Juvenile Protective Association Study stated that a lack of employment options in the city contributed to their delinquency. The study noted that "From the interviews with all the boys in the jail it was clear that the lack of congenial and remunerative employment had been a determining factor in their tendency to criminality." It also found that "because the colored boys suffered under an additional handicap [their race] and because the opportunities for work are the essentials for all economic progress, the entire investigation had much to do with the question of employment."[34] Earl Moses's 1935 study also revealed that black children's delinquency was tied to the "difficulty of securing jobs.... Even when a job is secured the level of income is so low that life for them is on a minimum subsistence level."[35]

Fourteen-year-old Wesley Harris, one of the first African American children to be processed in juvenile court, was apprehended for a crime of poverty. In 1899, he was arrested by police and brought into court by probation officer William B. Thorpe for stealing ten feet of lead pipe. Wesley, who lived on the South Side, came from a poor home, as his father, a porter who raised him alone, could not find work, and his mother, a "housekeeper," resided in Omaha, Nebraska. According to court records, Wesley and his father had "no income." Wesley was apprehended and brought into court again in 1900 for "stealing 35 cents." Poverty seemed to be the motivating factor in this instance as well, since records indicate that his father still could not find work. It is unclear how juvenile court judge Julian Mack ultimately decided his case.[36]

Harold and Walter, two African American boys who similarly found themselves before Judge Mack in 1906, also illustrate how poverty could incentivize delinquency. Harold and Walter, fourteen-year-old boys who lived just south of downtown, were arrested for larceny. Neither of the boys had access to meaningful employment or the full economic support of both parents, as Harold was an orphan and Walter's father was dead. They were arrested for stealing four revolvers for the purpose of selling them. Judge Mack pronounced both boys "delinquent" and sent them to the John Worthy School for Boys "until age 21 or until sooner discharged." Harold was ultimately transferred to the Illinois Training School for Boys at St. Charles in 1907.[37]

The surge in the number of African American children in juvenile court was also due to the lack of recreation options and community centers for black children. Very few community-based or child-centered Progressive-era reform innovations were located in black neighborhoods. Playgrounds, day nurseries, clinics, public baths, and relief stations were located primarily in native and immigrant white communities. Black working mothers who attempted to enroll their children in day nurseries outside of black neighborhoods found that even the youngest black children were either flat-out denied or lied to about child care availability. White adults and children alike protested the presence of black children on the city's playgrounds.[38]

Black Chicagoans were cognizant of this relative lack of recreational options in their communities and called attention to the problem. Clubwoman Irene McCoy Gaines wrote about this lack of public recreational opportunities for black children in an article in the *Chicago Daily News*: "One may find in the territory known as the black belt, more than 10,000 colored girls without recreational facilities." The Chicago Urban League's 1926 annual report similarly concluded, after conducting a study of recreational spaces in the city, that the "need for a small park in the second and third wards is so apparent that no argument is necessary." The second ward of Chicago, which was 87 percent black at the time, had only seven and a half acres of public parks and playgrounds. This translated to over eight thousand people per acre of playground space even though the ratio for the city as a whole was 508 people per acre.[39] In a 1925 speech before the Wabash Avenue YMCA, Judge Edgar Jones made a similar argument when he stated of African American boys who had appeared in juvenile court during the year, "almost all" reported that they had "no place for recreation except for pool rooms and streets."[40]

The *Chicago Defender*, citing a survey conducted by the Chicago Council of Social Agencies, made a plea for more community resources for children in black neighborhoods. This 1921 survey, which found 93,000 African Americans in the area of the city known as the Black Belt, reported that community resources for children reached only 737 boys. These institutions included the YMCA Lincoln Center, the Urban League, and four churches. Eleven thousand African American boys lived in the Black Belt. The survey also found that "The parks and playgrounds near this territory are used very little by Negro boys. The white boys are said to keep them out."[41]

Institutions for Delinquents as the Default Option for Dependent Black Children

By 1910, at least one-third of the African American children who appeared in court were labeled dependent because they were orphaned, abused, abandoned, or neglected. Abandoned black children, like the baby boy "about the age of two months" who was found in July 1921 on the doorstep of a home on the South Side, became wards of the juvenile court. The court published an adoption notice for the "Unknown Baby Boy" known as "John Doe" in local newspapers. The notice was addressed to the "Unknown Parents" and stated that the child would be declared "dependent" if they did not appear in twenty-one days. The juvenile court ultimately committed the infant to the Illinois Children's Home and Aid Society in the hopes that a black family would adopt him.[42]

Although they made up less than 3 percent of Chicago's child population in 1920, 7 percent of dependent children processed in Cook County Juvenile Court were black.[43] Poor or disabled children whose parents were unable to take care of them also appeared in juvenile court when they were apprehended by probation workers or taken to court by their parents. In 1913, 48 percent of the 378 African American children who appeared in juvenile court were dependent rather than delinquent. The proportion of African American children who appeared in juvenile court because they were dependent ranged between 22 and 45 through the 1920s.

The juvenile court's disposition of dependent black children's cases was often indistinguishable from its disposition of delinquent children's cases. The only institutions that readily admitted dependent black children were facilities for children who had committed crimes. Child welfare services were typically contracted to private and religious homes for dependent children that discriminated against African Americans. This included private maternity homes for pregnant and unmarried girls.[44] This problem persisted until the early 1950s. Rather than mandating that institutions that received public funds for the care of dependent children become more inclusive, the state legislature's response to the intertwined problems of black children's dependency and migration that were aggravated during the Depression was to pass a 1939 law requiring that recipients of relief prove they had resided in the city for three continuous years before receiving relief.[45]

As late as 1945, 38 percent of dependent African American children in social worker Rosetta Holland's study—much like Mary Tripplet, the first black child to appear in juvenile court and whose petition was amended to "delinquent" in 1899—had their juvenile court petitions amended from dependent to "truant" so that they could be placed in the Chicago Parental School.[46]

Sandy Littleton, a blind fourteen-year-old African American girl who was labeled "truant" in juvenile court, is another example of a dependent—and in this case disabled—black child who was criminalized. She first appeared before the juvenile court in 1926 because she did not have "proper parental care and guardianship." The juvenile court committed her to live with a relative, Mrs. Bigsby. She was residing with a sister, Nina, in 1931, when she appeared in juvenile court a second time for being a "truant." According to the Parental School report, two "older girls," ages nineteen and eighteen, "unduly influenced" Sandy and consistently talked her out of going to school. Although Sandy's sister attempted to persuade her to stop hanging out with the girls and missing school, she was unsuccessful. School officials concluded Sandy was "not normal mentally and physically," but her deportment in school was "good." Psychologists at the Institute for Juvenile Research and her school teachers also labeled her "subnormal," with "defective vision." Racial discrimination against dependent and disabled black children in Chicago ultimately led to the juvenile court's decision to ignore evidence of her mental disability and place her in a school for truants—as opposed to an institution for feeble-minded girls.[47]

Racial discrimination and resource deprivation in black communities led thirteen-year-old Frances to be committed to an institution for delinquents after her father sexually assaulted her. After losing her mother at the age of seven, Frances spent six years living in different family members' homes. Shortly after she moved in with her father, he physically and sexually assaulted her. After her father was imprisoned for incest in 1927, Frances became a "dependent" child under the 1899 Juvenile Court Act because she did not have "proper care or guardianship." Judge Mary Bartelme subsequently labeled Frances a "delinquent" and committed her to the Chicago Home for Girls—a public institution for girls who had committed crimes.[48] Like many other black children, the only institution available to give her "proper care or guardianship" was an institution intended for children who had committed crimes.[49]

The juvenile court's commitment of dependent black institutions for delinquents artificially inflated the number of black children labeled "delinquent" in juvenile court and the proportion of children that made up these institutions. Over time, this overrepresentation of black children in juvenile court and conflation of black dependency with delinquency led to a racialized process of criminalization as black children became increasingly associated with delinquency.

Sociologist Earl Moses's 1935 study of black juvenile delinquency in Chicago included the statements of a white probation officer who linked the dearth of community resources for black children with the overrepresentation of black boys at the Training School for Boys at St. Charles. The probation officer observed that African American boys "lack many facilities which make an institutional commitment necessary earlier than would probably otherwise be made." Moses's study was reinforced by the finding in the 1938 study that dependent black girls were more overrepresented than black boys in institutions for dependent children. He cited a chief probation officer who asserted that "The difficulty of providing adequate care for the dependent and neglected colored children constitutes one of the greatest problems with which the court has to deal. The situation is complicated by a lack of resources in the community comparable with those available for white children in the same circumstances. Practically no institutions are to be found in the community to which this group of colored children may be admitted. The situation with reference to community delinquent colored girls is even more desperate."[50] They also noted with particular consternation that African American girls had "frequently been held for periods as long as six months in the Juvenile Detention Home" even after the court had committed them to Geneva.[51]

The Juvenile Detention Home consistently complained about sheltering dependent African American children "out of all proportion to the rest of its population" throughout the 1920s.[52] By 1928, African American children made up 27 percent of inmates at the Training School for Girls at Geneva, 25 percent of inmates at the Juvenile Detention Home and Training School for Boys at St. Charles, 23 percent of those housed at the Chicago Parental School, and 30 percent of those at the Chicago and Cook County School for Boys.[53] A memo from the city's Joint Service Bureau Department of Child Placing of Negro Children—a referral agency that opened in the 1930s to help manage the large number of under-resourced black children—noted that "reformatories are housing unusually large percentages of Negro children where they had to be sent for lack of different facilities."[54]

This trend was not unique to Chicago, however, as a national 1923 study analyzing the distribution of black and white children across various types of institutions found a similar disparity. That study examined juvenile court records and found that 19 percent of white youths were sent to correctional facilities, compared with 50 percent of black youths.[55]

African American children's lives were profoundly affected by their exclusion from homes for dependent children and the lack of community resources for them in Chicago. The juvenile court's disposition of black children's cases reflected and reinforced racial discrimination in Chicago. By amending dependent black children's petitions and committing dependent children to homes intended for children who had committed crimes, the juvenile court played an active role in constructing the image of a "delinquent" child and associated delinquency with blackness. The juvenile court's racially inflected disposition of cases also meant that black boys and girls who were committed to the state training schools for dependent children were on average younger than native and immigrant white children.[56] This was a widespread phenomenon, as a national study conducted in 1930 showed that 84 percent of black boys and 79 percent of black girls in such institutions were under the age of sixteen. In contrast, 79 percent of white boys and 60 percent of white girls in homes for delinquent children were under sixteen.[57]

Black children and their mothers were the least likely of all racial and ethnic groups to be administered mothers' pensions in juvenile court, even though their poverty rates were among the highest. Mother and child, circa 1922. Courtesy of Schomburg Center for Research in Black Culture, New York Public Library.

Mothers' Pensions

Cook County Juvenile Court itself directly perpetuated discrimination against African American children through its administration of mothers' pensions. In 1911, the juvenile court established a "home-based" track as part of its effort to support dependents who found themselves in court. The juvenile court began to administer mothers' pensions based on the principle that the state should not take a child away from his or her mother simply because she was poor, and that a mother who cared for her children was performing a public good in the state's interest. Children—primarily the children of single mothers and widows—who were placed in the home-based track remained at home with their families and were partially supported by state disbursements paid to their mothers.[58]

The proportion of black mothers and children in the home-based track was very small. Although roughly one-third of all dependent children's families received pensions, a minuscule 3 percent of African American children's families received mothers' pensions in 1913. In comparison with European immigrants, this disparity was even starker. The percentages for the families of dependent Austrian, English, Irish, and Russian children were well over 40 percent.[59] In 1921, the proportion of black children receiving pensions increased to 14 percent; however, the proportion of native and immigrant white children receiving pensions remained at about 40 percent.[60] By 1925, when the number of needy African American families in the city had grown as a result of migration, the proportion of black children receiving mothers' pensions reached only 7 percent.[61] Juvenile court workers did not leave any evidence as to why African American children were so starkly underrepresented in the pensions' rolls, particularly since the majority of dependent black children had mothers with whom they could reside. Racist stereotypes about black people and black families' "cultural backwardness" or inability to properly care for their children may have contributed to this disparity.[62]

In addition to being much less likely to have the juvenile court administer pensions to their families, the parents of the few dependent black children who were committed to institutions for dependent children could be ordered to financially support their institutionalized children and be penalized for not doing so. Molly Fairchild found herself in juvenile court in 1912 and 1913 for not having "proper parental care or guardianship." She lived with her mother, and the whereabouts of her father were unknown. The juvenile court committed her to the Illinois Technical School for Colored Girls, a publicly funded Catholic institution that built a separate institution for dependent African American girls. In spite of the father's unknown whereabouts, the court ordered him to pay $7 a month to support her care. The juvenile court also ordered her mother to contribute $3 a month for her care. The court subsequently issued a "Notice of Contempt" because her father—whose whereabouts were still unknown—did not contribute any money to Molly's care. In *People of the State of Illinois v. Jim Fairchild*, Molly's father was sentenced "to the common jail of Cook County . . . there to remain, safely held until the expiration of thirty days." Rather than the juvenile court offering financial support to Molly and her mother in the form of a mother's pension, her mother was ordered to pay and her father sentenced to jail. Unfortunately, Molly's institutional experience did not end with the Illinois Technical School. In 1917, the juvenile court sentenced her to the Training School for Girls at Geneva based on the vague conclusion that she "was and is incorrigible."[63]

Cook County was not unique in having African American children over-represented in juvenile court. Within a decade of "courts for children" springing up across the country, this disparity had become a national phenomenon. The number of black boys labeled delinquent in New York City's Children's Court was three times the rate of native and immigrant whites, while in Baltimore it was more than four times the rate of native and immigrant whites. Midwestern cities such as Dayton and Indianapolis also mirrored Chicago in the racial gap between white and black boys appearing in juvenile court.[64] In 1941, 5 percent of the girls arrested in Los Angeles's South Central region were black even though African American girls comprised less than 3 percent of the child population at the time. Los Angeles resembled the Jim Crow South in the police department's treatment of black girls, as many of the girls were arrested as vagrants while they were looking for jobs.[65] Generally, disproportionality in the numbers of black children being processed in juvenile courts was much higher in northern cities, where the black rate was roughly one and a half times the white rate. This suggests that in Chicago, and many cities across the urban North, juvenile courts began to shape the life trajectory of a significant number of black children.

Black Children and the Juvenile Detention Home

The Juvenile Detention Home, which was established in 1901 by the same group of reformers who advocated for the creation of the city's juvenile court, was an essential part of the juvenile court's function and mission. For the child savers, the incarceration of young children right alongside adults in the city's jails and prisons provided the strongest evidence of the urgent need to create not only a separate court for children but a space where children awaiting their court dates or commitment to other institutions could be housed. The reformers' desire to protect children from the influences of hardened criminals for the purposes of future rehabilitation was a key component of their reform ideal. They helped form the Juvenile Protective

Association, an organized group of Chicago reformers who helped financially and politically execute their child-saving ideals. The JPA helped support the Juvenile Detention Home to aid the juvenile court in executing its function as prescribed under the 1899 Juvenile Court Act.[66]

The Juvenile Detention Home, which initially existed as a separate structure, was incorporated into the same building as the juvenile court in 1906. Juvenile courtrooms existed on the first floor, and the detention home's rooms occupied the second and third floors. African American children had their vital statistics recorded upon entering the detention home. Staff members, who believed the vast majority of children were in a "filthy condition, often having both head and body vermin," gave the children an "antiseptic bath" and physical exams as soon as they entered the premises.[67] Older and "rougher" boys were housed separately from "small and mildly delinquent" boys and dependent children.[68]

Delinquent girls were separated from the delinquent boys and dependent children. Administrators placed the girls on the third floor because they feared delinquent girls would spread sexually transmitted infections to the other children.[69] As the superintendent explained in the home's 1909 annual report, "The delinquent girls are kept apart from and are not permitted to associate with dependent girls. Many of the delinquents are infected with venereal diseases and these are separated from the others. These girls are segregated in two large dormitories, one being set aside for negative, the other, for positive cases. . . . The positive cases receive medical care twice daily, while very severe cases are, if possible, sent to the County Hospital." Administrators justified these actions based on their knowledge that "very few of the delinquent girls were there for reasons other than immorality."

By the 1930s, the Juvenile Detention Home regularly housed as many five to six thousand children per year. Children in the detention home were still required to attend school, and the Chicago Board of Education began to divert financial and human resources to children in the home. In 1926, the Board of Education reported accommodating 4,254 boys and 1,439 girls in class held at the detention home.[70]

Severe overcrowding plagued the Juvenile Detention Home from its earliest years. Because the home functioned as an intermediary institution, its overcrowding was a result of many factors: delayed court hearings, the need for psychiatric evaluations by the Institute for Juvenile Research, and court-mandated hospital evaluations of some of the children.[71] As early as 1910, Superintendent Rachel Blanchard complained in the home's annual report that "long delay[s] in transfers because of the overcrowded condition of the Training Schools to which the delinquent boys and girls are committed by the Court" were a chief source of the problem.

African American children, who had always been overrepresented in the home, were particularly vulnerable to the cramped and unsanitary conditions that accompanied overcrowding. The insufficient resources for dependent black children in Chicago was a key source of the problem of overcrowding in the institution. Superintendent Blanchard also noted in the 1910 report that the dearth of institutional resources for dependent black girls in particular aggravated overcrowding when she stated, "we feel particularly the need of such institutions for colored girls, as adequate school provision for them is lacking."[72] Probation and parole officers from Earl Moses's 1936 study also noted with particular consternation that African American girls had "frequently been held for periods as long as six months in the Juvenile Detention Home" even after the court had committed them to Geneva. African American boys waiting to be transferred to the Illinois Training School for Boys at St. Charles were also more likely to stay in juvenile detention for several months. In contrast, native and immigrant white children who had been committed to Geneva and St. Charles were held "one to three weeks."[73]

Black Children and the Institute for Juvenile Research

The Institute for Juvenile Research, like the Juvenile Detention Home, was founded by Progressive-era child savers. For reformers, it was a critical part of the rehabilitative vison they had for the many children who walked in to Cook County Juvenile Court. IJR was a child-study clinic that employed psychiatrists, psychologists, and physicians who studied and treated children. Named the Juvenile Psychopathic Institute when it opened in 1909, it initially sought to scientifically determine the cause of delinquency in individual children by evaluating, studying, treating, and supervising children who found themselves before the juvenile court. The very emergence of IJR in the realm of juvenile justice was a physical manifestation of Progressive reformers' reliance on "scientific" and "objective" data.[74]

Before receiving any treatment at IJR, the staff gave the children physical examinations and took their social histories. After the examinations, staff members made a diagnosis and recommended a method of treatment.[75] When "Louis L." was referred to IJR by a social worker who was friends with his mother, psychologists completed a detailed survey of his family and background. Louis was a thirteen-year-old African American boy whose "mother had complained that the boy showed no love towards her." IJR's psychologists concluded that Louis had "dull intelligence." They also described him as a "slow, methodical, retarded effeminate adolescent" even though he was "doing well in school." The diagnostic staff also felt that Louis's mother was to blame for some of his disturbances, as there was "an element of seduction on the part of the mother of which she was unaware." They also believed that part of the reason Louis's mother "was not aware of his being as interested in boys" was that she suffered an Oedipus complex in regards to her son. Louis did not take full advantage of IJR's (unspecified) treatment plan, however, because his mother ultimately decided to pull him out.[76]

African American children were well represented among children seen at IJR. For example, 8 percent of children treated at IJR between 1920 and 1930 were African American.[77] Most African American children were examined by IJR staff members as a result of their encounter with the juvenile court or other juvenile justice institutions.

School referrals were another primary means through which black children arrived at IJR.[78] The disturbing case of an anonymous "seven year old colored girl," who was mentioned in social worker Katherine Auer's 1938 study of the institute, is a good example of this. The girl, who was a victim of sexual assault, was referred to IJR "because of disobedience in school, sleeping and eating difficulties and masturbation." IJR psychologists noted that the "child had been taught to masturbate by a fifteen-year-old boy who later raped her." It is not clear what, if any, treatment IJR offered her. Her IJR case workers did recommend, however, that she be placed in a foster home "where there are no boys and . . . the foster parents would not be too emotional about her masturbation."[79]

For a variety of reasons, African American families were less likely than other racial and ethnic groups to take their children directly to IJR. As black psychologist Winifred Link suggested in her 1936 study of black children who were patients at IJR, a mistrust of "any service offered to them by white people, especially a psychological service" was a disincentive for black parents to seek out the institute's services. More specifically, Link argued, African Americans felt "keenly that their race has been exploited by psychologists who used test results to prove something about the inferiority of Negro children. They are slow to seek such a service, doubting if their children will receive an impartial study."[80] On the flip side, the institute, like many other child guidance clinics, found black families particularly "uncooperative" and difficult to work with because they were less likely to follow the advice given in clinics.[81]

Black parents' mistrust of the institute and reticence to have their children undergo psychological examinations are understandable. Beginning in the early twentieth century, the results of intelligence tests—often biased and methodologically unsound exams administered by professionals in the field of psychology—became one of the foremost markers of racial difference. Alongside new notions of black criminality in spaces across the urban North, statistics regarding black intelligence—particularly the intelligence of African American children—began to be held up as proof of black inferiority.[82]

In addition to a general mistrust of psychological services, economic realities made African American families less able to take advantage of the institute's treatment plans. Working mothers and fathers found it difficult to arrange and attend the frequent daytime meetings prescribed by the plan. For social workers such as Elizabeth Giddings, African American parents' lack of compliance with the treatment plans prescribed to their children stemmed from the reality that these parents were "far better able to visualize than the psychiatrist or social worker the fruitlessness of undertaking treatment." She noted that parents found "little value in the suggestion that a certain doctor might talk to the child" when they were well aware that "the dearth of institutions" available to black children set their children up for unique challenges. African American parents recognized that many of the perceived behavioral problems school administrators and other institutional actors identified were rooted not so much in a dysfunctional individual psyche that IJR workers sought to fix but in the racial and economic structural inequalities that shaped their experience. Louis L.'s mother, for example, said she pulled him out of treatment because she believed his behavior improved after she found a recreational space in their community for him to utilize.[83]

Black Children and the Chicago Parental School

Cook County Juvenile Court was a critical component of the state's enforcement of compulsory school attendance laws. Illinois's compulsory education law mandated that all children under the age of sixteen attend a public or private school. The Parental School Law, which the state legislature passed on July 1, 1900, created a boarding home for truant children. The school, which opened its doors on the north side of the city in January 1902, was initially for males only. The court committed thirteen boys there during its first year. The Parental School fell under the organizational umbrella of the Board of Education and was administratively treated like a city public school.[84]

Although the Parental School was intended to be used as a last resort for truant children under sixteen who failed to respond to correction and treatment, by 1920 as many as three-quarters of children labeled truant in juvenile court were committed there.[85] Between 1912 and 1913, 633 truant cases were heard in juvenile court. A total of 472 of these boys were committed to the Parental School, ninety-nine were released on probation, and sixteen had their petitions recategorized as dependent cases. Roughly three hundred boys would be held in the institution at a given time. They would stay in the school anywhere from a few weeks to several months.[86]

In 1919, the Board of Education began operating a girls' branch of the Parental School in an old school building on the North Side. The girls' branch was eventually relocated to another North Side building in December 1925. Even though the boys' and girls' schools were located in different buildings, they were referred to collectively as the Chicago Parental School.[87]

Children who were habitual truants or labeled as "problem children" in school found themselves in Cook County Juvenile Court. Victor Shields, a twelve-year-old African American who attended Chicago's Dante School, was hauled into court because his principal said his behavior was "very bad" and accused him of being a "habitual truant." In truant officer G. R. Wallace's opinion, Victor's mother, who was intoxicated on one of his home visits, created a "poor home and environment" that caused his behavior to become "beyond the control of his parents." The juvenile court committed Victor to the Parental School in 1926.[88]

The juvenile court began committing African American children to the Parental School as soon as it opened. By 1906, thirteen out of the 234 boys the juvenile court committed to Chicago Parental School, or 5 percent, were black. At that time, African Americans made up less than 3 percent of the city's population. The percentage of African American boys in the institution remained steady at roughly 5 percent through 1910.[89] As black migration into the city began to pick up during the world wars, the disproportionate numbers of African American children in the institution, just like in the juvenile court and Juvenile Detention Home, increased. By 1920, 15 percent of children in the Parental School were black. By 1925, the proportion of black children had increased to 25 percent.[90]

The number of black children committed to Chicago Parental School was not directly proportional to the number of black children who had been labeled truants or problem children in juvenile court. Because of racial discrimination in public and private homes for dependent children, and the inability of black-owned homes for dependent children to accommodate the increasing number of dependent children on their own, juvenile court officials were often forced to use Chicago Parental School as a dumping ground for black children. Similar to the state training schools in Geneva and St. Charles, the Parental School housed a significant number of poor and dependent African American children who did not belong there.

Juvenile court workers often amended black children's dependent petitions to truant petitions so that they would be eligible for admission to Chicago Parental School. In 1945, for example, social worker Rosetta Holland's examination of one hundred black children's juvenile court cases revealed that thirty-eight dependent children's cases in the sample had been reclassified as truant cases so that the juvenile court could commit the children to Chicago Parental School. The study also revealed that dependent children who had migrated with their parents from the South were particularly vulnerable to being committed to Chicago Parental School even though they had not violated any compulsory education laws. Twenty-four out of thirty-eight of the children's parents were "born and reared" in such states as Mississippi, South Carolina, Georgia, and Louisiana.[91]

Although the Chicago Parental School was not intended to be a punitive institution, and children committed there were not "delinquent" children but rather "truants," the commitment of dependent black children to the school was not an innocuous practice. Children who were dependent in fact but labeled "truant" were essentially branded with a legal term reserved for "problem children" in school, as children who violated state law by not attending school. Beyond being labeled as a type of "problem," children committed to the Parental School were necessarily subjected to the same vulnerabilities other children in confinement faced.

The *Chicago Defender* featured a story about the physical torture and abuse in the boys' branch of the school in 1923. The high number of black boys in the school made the scandal of particular interest to the *Chicago Defender*. The article reported that boys who testified in a criminal court hearing on September 1 told "shocking stories of inhuman brutality inflicted upon pupils of the Parental school." Eleven boys, four of whom were black, shared stories in court about "how badly they and others had been beaten and tortured almost to death and then placed in the guardroom . . . for days until their battered, bruised, discolored faces should again take on a normal appearance."[92]

Racially biased interpretations of children's behavior in schools functioned as an antecedent to the late twentieth-century "school to prison pipeline" by funneling black children into juvenile court and initiating a cascade of institutional interventions in their lives. In addition to the lack of public and private city resources for dependent children, teachers' and principals' racial biases contributed to the disproportionate number of black children in Chicago Parental School. Teachers and principals initiated the bulk of school referrals to juvenile court, giving them an incredible amount of power over the children in their care.

Teachers were not immune from the impact of a culture that consistently cast black children outside the bounds of childhood, conflated blackness with criminality, and perpetuated the notion that blacks were intellectually inferior to all other races. A 1936 study on school referrals to IJR found that the race of African American students' teachers influenced the way in which the students were perceived. "Indeed, the same behavior," social worker Rose Long noted in the study, "was sometimes construed by one teacher as indicating delinquent tendencies and by another as showing high spirits and promising talents." She used the case of a fifteen-year-old boy to illustrate her point:

A fifteen-year-old Negro boy, attending a school for truants, was referred to the Clinic by his white teacher with the comment that he was defiant, insolent, talked back when lessons were assigned, and was abusive or haughty when reprimanded, caused disturbances by drawing obscene pictures, by affecting a Charlie Chaplin walk, and by changing the pitch of his voice while reading. . . . The boy was changed to a class with a Negro teacher. To this teacher the boy presented no problems. In fact, she found him responding well to special help in reading. The art teacher . . . reported that the boy had real talent in drawing. . . . Instead of being annoyed by his impersonations she remarked that it would be wonderful to laugh and sing in the carefree manner he did.[93]

A 1940 study of African American girls in the juvenile court of Los Angeles also suggested that white teachers' perceptions of black children could lead to court referrals. The study noted that teachers frequently committed African American girls for having a "'perverse' attitude in school" and for engaging in "disruptive behavior."[94]

Some of Cook County Juvenile Court's existing case records include the Board of Education's supporting documents for truant petitions. These documents include a "History of the Case" and "Parental School Petition," revealing why some schools referred some children to juvenile court. Harold Cobbs, for example, a thirteen-year-old African American boy from Atlanta who was a student at the John Farren School, was referred to juvenile court by his teacher in 1926 because of "behavioral problems." His teacher indicated his "best work" was in arithmetic but that he was "incorrigible," "very persistently unruly," "dull," "energetic," and "ill-tempered." The superintendent of the school stated, "He loses control of himself and causes a great disturbance. His teacher wishes to have him brought before the Judge." As a result of Harold's teacher and principal referring him to juvenile court, he was committed—against his parents' consent—to the Chicago Parental School.[95]

These cases illustrate how many African American children's experiences in juvenile court were shaped by a relationship—which increasingly became symbiotic over time—between the state's compulsory education laws, schools, the juvenile court, and Chicago Parental School. Black children and their families, particularly those who were poor or southern migrants, were vulnerable to being caught in the institutional web of the Board of Education and juvenile court. The increasing mismatch between the cultural construct of the vulnerable, malleable, poor, and immigrant white child that had inspired the city's child-saving movement and the rising number of black children—who were constructed as insensate, un-malleable, and threatening beings prone to criminality—led to the unraveling of the legal principles on which the Cook County Juvenile Court had been predicated.

A Punitive Transition: Susie Lattimore and the Abandonment of the Rehabilitative Ideal

The Illinois General Assembly's passage of the Juvenile Court Act of 1899 marked the political ascension of the notion that children—because of their vulnerability, inherent innocence, and potential to be rehabilitated—needed a separate nonadversarial court. The Juvenile Court Act gave the court jurisdiction over boys under seventeen and girls under eighteen. However, the state constitution followed common law tradition and fixed the age of criminal responsibility at ten years. In effect, after the passage of the 1899 act, the juvenile court and criminal court had concurrent jurisdiction over persons under the age of eighteen.

The rise of Prohibition fueled organized crime, and the notoriety of well-known Chicago gangsters like Al Capone, the Great Depression, labor unrest, and continuing racial hostility surrounding migration led to a general sense of unrest in Chicago by the 1930s. It was the disproportionate number of black children in juvenile court and the artificial inflation of the number of black children sent to homes for delinquent children, however, that racialized delinquency and helped fuel a public hysteria over "dangerous" children in the juvenile justice system. An African American minister who was interviewed by black sociologist St. Clair Drake recounted a statement white city officials in 1931 made about crime among black youths: "They told me that the Negro youth of Chicago were committing more crimes than ever in the history of Chicago."[96]

In addition, the muckraking journalism that increased public support for the notion that children were inherently innocent and needed a separate court system at the turn of the century had shifted by 1930. The current flowed in the opposite direction, as the city's major newspapers paid new attention to black crime and advocated a more punitive stance to children in court. The *Chicago Tribune* published several articles squarely opposed to the juvenile court. One article, "Social Workers Defend Young Toughs," criticized the "citizens committee on the juvenile court" for "asking the legislature to take jurisdiction of even the most hardened young criminals away from the Criminal court and hand it over exclusively to the juvenile court."[97] As the image in the public mind of the type of child that would be in juvenile court transformed because of migration and demographic change, the popular and political sentiments that had made the juvenile court movement viable during the Progressive era began to wane.[98]

In 1935, the chief justice of Cook County's Criminal Court, Dennis Sullivan, launched a campaign to wrest power over children accused of crimes from the juvenile court so that all of their cases would be heard in criminal court. A *Chicago Tribune* article noted that Judge Sullivan "criticized the juvenile court, asserting that it attempted to take jurisdiction of young offenders, no matter how hardened and criminal minded they were," and gave these offenders such "light sentences" that they could pursue their "criminal careers" upon release.[99] Judge Sullivan began agitating for a series of amendments to the Juvenile Court Act that would give adult criminal court judges not only sole jurisdiction over children age ten and above but also the right to sentence them to adult correctional institutions. He argued, "The outdated Juvenile Court Act permits highly dangerous gunmen and thieves, or even murderers, to be accorded leniency intended only for bad boys or bad girls who have committed no serious crime and are not habitual offenders. The act is clearly in conflict with the legal rights of the criminal court." The JPA worked tirelessly to defeat the amendment, and as a result Judge Sullivan's efforts to amend the Juvenile Court Act did not succeed. Susie Lattimore, a fifteen-year-old African American girl accused of murder, had the misfortune of having her case assigned to Judge Sullivan that same year, and Sullivan successfully used her case to buttress his arguments in his campaign against the juvenile court's jurisdiction.[100]

Susie Lattimore, the youngest of seven children, migrated to the city with her family from Atlanta, Georgia, when she was four. Like many migrant black families whose poverty was exacerbated because of the Depression, the Lattimores struggled financially while her father was unable to find suitable employment for five years. On the night of February 23, 1935, Susie, age fifteen, stabbed sixteen-year-old Ruth Robinson during a fight at a tavern. The *Chicago Defender* described the fight as a rivalry "for the affections of a married man." During her trial, Susie described the fight this way: "One night we were in the beer tavern on Racine and she did not want me to dance with her boyfriend and she came and pushed me away from him and she jerked him." Susie then asked to borrow a knife from a friend at the tavern "just in case" and proceeded to fight with Ruth. Ruth died that night as a result of a stab wound to her chest.[101]

After her arrest, Susie was taken to juvenile court and, following routine procedure, taken to the Institute for Juvenile Research to be examined by a psychologist. The psychologist concluded that she was a "high grade mental defective" with a mental age of only ten years and one month, despite her chronological age of fifteen. On the basis of this finding, IJR recommended that the juvenile court commit her to Dixon State Hospital for psychiatric treatment.

Franck Bicek, presiding judge of the juvenile court, ignored the institute's recommendations and transferred Susie's case to criminal court instead, where she pleaded not guilty and waived her right to a criminal trial. Her attorney, public defender Benjamin Bacharach, contended that the criminal court did not have the jurisdiction to try her because the juvenile court had already declared her delinquent. He also filed a motion to transfer her case back to juvenile court.[102] Susie then appeared before Judge Sullivan, who rejected her attorney's motion to transfer her case and found her guilty of first-degree murder. Judge Sullivan then awarded Susie the penultimate sentence of twenty-five years at the Illinois State Reformatory for adult women in Dwight, Illinois.[103] Local newspapers such as the *Chicago Tribune*, which followed the case closely, largely sided with Judge Sullivan and referred to Susie as a "colored murderess" and "juvenile court graduate" even though this was the first time she had appeared before the court.[104]

Her lawyer ultimately appealed the case to the Illinois Supreme Court. For unknown—but perhaps political—reasons, the state's attorney provided the court with an incomplete record of Susie's trial. The incomplete record allowed the state's justices to create an issue by behaving as if the juvenile court contested Susie's transfer to the adult criminal justice system, even though it never had. This allowed the judges to decide the then controversial issue of concurrent jurisdiction between the juvenile and criminal courts.

The "sole question" on appeal, then, was "whether the defendant, a ward of the juvenile court, who had been indicted for murder, can on such an indictment be tried in the criminal court without the consent of the juvenile court." The Illinois Supreme Court overturned the 1926 *People v. Fitzgerald* decision, which had held that the juvenile and criminal court did, indeed, have concurrent jurisdiction over persons under eighteen. In *People v. Lattimore*, the Supreme Court ruled that the criminal court had final jurisdiction over any child age ten or above. The court explained that the state constitution, which granted criminal courts jurisdiction over persons above the age of criminal responsibility, could not be divested of power by an "inferior court" created by an act of the legislature. The court, occluding the intent of the drafters of the Juvenile Court Act, concluded that "by no stretch of the imagination" was it conceivable that the legislature had intended to give the juvenile court such power and turn the juvenile court "into a haven of refuge where a delinquent child of the age recognized by the law as capable of committing a crime should be immune for punishment for violation of the criminal laws of the State."

This stance was ironic, because the statute that gave birth to the juvenile court was formally titled "Act to regulate the treatment and control of dependent, neglected and delinquent children," a title that on its face was intended to include "delinquent" children. Progressive reformers and state legislators who signed the act into law fully intended that the juvenile court have original—if not exclusive—jurisdiction over all children.[105]

A year later, the JPA made an unsuccessful attempt to get around *Lattimore* with an amendment to the Juvenile Court Act. Some JPA members proposed that there be "an amendment to the criminal code" raising the age of criminal responsibility from ten years to sixteen years of age. The JPA and other child advocates felt that such an amendment was "necessary because of the Supreme Court decision in 1935 . . . which definitely placed the trial of children in criminal court."[106]

In 1938, the JPA tried to soften the blow of *Lattimore* again by proposing an amendment to the Juvenile Court Act that would increase the age limit of children who could be tried in juvenile court. Chief Justice Cornelius Harrington of the Criminal Court and state attorney's office "expressed strong opposition" to the proposed amendment.[107] This attempt to get around the 1935 decision also failed, however, as there was not enough political will to reconstruct the image of a vulnerable child in need of "saving." *People v. Lattimore* continued to inform the handling of juvenile delinquents in Illinois through the twentieth century.

People v. Lattimore, which rejected the notion of children's inherent innocence and malleability—principles the juvenile court movement had been built on—crystallized the state's transition to a more punitive juvenile justice system. In effect, Susie Lattimore's case gave the Cook County state's attorney the sole authority to prosecute any child he chose in criminal court and sentence him or her to an adult penitentiary. *Lattimore* also gave prosecutors an incredible amount of discretion, as they could decide which children would be tried as adults. This provided another means through which racial biases against blacks could thrive in the justice system. Four years after *Lattimore*, another watershed decision marked how far the political mood had shifted since the General Assembly passed the Juvenile Court Act in 1899. Spurred by local concerns over "dangerous" youths of a different "racial stock" increasingly filling the Illinois State Training School for Boys at St. Charles, the state legislature approved the construction of the state's first maximum-security prison for boys in Sheridan, Illinois, in 1939.[108]

Lattimore began a precedent for the treatment of many black children who found themselves in Cook County's juvenile—and now adult criminal—justice systems. It is not coincidental that the watershed decision that marked the beginning of the state's more punitive treatment toward youthful offenders, and the divestment of the juvenile court of its primary jurisdiction over children, involved the case of an African American girl. The *Lattimore* decision is an important marker and manifestation of the way in which perceptions about children inhabiting Cook County's juvenile justice system had changed.

Notions of juvenile justice, childhood innocence, and rehabilitation have always been contested. When Progressive reformers successfully advocated for and brought about the existence of a juvenile court, the children whom reformers and laypeople imagined would fill the court were children they believed had the potential to be reformed. Juvenile justice was created for

poor native and immigrant white children, who in spite of their perceiv
flaws were viewed as pliable beings deserving of protection. African Ame
ican children, in contrast, had a long history of being constructed outsic
the bounds of childhood innocence and purity. As the numbers of black
children in Cook County Juvenile Court skyrocketed as a result of both the
Great Migration and private child welfare agencies' discrimination against
dependent black children, the notion that white children alone—the intended beneficiaries of the rehabilitative ideal—were, in fact, the beneficiaries was disrupted. The demographic changes that led to an increasing
presence of black children in juvenile court and the *Lattimore* decision
changed the relationship children had with the justice system. Rather than
entering the justice system for help and rehabilitation, children accused of
committing crimes would now enter a system rooted in retribution.

The adaptation of state institutions for delinquent children at Geneva
and St. Charles to the mere presence of black children also played a critical
role in the eventual dismantling of the rehabilitative ideal and the juvenile
justice system's transition to a more punitive system. For black children
in Chicago, youthfulness—far from being a marker of purity or inspiring
protection—subjected them to particular institutional, social, and economic
vulnerabilities that shaped their encounter with the justice system. There,
too, blackness overrode the potential protections their legal status as "child"
could have bought them.

CHAPTER THREE

Constructing a Black Female Delinquent

Race, Gender, and the Criminalization of
African American Girls at the Illinois Training
School for Girls at Geneva

The inhumanely stifling and overcrowded state of Lincoln Cottage, the only residence for African American girls at the Illinois Training School for Girls at Geneva, must have compounded the devastation sixteen-year-old Mary Ellen felt when the juvenile court sent her there in 1928. After quarrelling with her father, Mary Ellen made the fateful decision to flee her home and seek solace with thirty-eight-year-old Perry Daniels, who took advantage of her vulnerability when he invited her to his home. Daniels raped and imprisoned Mary in his home until her father and a police officer rescued her six days later. Like a number of African American girls in Chicago who were unfairly labeled "sex delinquents" in juvenile court after they had been sexually assaulted, Mary was sent over fifty miles away from her home to the Illinois Training School for Girls (hereinafter "Geneva"). After being screened for a sexually transmitted infection and quarantined like other new admits so that the school could ensure she did not have an infectious disease, she was relegated to Lincoln Cottage. Even though Lincoln Cottage was built to house no more than thirty-two girls, and there were vacancies in other cottages, staff members packed over sixty African American girls into the residence.[1] Geneva was an outgrowth of the child-saving movement, and staff members were generally guided by their belief in the innocence and rehabilitative potential of their charges. Mary and other African American girls were placed at the margins of those commitments, however.

Intersecting notions of race, gender, and sexuality shaped reformers, and practitioners' understandings and applications of the rehabilitative ideal. African American girls at Geneva were blamed for the interracial sexual relationships abhorred by staff members and professionals and were considered the most violent girls in the institution. Staff members, social scientists, medical professionals, and lawmakers, although they had different agendas and did not all speak with the same voice, contributed to a milieu that fostered the exclusion of African American girls at Geneva from notions of innocence and femininity. More important, they participated in the construction of a race-specific image of female delinquency. Unlike the image of a fixable, inherently innocent delinquent that spurred the child-saving movement and brought all persons under the age of eighteen into the protective and rehabilitative folds of the juvenile justice system, images of African American girls connoted an inherently deviant, unfixable, and dangerous delinquent whose negative influences resulted in the contamination of other children in the institution.

Within this milieu, a distinction between girls was made based on race, and African American girls' delinquency was viewed as a symptom of their innate and unfixable deficits. This chapter, which begins in 1893, when Geneva opened, and extends beyond the Progressive era through World War II, is centered on African American girls' experiences in the institution within the context of constructions of delinquency and black girlhood in the larger society. The first part of this chapter contextualizes the institutional environment African American girls found themselves in by introducing Geneva, describes the different reasons girls were committed to the institution, and provides a glimpse into the girls' daily lives. The next sections reveal the ways in which Geneva staff members' perceptions of African American girls, which were filtered by popular intersecting notions of race and gender, contributed to the formation of a race-specific construct of delinquency. This chapter also details black Chicago's rejection of and agitation against this racialized construction of delinquency.

Reforming "Immoral" Girls: Daily Life and Surveillance at the Training School for Girls

Reformers began exerting a substantial amount of effort in solving what later became known as the "girl problem" in the late nineteenth and early twentieth centuries. Female adolescents' sexuality became the focus of intense public anxiety and the target of new reform and control. The phrase "the girl problem" encapsulated reformers' anxieties surrounding the generational tensions occasioned by young women and girls' sexual and reproductive behavior, less conservative style of dress, and the increasing economic and sexual exploitation of young women and girls in newly industrialized cities. The new autonomy of young women in urban areas became a source of alarm for experts and reformers.[2]

In the first stage of reform efforts, which began in the 1880s, women reformers worked to criminalize sex with young girls by raising the age of consent. These efforts were framed as protective, as they challenged the widespread perception of "fallen women" as depraved and dangerous by portraying them as victims of male lust and exploitation. During this period, reformatories and maternity homes to redeem and reclaim these "fallen women" began to spring up around the country. During the Progressive era, a second stage of reform evolved, focusing on the familial, social, and economic roots of "immorality" among young women. Adolescence began to be seen as a distinct stage of development characterized by a crisis of identity, increased sexuality, and antisocial conduct. Reformers engaged in a series of preventative and protective reforms to control young women's and girls' behavior. In both stages of reform, institutions and the strong arm of the law were used as part of reformers' attempts to "fix" and control young women and girls. During the Progressive era, however, juvenile courts, which emerged as a result of reformers' arguments that children (in most states persons under the age of eighteen) were inherently innocent and should be treated differently than adults, became another means through which girls' behavior, particularly their sexuality, could be controlled. Delinquent girls' experiences of these reform movements reflected reformers' and professionals' varied and vacillating views about them, as there were always competing conceptions of female delinquency.[3]

These institutional and legal reforms to control young women and girls' behaviors revealed that the notion of a "girl problem" was racialized. Many experts and reformers focused on poor and immigrant girls of European descent because they believed there was, in fact, a "problem"—a deviation from a normal and ideal standard of behavior that could be addressed through legal reforms and institutions. Antisocial conduct, promiscuity, and illegitimacy were not seen as behaviors that were outside the norm for African American girls, however. The Mann Act of 1910 was intended to protect young white women and girls from sexual exploitation by adult men. Reformers' advocacy was inspired not by the long-standing and rampant sexual abuse of black women and girls at the hands of white men in domestic spaces but by concern about native white and European immigrant girls. The act made it a federal crime to transport women and girls from across state lines "for the purpose of prostitution or debauchery, or for any other immoral purpose."[4] The purpose of the act was to prevent "white slave traffic" and protect young white women.[5] The modification of the word "slave" with "white" was meant to distinguish the trade from black slavery and thus rendered the sexual abuse and trafficking of black girls and women both normal and invisible.[6]

African American girls at the Illinois State Training School for Girls at Geneva were caught up in the milieu of this implicitly racialized understanding of protection and delinquency. Geneva, founded as the State Home for Juvenile Offenders (an outgrowth of the first reform movement), opened its doors in December 1893. Its original purpose was to protect young girls from the perils of city life, as well as from their own sexuality. Once Geneva began working hand in hand with Chicago's juvenile court, it became integrated into the new juvenile justice system's ideological and administrative program. State officials renamed the Juvenile Home for Female Offenders the Illinois State Training School for Girls at Geneva in 1901 to emphasize its new rehabilitative focus. Although Geneva began with only one building, by 1925 it boasted 240 acres of land and thirty buildings.[7]

The majority of girls at Geneva were committed for "sex delinquency," which was also referred to in court records as "incorrigibility" or "immorality." These labels were applied to girls who violated middle-class notions of female propriety because they associated with men or engaged in any type of sexual behavior with them.[8] The broad definitions of the terms allowed girls to be brought before Cook County's Juvenile Court for behaviors ranging from accepting a ride from a male stranger, to flirting, standing on a street corner, or having sex.[9] In 1912, Progressive reformer Sophonisba Breckenridge estimated after her visit to Geneva that 80 percent of the girls were sent there for sexual "immorality," whereas social scientist Beth Corman estimated that the proportion was closer to 85 percent in 1923. The proportion of girls committed to the school for sex delinquency decreased steadily throughout the period but never reached below 50 percent. A 1953 survey conducted by the Illinois Youth Council found that 54 percent were sex delinquents.[10]

From its inception, the demographic profile of girls at Geneva was diverse in age, race, and ethnicity. Between 1893 and 1950, most of the girls at Geneva typically fell between the ages of thirteen and eighteen, although it was not uncommon to have girls as young as nine or as old as twenty-one there. The majority of girls at the institution, who came from various cities around the state, were American-born whites or European immigrants.[11] There is no evidence that girls of a race other than black or white resided at Geneva during this period.

Of the fifty-nine girls present at the institution when it first opened, institutional reports indicate that ten were African American. The total number of girls at the institution increased steadily over the years. In 1920, Geneva housed a total average of 450 girls and by 1950 as many as 529 girls. The total number of girls at the institution usually ranged between 250 and 523.[12] On a daily basis between 1896 and 1920, African American girls made up 10 to 15 percent of the population. Their percentage steadily increased during the 1920s, forming about 20 percent in 1920 and 35 percent in 1928, even though African Americans made up only 1 to 2 percent of Illinois's population at the time. In "A Study of Negro Girls Committed to the Geneva State Reformatory," Joyce Letty Grossberg revealed that although Census Bureau statistics indicated that African American girls made up no more than 5 percent of girls in Chicago between the ages fifteen and nineteen, they comprised a staggering 75 percent of the girls Cook County Juvenile Court sent to Geneva between 1937 and 1938. A larger 1949 study of the population in state institutions found that 50 percent of all Cook County girls the juvenile court sent to Geneva were black.[13]

Although this steady increase in the number of African American girls certainly reflects the impact of the Great Migration, their stark overrepresentation in the number of girls both sent there by the juvenile court and among Geneva's inmates is also a function of the lack of other institutional options for pregnant, poor, sick, neglected, and abused dependent girls in Chicago. The court committed girls like Mildred Davis, a "very thin" seventeen-year-old African American girl who was "pregnant out of wedlock for the first time" and "severely deprived both emotionally and materially" as a "sex delinquent" because of this dearth of resources. Her parole officer, who documented in her report that Mildred desired "very much to return to her mother's house" and that her mother wanted Mildred home as well, ultimately decided to parole her to Provident Hospital when Mildred was eight months pregnant.[14] Between 1937 and 1938, for example, juvenile court records indicate that forty-nine of the seventy African Americans girls committed to Geneva—over two-thirds of the girls—were sent there because they were in need of "medical attention." The majority of the other girls, however, were sent there after being labeled sex delinquents or truants in juvenile court. Eight of the African American girls in the study were pregnant, thirty-eight were suffering from some sort of sexually transmitted infection, and three were listed as having a mental disability. The lack of institutional resources for African American girls in Chicago had an impact on the demographic age range of girls in Geneva. Black girls were on average one and a half years younger than white girls.[15]

Geneva's staff members' and administrators' primary rehabilitative goal was "to help correct" and prepare the girls for the "re-adjustment as citi-

Group photo of girls at the Illinois Training School for Girls at Geneva, circa 1905.
Courtesy of the Geneva Historical Society.

zens" by "educating the girls to a high standard of womanhood." They utilized the family-style cottage system to make the institution less prison-like
and to give the residences a "home-like atmosphere." By placing a house
mother, managing matron, and housekeeping matron in each cottage, Geneva's trustees hoped to provide the girls with "reputable" examples of womanhood by fostering a "mothering spirit" and "enabling some of the girls to
enjoy for the first time . . . the advantages of a home and its influence." The
girls were trained in the domestic arts and were responsible for helping with
the housework and making their own stockings and clothing. Vocational
training, which boasted "modern and efficient equipment" and certifica-
tion from the State Department of Registration and Education, included
courses in "beauty culture," cooking, and sewing.[16]

Geneva administrators instituted a "cottage plan" to create a home-like
atmosphere to comfort the girls, many of whom were "overwhelmed with
grief because of separation from their home and mother." Under the plan,
fifteen to thirty girls were to live in a cottage, which a 1946 Department of
Welfare report described as being "reminiscent of a southern planta-
tion house," along with a matron and two assistants. Early administrators

envisioned each girl having her own room with a bed, chair, nightstand, and mirror. The girls were placed in the cottages "according to their age, ability and type" and cooked and prepared their own meals. Because staff members and administrators believed the "majority of these girls came to Geneva in a bad condition mentally, morally, and physically," their rehabilitative aim was "to build them up and in every way to help them to become good, self-supporting women."[17]

Resident physicians, psychiatrists, psychologists, counselors, and nurses determined each girl's rehabilitative program. After arriving at the institution, each girl was put in isolation, screened for sexually transmitted infections, given an IQ test, psychologically evaluated, and assigned a counselor.[18] On average, African American girls were judged to be worse than white native and immigrant girls on almost every conceivable test administered at the institution. For example, researchers concluded that African American girls at Geneva had a more disorganized family structure than white girls as well as parents who were younger at birth, and researchers perceived a lack of "affection" between parent and child.[19] As soon as African American girls crossed Geneva's doorsteps, admissions tests reinforced the notion that they were more sexually promiscuous and diseased than their white counterparts, as their rates of pregnancy and venereal disease were higher than those of white girls. These relatively high numbers of African American girls who needed medical treatment were linked to racial discrimination and a lack of available institutional care for them in Chicago.[20]

Once a juvenile court judge decided to sentence a girl to Geneva, she was not sentenced for a specific length of time. Rather, she was given an indeterminate sentence, which tasked administrators and staff with making individual determinations of whether and when each girl would be released. Girls could be committed up to the age of eighteen and held at Geneva until age twenty-one. Girls who were released were promptly put on parole for a length of time that was determined by their parole officer. Girls who, like Mildred Davis and Mary Ellen, were committed to Geneva because they happened to be poor, pregnant, or sexually assaulted were also put on parole upon being released from the institution. Pregnant girls who were not released on parole before the birth of their babies were brought back to the school and expected to take an active part of school life while the baby was kept in a hospital nursery on the grounds. They were allowed to keep their babies with them for eight months. After that, the girl decided whether she wanted the baby placed with family members or in foster care.[21]

Many girls, as well as their parents, attempted to influence how long they stayed at Geneva and shape the nature of their parole. The juvenile court committed Flora Matthews, a fifteen-year-old married transplant from Georgia, to Geneva in July 1931 for being "incorrigible." Throughout her stay at Geneva, Flora attempted to convince administrators to release her so that she could help her mother, who had suffered a serious leg injury. Staff notes also documented the school's receipt of letters from Mrs. Matthews, Flora's mother, asking that Flora be released because her "mom has been in an accident and wants the girl home." Flora was ultimately released on probation in September 1932. After visiting Flora and her mother, her probation officer noted that Flora was "happy at home and her mom is happy to have her."[22]

Some parents whose children were paroled to them refused to let their ensuing relationship with Geneva's parole officers be defined simply by surveillance. They believed that the school had a responsibility to ensure their children's well-being and provide for them even as the institution monitored their children's behavior outside its walls. Della Little, a sixteen-year-old African American girl and native of Illinois, was committed to Geneva in June 1930 by the juvenile court as a "delinquent" for reasons the records do not make clear. Her parole officer noted that she was "anxious to get home to her mother" and gave written support of Della's release from the institution in November 1931. Throughout Della's parole, which lasted for four years, Mrs. Little sent letters to Della's parole officer and visited the school's Chicago parole office to ask them to actively support Della—not simply send parole officers to their home to monitor her. In December 1932, Mrs. Little sent Della's probation officer a letter to ask whether there was a "possibility of a Christmas basket or winter coat that would be suitable" because she could not afford one or locate other resources in the city to provide for her daughter. In 1935, Mrs. Little contacted the parole office and reported that Della, who had been having severe headaches after receiving "x-ray treatments" from the Illinois Research Hospital that "made her hair fall out," was very sick. Mrs. Little "wanted to know whether something could be done" because the "County Hospital refused to take her." It is not clear whether Della's probation officer helped her resolve the problem.[23]

Despite staff members' and administrators' attempts to make Geneva a home-like institution, harrowing stories about the nature of confinement and reports of cruelty there tainted its reputation.[24] Its notorious reputation had been solidified as early as 1909 when superintendent Ophelia Amigh was forced to resign following publication of stories in the local newspapers about her cruelty to the girls.[25] Although school reports indicate that "cases of extreme irritability, over-excitement, or hysteria" were "treated" by the resident physician, and corporal punishment was prohibited, Amigh tortured the girls in her charge with a strong chair and whips.[26] Although Amigh denied these accusations and asserted "that no girl was ever punished unless she richly deserved it, and then not in a cruel manner," a chest full of leather handcuffs and whips worn from overuse was found after her ouster.[27]

Geneva's reputation was so bad that it led some young women to take drastic steps to avoid being sent there. In 1912, the *Chicago Defender* featured a story about a sixteen-year-old African American girl who went to extraordinary lengths to escape being taken to Geneva. She used her bed sheets as rope and jumped three stories from a police station window, dislocating her knee and fracturing her arm in the process. Her companions at the police station said she cited not wanting to be taken to Geneva as the reason for her escape attempt. When she was questioned directly, she stated that she just wanted to "get out of there to show them that they could not keep me locked up like a criminal."[28]

Once they were in the school, many girls balked at the disciplinary regime, corporal punishment, and their very confinement by trying to escape. In July 1924, Sadie Cooksey, a nineteen-year-old African American mother from Arkansas who had been an inmate at Geneva for at least five years, died during her attempt to escape from the institution. Although the circumstances surrounding how Martin Hopper, a thirty-four-year-old white school maintenance man, impregnated Sadie are unclear, Sadie had given birth to a daughter, Elizabeth Marie Cooksey, in September 1923. Elizabeth, who died from "convulsions" when she was only four and a half months old, was buried on the school grounds in February 1924. When Sadie decided to take matters into her own hands and end her confinement by running away, it was likely that her daughter's death was only one among a myriad of reasons that compelled her to escape and ultimately meet an untimely death. An article published in the *Batavia Herald* reported that Sadie "stumbled and fell over a third rail of the C.A.&E. railway near a power plant" on a Thursday night. "The electrocuted young woman was found Friday morning lying across the charged rail."[29]

Other girls protested Geneva's disciplinary regime by taking over the spaces they were confined in and barricading themselves in cottages. When staff members reprimanded seven African American girls and asked that they be "confined to their quarters" because they "shouted encouragement to three white girls who were trying to escape," the black girls protested their punishment. The *Geneva Republican* reported that the girls "barricaded themselves in the living room of Hope cottage and were only quieted after Sheriff Damisch and his deputies had removed them to county jail." Institutional administrators responded to the girls' protest against their punishment, dubbed a "Prison Riot" by the newspaper, by giving them over to the state's attorney Charles Seidel. The state's attorney subsequently put them on trial. Six of the seven girls were sentenced to the state prison for women in Dwight, Illinois, for one year. The only reason one of the girls remained at the institution and was not sentenced to Dwight was because she was under the age limit for the prison.[30] Although it is not clear what, if any, punishment was received by the white inmates the African American girls had encouraged to escape, Geneva's official policy was to discipline escape attempts. An Illinois Association for Criminal Justice 1938 study reported, for example, that "girls found planning or helping to plan escapes are given individual attention." This "individual attention" included transfer to another cottage, withholding of privileges, or a conference with a matron. Runaways who had "been gone more than twenty-four hours were sent to the Disciplinary Cottage." In light of this, the black girls' prosecution by the state's attorney and commitment to state prison for simply cheering on potential runaways was an extremely harsh punishment that was out of line with the institution's policy toward girls who actually escaped.[31]

The "Tendency on the Part of the Colored Inmates Toward Violence": Constructing a Masculine and Aggressive Black Female Delinquent

Although African American girls were admitted into an institution with the stated purpose of protecting and rehabilitating young girls because of their legal status as children, their experiences expose the implicit belief that they were a different sort of "child" or "girl." African American girls' intersecting racial and gender identities influenced both their experiences and the ways in which staff members at Geneva perceived them. Staff members masculinized African American girls and constructed them as the most violent and aggressive residents at the institution. In spite of the reality that African American girls were typically younger than white girls and the fact that a disproportionate number of them were sent to Geneva not because they had committed any crimes but because there were no institutions available for dependent African American children, staff members believed that they were the most violent, sexually deviant, and uncontrollable girls at the institution. Staff members' and administrators' beliefs, which they reflected in school policies, reveal how embedded intersecting notions of race, gender, and sexuality were in juvenile justice practice at the institution.[32]

This belief that African American girls had an innate proclivity for violence and aggression had material implications for their experiences at Geneva, as it rationalized the institution's racial segregation and structured its administration of rehabilitative programs. Geneva's staff members articulated their belief that African American girls had a more natural inclination for violence in their notes, in state institutional reports, and in studies by external reviewers. For example, Dr. Clara Hayes, one of the physicians who worked at Geneva between 1912 and 1920, echoed other staff members' feelings when she stated in a 1922 report of the Chicago Commission on Race Relations that "there is a little more tendency on the part of the colored inmates toward violence than there is among white girls."[33]

Unlike staff members and administrators at the state home for delinquent boys at St. Charles and other juvenile justice institutions, administrators at Geneva racially segregated the girls through the 1950s. Institutional reports between 1910 and 1953 include several references to segregated cottages, choruses, musical quartets, Christmas programs, piano and voice recitals, glee clubs, academic classes, and vocational training courses. Courses also met at different times, with "the colored girls meeting for a period of three hours in the morning and white girls for a similar length of time in the afternoon" to further ensure the separation of white and black inmates.[34] Eugene Lies, a representative of the National Recreation Association who was hired by the Department of Public Welfare to study leisure programs in the state's prisons, St. Charles, and Geneva in 1937, noted that recreation programs were segregated at Geneva: "at the time of the survey one [class] of forty white girls and one of twenty colored girls" participated in a drama program. The representative, like staff members in institutional reports, made no mention of racial segregation in the boys' school at St. Charles.[35] Geneva's administrators even thought it necessary to keep separate black and white girls sent to the school's disciplinary cottages, which the girls referred to as "dungeons." The Illinois Association for Criminal Justice similarly reported "in the cottages for white girls, each has a separate room, while in the colored cottages some of the rooms are shared by two girls.... There were from twenty-two

Segregated vocational class at the Illinois Training School for Girls at Geneva, circa 1940. Courtesy of the Geneva Historical Society.

to thirty-four girls per cottage, while in the cottages for colored there were fifty per cottage."[36]

Staff members and administrators explicitly stated that they attempted to manage the perceived aggression on the part of African American girls by instituting racial segregation. This meant that although African American girls participated in a similar range of domestic, club, and cultural activities as white girls, and although black and white girls alike were sometimes subjected to harsh physical treatment, African American girls were marginalized and separated from white girls because of their race. Staff members and administrators went through the motions of including African American girls in the institutions' rehabilitative activities—activities that were more than likely not separate but equal—at the same time that they articulated and demonstrated their belief that black girls were beyond the purview of the stated rehabilitative purpose of the institution. Their decision to racially segregate the girls, then, was not simply a replication of wider societal practices. Rather, it reflected staff members' and administrators' beliefs that African American girls had a unique set of problems that could be recognized and anticipated because of their race and that they needed to be segregated from other girls because of it.

Margaret Elliot explained in her 1912 and 1913 superintendent's report for the Illinois State Board and Charities Commission, for example, that African American girls' perceived violent and unruly nature guided administrators' cottage assignments. After noting the disciplinary challenges in Faith and Lincoln—cottages inhabited by African American girls—Elliot relayed staff members' decision to locate the "two cottages for colored girls . . . on opposite sides of the grounds" because "the effect [of having them next to each other] upon discipline has not been good." Elliot noted that Lincoln, "the cottage that had been used by the older colored girls," seemed to be a particularly long-standing problem for staff members, as "it had always been a problem to maintain order there," and "disorder had at times assumed the character of mob rule and violence." Lincoln residents' attack upon one of its cottage matrons, who sustained such severe injuries that she was unable to work for two months, was used as evidence of the violent tendencies of African American girls. Attacks upon staff members in white cottages, however, did not result in these cottages being described as having an air of "mob rule and violence."[37]

The only recorded episode of racial integration in cottages during this period occurred as a result of a fire destroying Lincoln, one of the African American girls' residences, in 1912. Although some staff members initially objected to integration, it was looked upon favorably once they concluded that it aided in controlling African American girls' behavior: "The colored girls being only two or three to a ward, have realized that they were outnumbered and that in any attack upon their matron, they might expect the white girls to take her part." Despite these perceived benefits, integration was temporary and staff members continued to racially segregate girls after the cottage was restored because of African American girls' perceived violence and unruliness.[38]

Staff members' behavioral characterizations are peculiar not only because a higher proportion of African American girls in the institution were younger, pregnant, or in need of medical attention but because those who were, in fact, "delinquent" had committed crimes for the same type of offenses as those committed by white girls. As Judge Mary Bartelme observed of girls sent to Geneva when she was questioned by the Chicago Commission on Race Relations, "the offenses of white and colored are very much the same."[39] Moreover, administrators' and staff members' decision to racially segregate Geneva's cottages often led to severe overcrowding in African American girls' residences. It was not uncommon to have the number of African American girls residing in disciplinary and nondisciplinary cottages be more than twice the occupancy rate the cottage was designed to hold. Nevertheless, staff members failed to make logical links between what they perceived as an air of "mob violence" or the "tendency on the part of the colored inmates toward . . . aggression" and the severe overcrowding.[40]

Staff members and administrators at Geneva were not alone in believing that young black women and girls were innately more violent than white women. This belief was present in other punitive and corrective institutions for women. In her book *Society's Misfits*, reformer Madeline Doty revealed her anxiety over being imprisoned with black women before her weeklong venture as an undercover inmate at New York State Prison for Women at Auburn in 1916. The prison warden and commission members reinforced her anxiety when they questioned her strength and warned her that she "might suffer harm from the convicts for some were colored women of a hard and vicious character" and that she must "look out for blows" because the black women were "occasionally violent."[41] L. Mara Dodges's examination of the history of women's imprisonment reveals that in the early twentieth century, African American women at Joliet Women's Prison in Illinois were "popularly regarded as the most vicious and most depraved" group of inmates there as well.[42]

Staff members' belief that African American girls at Geneva were the most violent and aggressive occurred within a matrix of local and national popular images about black women. In *Chicago by Day and Night*, an 1892 travel guidebook that outlined the landscape of sexual commerce in the city, Harold Vynne issued a warning to visiting white men: "There are dark forms lurking in the alley-ways and doors . . . dusky female characters of whom the police have a wholesome dread. . . . They are Amazonian in physique . . . and of such marvellous strength that no officer" could arrest them alone. Clifton Wooldridge, a retired police detective, also titillated turn-of-the-century Chicagoans with newspaper stories about his encounters with brutish black prostitutes. He described one black prostitute as standing "over six feet tall" and "weigh[ing] about two hundred and twenty pounds"; she had "muscles of steel" and was "as fearless as she is ferocious." Historian Cynthia Blair noted how these composite sketches various city writers pulled together connoted an image of black women who were "extraordinarily large in height and girth and possessing brutish strength and cunning" and were "prone to violent rages," with an "insatiable appetite for criminal activity." Black women were referred to as "Amazons," "African giantesses," and "gigantic Negresses."[43] Sensational newspaper reports continued to produce images of dangerously violent black prostitutes as late as 1936. In her 1931 text *Reformatories for Women in the United States*, Dutch legal scholar Eugenia C. Lekkerkerker noted that this perception of black women's brutish strength and proclivity for violence was a national one. Like other academics of her time, Lekkerkerker supported this viewpoint and asserted that the tendency for criminal behavior among black women was partially due to the "inadequate cultural adjustment of the Negro race to modern Western civilization."[44]

Notions of African American women's masculinity and strength originated during slavery. In the late eighteenth century, femininity was increasingly linked with physical weakness and strong morality. Black women's alleged ability to bear the backbreaking work of enslavement—as well as their sexual violation by white men—made them the antithesis of this new definition of femininity: physically strong and immoral.[45] Historian Cheryl D. Hicks notes that this notion of black women's masculine strength continued after emancipation, and the perception of black female offenders was filtered through this racial lens.[46] In *The Female Offender*, for example, Cesar Lombroso's 1895 pseudo-scientific study on female criminality, "the father of modern criminology" illustrated this point when he stated that African American women were mannish and prone to criminality: "[they are] difficult to recognize as women, so huge their jaws and cheekbones, so coarse their features. And the same is often the case in their crania and brains."[47]

"Perversions" and "Wild Affections": Manufacturing Sexually Deviant Black Female Delinquency

These negative representations of black womanhood were also embedded in administrators' and staff members' constructions of sexual deviance in African American girls, whom they believed were the catalysts of interracial sex. Staff members were unsettled by sexual relationships among the girls as they believed the girls' "efficiency and deportment in school, cottage, and the industrial room all suffer[ed]" as a result of it. Girls who were found engaging in sexual relationships were "taken immediately out of school and kept away from all group contacts," encouraged to read and sew, and given "plenty of exercise" along with a "new diet which had some of the richer foods removed" in an attempt to "build up interests which would be substituted for homosexual activity."[48] Their paranoia over the specter of interracial sexual relationships in particular, however, served as another impetus to institute and maintain racial segregation to protect white girls from the alleged contaminating influences of black girls.

Interracial sexual relationships, which staff members believed were largely precipitated by black girls at Geneva, provoked a great deal of anxiety and consternation. As visiting psychologist Margaret Otis noted in her 1913 report, "the difficulty [of interracial sex] seemed so great and the disadvantage of intimacy between the girls so apparent that segregation was resorted to.... The girls were kept apart both when at work and when at play ... and the white girls were absolutely forbidden to have anything to do with the colored." An anonymous matron interviewed by Early Myers for the Illinois Association for Criminal Justice stated that the "homosexual manifestation which is particularly difficult is that between colored and white girls" as it was "the one thing they could not control.... Frequent crushes occur, and when they do the writing of what are known among the girls as 'honey notes' begins."[49]

In her memoir *Women in Crime*, Florence Monahan said this of her time as Geneva's superintendent during the 1930s: "It is pretty well known that homosexuality and perversion thrive in places where the population is all of one sex. I came face to face with the problem at Geneva.... Our biggest difficulty was the Negro and the white girls.... By segregation we were able to eliminate the major portion of the trouble."[50] Geneva's staff members were not alone in their fear of interracial sex, however. Staff members and administrators at other institutions for delinquent women and girls were also anxious about the "love-making between the white and colored girls" and viewed it as an extension of their "perversion."[51] Criminologists, psychologists, and state officials also encouraged prison and reformatory administrators to stem interracial relationships between black and white women for fear that they would disrupt prison discipline.[52]

In nearly all the descriptions of relationships between Geneva's black and white girls, staff members and visiting professionals suggested that African American girls both embodied masculinity and forcefully initiated these relationships. Their construction of these interracial same-sex relationships, which they referred to as the "honey-girl" phenomenon, masculinized African American girls by portraying them as the sole sexual aggressors even in the face of clear evidence of white girls' non-passivity and excluded African American girls from notions of femininity.[53] For example, psychologist Margaret Otis argued that interracial sex was different from the "ordinary form that is found among girls in high-class boarding-schools."[54] Unlike same-sex relationships among white girls, where both participants retained a feminine identity, for Otis "difference in color . . . took the place of difference in sex." The black partner, in contrast to the white one, was not "ordinary" and embodied the characteristics of a different—nonfeminine and masculine—sex. Moreover, Otis believed that an "animal instinct" was "paramount" to black girls' constitution and influenced their sexual relationships.[55] Social scientist Ruth Klein made a similar argument after conducting a study at Geneva in 1918: "The violent attachment of one girl for another takes on a heterosexual character, the aggressor adopting the masculine role and the other girl playing the feminine part. . . . When the attachment occurs between a colored and a white girl, the former invariably assumes the masculine role."[56] An administrator interviewed as part of the Illinois Association of Criminal Justice's 1928 report suggested that "in every case in which colored and white girls became attached to each other, the colored girl is considered the male, and is called 'daddy' or sometimes 'uncle.' " Staff members' and experts' positing of these relationships as heterosexual in character, where a difference in color took the place of difference in sex and black girls "invariably" assumed a "masculine role," while white girls played a more passive, "feminine part," revealed a race-specific construction of sexual behavior in the institution.

Psychiatrist Elizabeth Stone also concluded that African American girls "were usually more aggressive" and "appealed to the weaker white in a masculine sense." Stone asserted that African American girls' aggressive procurement of interracial sex was sought through "vulgar pantomime and suggestive acts, even in broad daylight, and at school." She then stated that African American girls' desperate attempts to gain the sexual attention of white girls even took on a violent and physical form, as a "colored girl, to attract the attention of the white, will surreptitiously expose her person" or resort to assault. To support her point, she relayed the story of an African American girl who allegedly "choked her sweetheart into submission if she resisted, and threatened to kill her and do her all manner of bodily injury if she told of these visits."[57] Otis similarly connoted an image of desperate African American girls who went to extraordinary lengths—by using "curious love charms made of locks of hair" and other "superstitious practices"—to gain access to white girls.[58]

Stone's and Otis's depictions of African American girls as desperately crazed, aggressive, oversexed beings who resorted to violence as a result of their desire to have sexual relationships with white girls bore an uncanny relationship to the propaganda used to justify the lynching of black men who were charged with raping white women.[59] White girls at Geneva typically appeared as devoid of any agency in their relationships with black girls and were understood to assume a passive role in these relationships at best. These depictions of African American girls who resorted to extraordinary lengths, by exposing "their person," overcoming any objections against their affection with strength, or resorting to violence to satisfy their sexual desires, discursively linked them to the popular images of violently hypersexual black men.

Researchers and staff members unwittingly revealed the falsity of these constructs, however, as the same descriptions used to highlight black girls' violent and aggressive efforts to obtain relationships with white girls contained examples revealing white girls' agency in these relationships. Several offered examples of white inmates actively seeking relationships with black girls and defying staff members' rules in order to do so. Stone described a superintendent's frustration at a Geneva dance because "the white girls insisted in dancing with the colored."[60] She also relayed the story of a white girl who carried her black "honey's" soiled napkin in her bosom for a week as a mark of devotion. Psychologist Margaret Otis also noted that white girls, who had this "habit of 'nigger-loving' . . . would congregate in one part of the dormitory to watch at the window for colored girls to pass. . . . Notes could be slipped out, kisses thrown and looks exchanged . . . just 'to see the coons get excited.'"[61] Klein also relayed an incident where the white girls precipitated a "minor scandal" because they "moved into the cottage of the colored girls" despite the matrons' attempt to prevent the development of same-sex relationships between them.[62]

Descriptions of white girls who carried around black girls' soiled napkins, defied orders to move into black girls' cottages, and stood by windows to blow kisses as black girls walked by—behaviors that could also be read as assertive—belie the notion that African American girls were the sole aggressors while white girls were completely passive. The girls' own statements when discussing the honey-girl phenomenon also confirmed that African American girls were not the sole aggressors. When Otis asked one of the African American girls which race initiated these relationships, she responded, "It might be either way."[63] Given the extraordinary effort administrators and staff members made to keep white and black girls separate from each other, their persistent attempts to interact with each other was certainly a form of institutional resistance among black and white girls.

The discontinuity between the researchers' and staff members' own descriptions of interracial relationships and their conclusion that African American girls invariably occupied an aggressive, "masculine" role reveals how their preexisting notions about African American girls were clarified and rearticulated within the framework of the institutions' protective and rehabilitative goals. They also replicated and took part in a long history of masculinizing black women. The same behavior among black and white girls led to drastically different conclusions. Unlike black girls, white girls were able to retain their feminine identity despite engaging in behaviors that were considered stereotypically masculine, such as procuring a dance partner, boldly watching a potential lover walk by, and disobeying orders.[64] By constructing the image of an inherently deviant, masculine, and unfixable hypersexual black girl delinquent, staff members and administrators injected the color line into their rehabilitative discourse and practice. This explicit and implicit manufacturing of a violent sexual deviant, whose negative influence contaminated other girls in the institution, simultaneously reified white girls' inclusion in the rehabilitative project and excluded black girls from it.

The descriptions of Geneva's interracial sexual activity in terms that portrayed black girls as masculine and sexually aberrant deviants were replicated at other homes for delinquent girls, where staff members and researchers blamed African American girls for sexual "perversion" throughout the first half of the twentieth century. In her report of a 1941 study she conducted at a home for delinquent girls, psychologist Theodora Abel argued that white girls interpreted the "Negro aggression and dominance" as "maleness" and that their "physical characteristics seem to enhance [white girls'] attraction to Negro girls."[65] In a 1920 study of inmates at the New York State Reformatory at Bedford, psychiatrist Elizabeth R. Spaulding also concluded that homosexual sex occurred because African American girls "represented a substitute for unattainable heterosexual" relationships that many white girls at the institution craved.[66]

Staff members and professionals at Geneva also revealed the double standard for white and black girls by the ways in which they held white girls at the center of analyses about interracial relationships. They were more interested in understanding the implications of white girls' participation in these relationships and relayed the idea that white girls' same-sex activities were only temporary. For example, Klein speculated about the likelihood that white girls who had relationships with black girls would be more likely to have relationships with black men upon release when she argued that "having a colored 'honey' may make it easier for white girls to have intercourse or live with colored men after they are paroled."[67] Clearly, the possibility that white inmates were naturally attracted to other girls was not a possibility for Klein. She assumed that the white girls' attractions were only temporary, as they would inevitably have relationships with men upon release—even if these men happened to be "colored." Otis similarly implied that white girls engaged in these relationships temporarily, as she reported that many of them "had never seen anything of the kind outside" and engaged in the behavior only "when they saw other girls doing it."[68]

There is no evidence that Klein, Otis, or any other staff members attempted to analyze why black girls engaged in same-sex relationships, portrayed them as temporary, or reframed them in terms that included them within the heteronormative feminine categories of the time. This differential analysis indicates an assumption that black girls were already sexually "deviant," so there was no motivation to analyze and explain their participation in sexual behaviors they deemed "perverse." What is important is not whether their descriptions were accurate but the way in which their analyses resulted in the construction of a racialized female delinquent that put African American girls beyond the scope of any meaningful rehabilitation.

The images created by institutional administrators, staff members, psychiatrists, and medical professionals at Geneva and other institutions for young women were linked to contemporary theories of homosexuality. Homosexuality was largely considered a form of "gender inversion." However, their account of these relationships can be characterized as what historian Regina Kunzel has labeled "racialised gender inversion."[69] When staff members assigned the masculine "aggressor" role to black girls while preserving white girls' feminized role, they racialized African American girls' sexuality. By assigning the masculine role only to African American girls in the process of applying this theory of racialized gender inversion, staff members and researchers simultaneously excluded black girls from the bounds of traditional femininity and heteronormativity.[70] Social scientists' practice of casting black women and girls as aggressors in interracial prison sex continued through the latter half of the twentieth century. In her 1974 study of homosexuality among prison women, Catherine Nelson mapped masculinity and prison sex onto black working-class women and concluded, "Because of greater aggressiveness and domination in the general socialization process, lower class black females appear more likely to take on a male heterosexual role."[71]

The depiction of African American girls at Geneva as black delinquents with sexual desires that were strong, fervent, and insatiable evoked the image of Jezebel. Jezebel, an archetype that originated during slavery, connoted the image of a sex-starved black woman who was promiscuous and hopelessly consumed by her lustful passions. This alleged fervent lust and promiscuity justified the rape of enslaved black women by white men and sanctioned their use as breeders.[72] Despite their evocation of Jezebel, staff members' and professionals' descriptions represented the construction of a new intersecting racial and gender stereotype that denigrated young black women by portraying them as innately deviant, masculine, and hypersexual delinquents.

Nascent juvenile justice institutions around the country—though with regional variation—were engaged in the process of constructing racialized forms of black female delinquency. Historian Susan Cahn, for example, described the southern iteration of beliefs about African American girls' inherent sexual deviance through her description of debates surrounding race and juvenile justice in *Sexual Reckonings: Southern Girls in a Troubling Age*. Although southern states established racially segregated institutions for black boys, white boys, and white girls, public institutions for black girls were virtually nonexistent through World War II. Rehabilitative and protective work for African American girls was left up to black communities because of the widespread opposition to the state-sponsored building of institutions for black girls in particular.[73]

Some state legislators even argued that a reformatory for delinquent African Americans would be a waste of state funds, because such an institution would be unable to contain the number of black female sex delinquents in their communities. A North Carolina congressman stated in front of the state legislature in 1930, "In my opinion it would take the United States army to correct the morals of all Negro girls in the state." A writer for the *Charlotte Observer* similarly argued that "such a large proportion of the Negro girls might fall within the scope of such a correctional institution that the state would simply be overrun with inmates."[74] The implication was that "deviant" sexual behavior among white girls, who constituted the majority of girls in many southern states, was an uncommon correctable condition, whereas in African American girls, it was a deeply rooted, widespread phenomenon beyond the scope of any institutional rehabilitation program.

Historian Jennifer Trost's study of Progressive-era juvenile justice in Memphis also found that juvenile justice practitioners' perception of black girls' sexuality racialized their views of delinquency. Juvenile court officials were more concerned with white girls' sexual—as opposed to criminal—behaviors. For black girls, however, juvenile court officials were less concerned with their sexual behavior and more concerned with their criminal activity. Like many African American girls in Chicago, black girls in Memphis who were charged with "sexual misconduct" were on average younger than white girls and more likely to have been sexually exploited. In juvenile courts and institutions for delinquent children both north and south, then, black girls' sexual vulnerability was erased and constructed as sexually deviant.[75]

At Geneva, a northern institution, African American girls were not excluded from the training school but were subject to a different kind of segregation: a conceptual and discursive within-institution segregation from white girls that structured administrative decisions within the school and resulted in the construction of a race-specific image of black female delinquency. Because the construction of crime and delinquency was gendered, and sexual behavior was criminalized in girls but not boys, reformers and legislators around the country focused on a singular issue when it came to the rehabilitation of girls: sexuality. The impact this had on African American girls' relationships with juvenile justice institutions was reflected in southern state legislators' and reformers' refusals to establish homes for black girls and staff members' racially motivated sequestering of black girls from whites at Geneva.

Administrators at the Illinois Training School for Boys at St. Charles, only three miles away from Geneva, did not consider racially segregating boys until the mid-1930s. The demographic profile of boys in the institution was similar to that of Geneva through the 1950s. Although this does not indicate that the rehabilitative ideal fully applied to African American boys or that racial biases did not exist at St. Charles before 1930, it does reveal how intersecting notions of race and gender were embedded in constructions of delinquency and the administration of rehabilitative programs. Geneva, which may have appeared integrated on the surface because it accepted both white and black girls, was, in fact, racially segregated within its walls from its inception. Since the rehabilitative program at Geneva focused on curing sex delinquency and creating "proper women," staff members' discursive and practical segregation of African American girls because they believed black girls were innately violent and aggressively hypersexual whitened the rehabilitative ideal and cast blackness as delinquency.

Contested Constructions: Black Chicago and the Training School for Girls

Chicago's black community was aware of the emergence of this construction of black girls' delinquency as highly masculinized, deviant, and sexually aberrant and how those understandings shaped African American girls' experiences in the state's flagship institution for delinquent girls. Black community activists in Chicago challenged this construct by attacking the most visible and tangible manifestation of racialized criminalization at Geneva: racial segregation. A 1917 *Defender* article, for example, noted the emerging criminalization of black girls in the justice system and chastised the African American community for not doing more to protect black girls from dangers of the city: "Young schoolgirls in their teens are caught in disorderly houses. . . . Who cares? Few of our Race. But the white people do, for their girls who have fallen by the wayside. . . . I am sorry to say for in the past few days that I busied myself around the courthouse I have failed to see but three members of our Race."[76] By 1920, however, Chicago's black community was engaged in a fervent struggle to desegregate Geneva that lasted until 1953.

Black clubwomen, community organizers, and state legislators joined in the effort to desegregate Geneva. For these community activists, the racial segregation of girls became the focal point of their efforts, because it represented a racialized construction of delinquency that compromised Geneva's rehabilitative program. Evangeline Roberts, a *Chicago Defender* journalist, spoke for reformers in her coverage of a 1928 struggle against segregation at Geneva: "the general opinion of the group was that segregation was a primary cause of trouble there and that if all the delinquents were given the same correction and accommodation there would be no cause for complain."[77]

By directly advocating against racial segregation at Geneva and insisting that its rehabilitative programs be integrated and administered without regard to race, Chicago's black community rejected and challenged the belief systems that rationalized segregation in the institution. Clubwomen, who were often at the forefront of these efforts, periodically launched investigations into the conditions facing African American girls at Geneva and made specific recommendations to improve their experiences. A 1922 *Defender* article mentioned clubwomen's attempt to end segregation after their investigation at Geneva revealed that "the girls of Color [were] all thrown together in one cottage." Clubwomen noted that a significant proportion of the girls, particularly the younger ones, were there only "for truancy and some because parents are separated and they have no homes so are daily in contact with older girls who are sent there for more serious charges." After noting the deleterious consequences of racial segregation on young black girls who had not committed any crimes, clubwomen strongly asserted, "this practice should be broken up. Don't delay."[78]

Community activists also agitated against the severe overcrowding in African American girls' cottages. In 1928, a cottage matron told visiting community members that racial segregation had led to 104 African American girls being forced into two cottages, each of which had a maximum capacity of thirty-two. Community members found this overcrowding particularly egregious as there were several vacancies in cottages inhabited by white girls. Activists like Ida B. Wells, Morris Lewis of the NAACP, A. O. Foster of the Urban League, Senator Albert Roberts, state representative George S. Kersey, Susie Myers, and Lula E. Lawson of the YWCA collectively visited Governor Len Small during his stay at the Sherman Hotel in Chicago. They demanded that he launch an official investigation into the conditions facing African American girls at Geneva. They argued, "segregation was the primary cause of their trouble and that if all the delinquents are given the same correction and accommodation there would be no cause to complain." After listening to the community activists' concerns, Governor Small decided to launch an investigation and "promised to direct the building of more cottages to relieve the overcrowded conditions."[79]

Although this activism did not result in immediate racial integration at Geneva, community members continued to launch their own investigations and advocate against racial discrimination at the institution. For example, the *Chicago Defender* published the results of a 1930 investigation by clubwomen that revealed "a shocking state of ignorance and filth at that institution ... where women in charge are usually untrained and for the most part, mental equals of the girls they are supposed to teach." They recommended that the school recruit a "faculty of highly trained teachers and matrons who are qualified."[80]

Black state representative Charles J. Jenkins, at the behest of African American community members, made an attempt to oust Geneva superintendent Mary W. Pickerill in 1940, "for discriminatory and Jim Crow practices at the institution." Representative Jenkins, who simultaneously opposed the emergence of new attempts to institute racial segregation at the Training School for Boys at St. Charles, met with the governor and schools' managing officers A. L. Bowen and William Harmon. He called the meeting "for the express purpose of pointing out to them the un-American customs of segregation . . . [and] insisted that the school maintain the philosophy that no attention be paid to race." Representative Jenkins also pointed out that racial segregation at Geneva was a violation of the 1937 Civil Rights Act, where nondiscrimination orders were issued to every state institution and the heads of all departments. The instructions included an order to "cease and desist any discrimination wherever found in the state of Illinois and to treat all alike, with like accommodations."[81] Community members' advocacy on behalf of African American girls and attempts to desegregate Geneva began to pay off in the 1950s. Institutional records in Illinois's Department of Public Welfare mentioned attempts to integrate Geneva for the first time in 1951. Geneva did not fully integrate its curriculum and facilities until 1955.

Black Chicagoans also advocated for the employment of African American women in the institution, because they believed it would help ameliorate racial discrimination there. Women such as Gertrude Davis, former matron of the black community–sponsored Phyllis Wheatley Home for Girls, former school teacher Lulu Blowe, and educated women like Lucy Johnson and Mattie Gaines were appointed as matrons and staff members at Geneva as a result of community pressure and the special work of black policewoman Grace Wilson. Officer Wilson had firsthand knowledge of the impact the dearth of community resources, racism in the police department, and overcommitment of black girls to Geneva created.[82]

Segregation meant that black matrons and other staff worked only with African American girls. Although racial discrimination limited employment options for professional black women, many sought work at Geneva because they viewed it as an opportunity to target and provide service toward the care of vulnerable black girls. Mary Foster, for example, who began her work at Geneva in 1923 as a matron of Willard, one of the school's cottages for African American girls, relished her work because she could teach "her girls how to love and be loved." A Department of Public Welfare 1946 report noted of Foster, known affectionately by the girls as "Mother Foster," that "when a girl comes to live at her cottage, Mother Foster begins her unconscious campaign to win her as a friend."[83] Black Chicagoans' activism surrounding the State Training School at Geneva was part of their larger effort to deal with the issues of poverty, dependency, and delinquency. It also represented a rejection of racialized constructions of childhood innocence and delinquency. Black women were often on the frontline of this struggle.

Erasing Black Girls' Vulnerability and Constructing a Black Female Delinquent

Although racial segregation in new juvenile justice institutions that symbolized the ascendancy of notions of universal childhood innocence assumed different forms in the North and South, they all participated in the discursive and practical exclusion of African American girls from notions of innocence and rehabilitation. The connections between the white reform community's silence over African American girls' sexual victimization, reformers' beliefs that black girls were morally inferior to white girls, as well as black girls' experiences at Geneva were further laid bare when a scandal surrounding a prostitution ring of escaped Geneva girls erupted. This 1934 incident led to a flood of newspaper articles and litigation. Although African American girls were a part of this prostitution ring, later dubbed a "white slavery" vice scandal, reporters erased their victimization. The escapees were described as "little white girls" or "helpless girls" whose "harrowing experiences . . . in the hands of white slave barons" included being "threatened and whipped into silence by inhuman beasts," many of whom were described as being black men.[84] The erasure of black girls' victimization in major city newspapers of the incident, as well as the prosecutors' failure to prosecute men who prostituted African American girls, reinforced the notion that black girls were not as sexually exploitable as white girls because of their presumed sexually deviant and promiscuous nature. The *Chicago Defender*, however, which highlighted black girls' victimization in the 1934 scandal, used the incident as another opportunity to lambast "the wholesale trafficking" of black women and girls by "well organized" rings of racketeers in general.[85] This erasure of black girls' vulnerability was a necessary ingredient in the creation of a dangerous black female delinquent.

Whether the rehabilitative ideal was ever fully put into practice at the Illinois State Training School for Girls is certainly debatable. Of concern here, however, was to whom reformers anticipated the ideal would apply. Negative depictions of black women had tangible implications for black girls' experiences in northern juvenile justice institutions like Geneva. Because women and children are theoretically the most vulnerable and sympathetic members of a population, the construction of black children, particularly black girls, as innately violent, hypersexual beings further marginalized all African Americans and supported emerging beliefs about their innate criminality and proclivity to violence. Moreover, it perpetuated and reinforced the historical exclusion of black women and girls from notions of femininity.

By relegating Geneva's African American girls to a fixed, immutable, naturally deviant category of delinquency, staff members demonstrated how notions of the "girl problem," innocence, and rehabilitation were circumscribed by race. African American girls were rendered naturally aberrant because of their masculine, sexualized construction and were considered sexually deviant because of their race. Geneva's staff members and administrators believed that African American girls had a deleterious and contaminating influence on white girls and made institutional decisions based on this belief. Black and white girls were subject to different experiences in the institution in spite of its public rehabilitative goals simply because of their race. Although on the surface it may seem that African American girls were included in rehabilitation programs in northern institutions like Geneva simply because they were admitted to the institution, and that they did not suffer any "real" harm because there are few public stories of sadistic brutality or "southern-style" racialized violence on black girls' bodies, their construction as a different type of child influenced the juvenile justice practice in a lasting and tangible way. The symbolic purchase of this image helped facilitate the abrogation of the rehabilitative ideal and divestment of the juvenile court in fifteen-year-old Susie Lattimore's 1935 case.

It is not coincidental that the political campaign to eliminate the rehabilitative ideal—the notion that all children who commit crimes should be reformed, not punished—by divesting the juvenile court of jurisdiction over all children who broke the law was brought about using a black child as a vehicle. The decision in Susie's case was a watershed moment in the history of juvenile justice in Illinois. It was quickly followed by another punitive turn instigated by institutional change following an increase in the number of African Americans at the Illinois State Training School at St. Charles. A threatening construction of black boyhood was a critical component of the legislature's decision in 1941 to build the state's very first maximum-security prison for boys deemed incapable of reform at St. Charles.

CHAPTER FOUR

Flight, Fright, and Freedom

Delinquency and the Construction of Black Masculinity at the Training School for Boys at St. Charles

Rick Andrews, an eleven-year-old African American boy from Chicago, wound up at the Illinois Training School for Boys at St. Charles in 1933 because he stole an eight-year-old boy's shoes. After trying to sell them to a shoe repair shop, he was arrested and sent to Cook County Juvenile Court. By the time Rick ended up at the Training School, he had already gone through the ordeal of being separated from his mother and brother and being placed in foster care after his father abandoned them and they were evicted because they could not pay rent. They had moved into a one-room kitchenette apartment with two other relatives and slept on the kitchen floor.

Juvenile court caseworkers noted in Rick's file that he stole the shoes because he needed the money and that his crime was a result of the extreme poverty of his family. They ultimately concluded that separating him from his family and putting him in foster care would be in his best interests. For reasons that were not made apparent in his case history, his placement with the foster care family was unsuccessful, and he was ultimately committed to the Illinois State Training School for Boys.[1]

When Rick arrived at the school, he entered an institution that was in the midst of a dramatic upheaval. The Illinois State Training School for Boys at St. Charles became a site through which social and political contestations over delinquency, demographic change, and black freedom were fought. African American boys' experiences at the Training School for Boys at St. Charles elucidate the ways in which intersecting notions of race, age, gender, and sexuality shaped the administration of justice. The increase in the number of black boys, along with their relegation to a dangerous and unredeemable category of delinquency, led institutional administrators to implement new policies that removed black boys from the general white population and instigated the state's very first construction of a maximum-security prison for boys.

The Training School for Boys at St. Charles, like the Training School for Girls at Geneva, was born out of the Progressive child-saving movement, and was an integral part of Cook County's juvenile justice system. The state's founding of the Training School for Boys at St. Charles (hereinafter "St. Charles") marked the political viability and ascendance of the idea that children who committed crimes—unlike adults—were inherently innocent and entitled to a separate justice system that would rehabilitate them.

Notions of childhood innocence were rooted in notions of whiteness, however, and by 1930 it was clear that the demographics of St. Charles—like the state's juvenile justice system in general—were experiencing a dramatic transition that paralleled population change in Chicago. Early twentieth-century racist pseudoscience, cultural fiction, and purportedly "objective" crime statistics increasingly associated African Americans with criminality even as Jim Crow segregation crystallized. This association between African Americans and criminality, in addition to white Chicagoans' racial hostility toward the new migrants, shaped African American boys' experiences at St. Charles. The Chicago Commission on Race Relations' 1922 report found widespread beliefs among white Chicagoans that "the Negro is more prone than the white to commit sex crimes particularly rape . . . [and] that he commits a disproportionate number of crimes involving felonious cuttings and slashings."[2]

White Chicagoans' belief that black men were inclined to commit sexual crimes is significant, as the cultural fiction that black men were inclined to rape had tangible consequences that manifested itself through the lynching of over two thousand African American men between 1880 and 1930. This cultural fiction also helped ignite a 1949 scandal at St. Charles, which involved an African American boy accused of raping a white boy at the institution. The controversy over the scandal loomed so large that the state began to directly intervene in the management of the institution.

The increasing number of African American boys at St. Charles caused staff members, state legislators, and residents in cities surrounding the institution to refine their notion of what kind of boy St. Charles was originally intended for. Newspaper articles about boys at St. Charles fueled neighboring whites' anxieties over demographic change in the institution and ultimately fueled a backlash against its initial rehabilitative purpose. Within the institution itself, the increasing number of African American boys and notions of black maleness—which were increasingly represented through a hypermasculine trope that embodied danger, criminality, and menacing sexuality—triggered racial segregation and more punitive school policies. Widespread notions of black male criminality as well as white residents' discontent over black migration shaped the way in which the school administrators and state legislators addressed seemingly new challenges—like the problem of inmate escapes.

"Training Boys for Manhood and Citizenship": Gendered Rehabilitation, Race, and the State's Attempt to Eliminate "Perversion"

The St. Charles Home for Boys was created in 1901 by the Illinois legislature's Act for the Treatment and Care of Delinquent Boys. When the institution opened in 1904, 365 boys under the age of thirteen at Pontiac State Prison and inmates from other institutions for delinquent children, such as the John Worthy School and Chicago Parental School, were among its first inhabitants. Representing the legislature's commitment to the care and protection of dependent and delinquent children, the act was part of Progressives' efforts to separate delinquent children from adult criminals.[3] The Illinois Home for Delinquent Boys, which was renamed the Training School for Boys at St. Charles in 1905, was located forty miles from Chicago in Kane County. In the founders' vision, it would serve as both a reform institution for delinquent boys and a haven from the "vices of the city." Like other industrial schools and reformatories that sprung up around the country, the school's site was purposely located in a rural area to prevent boys from being drawn back into the dangers of city life. The initial campus was made up of 898 acres and seven farms. At that time, no other state public institution in the United States owned as much land as St. Charles.[4] The local newspaper, the *St. Charles Chronicle*, noted the school's opening with pride and affection, referring to it as "the greatest institution of its kind . . . that has ever been attempted in America, if not in the known world."[5] Like the Training School for Girls at Geneva and other institutions for delinquent children that emerged in the context of the child-saving movement, administrators utilized a "family-style" cottage system. Residential staff in the cottages included a "housemother" and "housefather" to make the institution seem less prison-like.[6]

St. Charles boasted extensive medical and dental departments with fully licensed professionals that helped maintain the health of boys in the school. The Institute for Juvenile Research maintained a close relationship with St. Charles and furnished counseling and assessment services for the boys. Unlike girls who were generally committed to the Training School in Geneva because they violated gender norms, boys at St. Charles were committed to the institution because they committed crimes in the traditional sense of the word. Theft, physical assault, robbery, and murder were the crimes that funneled boys into St. Charles.[7] Upon admission they were given a battery of physical, psychological, and intellectual tests. They were not subject to invasive medical exams that screened them for sexually transmitted infections like at Geneva because the impetus for the boys' "rehabilitation" was not their sexuality.

St. Charles instituted a number of programs to educate the boys and ease their transition into the outside world once they were released. In its early years, school administrators instituted vocational programs centered on agricultural work. The boys spent much of their time in the dairy barn, creamery, horse barn, and farm. By 1911, the school had added four more cottages, introduced new programs, and expanded to include a printing plant, carpenter shop, paint shop, wagon shop, and blacksmith shop. At the Training School for Girls at Geneva, residents were taught sewing, cooking, beauty culture, and other domestic arts to prepare them to lead a "proper home life." Boys at St. Charles were exposed to a more varied curriculum, including a diverse sample of trades intended to teach them to be carpenters, blacksmiths, tailors, printers, painters, barbers, and mechanics.[8] The boys typically spent half of their day learning these occupations and the other half in an academic program. In 1925, administrators approved the building of a student-run zoo with two bears, four foxes, two monkeys, a wolf, a swan, and other small animals with the support of "friends of the boys' school." All these amenities gave St. Charles the reputation of being a premier home for delinquent boys.[9]

During the Progressive era, reformers viewed delinquency and crime in cities as a predominantly male problem, and the "rehabilitation" of boys lay at the heart of the institution's early mission. Administrators and staff members at St. Charles believed they were engaged in the important task of separating boys from adult criminals in prisons and saving delinquent boys from engaging in a life filled with crimes. The first superintendent, N. W. McClain, described the important service staff members were providing to the state by taking on the "hard" task of "saving neglected and delinquent boys." For him, finding the "cure for delinquency" required a specialized "knowledge of the causes of delinquency." McClain urged state officials to continue financially supporting the school by warning them of the dangers that could accompany "sending a boy, who has committed some minor offense into confinement involving . . . intimate association with older and hardened criminals." He argued that an "ounce of prevention" and protection from the influence of vice and poverty was the most potent method of curbing delinquency, as "bitter poverty" could make "thieves of young men." As late as 1931, when the Progressive impetus for reform and child saving had waned, in its institutional reports St. Charles continued to embrace an explicit mission to protect "boys" and "correct and rebuild them for a useful and proper place in society."

In most cases, St. Charles continued to monitor former residents even after they were released. School administrators—through their own discretion or by order of juvenile court officers—put boys on parole or in foster care. Like other institutions that housed children and adults convicted of crimes, St. Charles had a high recidivism rate. Poverty, the stigma of having been committed to an institution for a crime, the temptation to fall back into the same behavior patterns, or conflict with host families often overwhelmed newly released inmates and caused many to be recommitted to institutions. African American boys who were paroled from St. Charles faced extra challenges as they experienced additional stigmatization because of their race.[10]

St. Charles took a gendered approach to training "healthy males" for citizenship by instilling military-style discipline and rigorous athletics. Administrators and staff members saw building and teaching citizenship as a critical component in their efforts to "rehabilitate" and "save" delinquent and "potentially delinquent" boys. As McClain noted in the first biennial report, "changing ignorant bad boys into intelligent manly youth" who could become useful citizens was a central part of the institution's mission. Military training became part of the boys' daily regimen to facilitate this mission and promote "obedience and respect for authority." The military training was also meant to foster "patriotism, civic duty, and individual responsibility." For staff members and administrators of the institution, rigorous athletic and recreation programs played a critical role in "training boys for manhood and citizenship."[11]

Official school policies prohibited corporal punishment at St. Charles, but external investigations and newspaper stories revealed that staff members' use of physical violence as a form of punishment was not uncommon at the institution. In a letter to the director of the Bureau of Juvenile Research, Calvin Derrick, an investigator the bureau hired to assess St. Charles, reported in 1928 that when he visited the guard house, he "found eleven boys. One large colored boy had his arms thrust through the bars of the door and handcuffed." When Derrick inquired about the offense that had led to the African American boy's punishment, the officer in charge "stated that he was thus secured because he had been 'fresh' and not obeyed promptly.

The other ten boys were standing 'on line' at attention."[12] A *Tribune* writer who interviewed thirteen boys at St. Charles in 1939 reported that the boys "declared that they would prefer Pontiac reformatory or state prison to St. Charles because of the beatings." One of the black escapees "said that a guard nicknamed 'Killer' took delight in striking him whenever he was within reach and in forcing him to do squatting exercises for punishment." Another African American escapee "showed marks he said were inflicted by beatings . . . . which were undeserved."[13]

Staff members and administrators at the school closely monitored the boys' sexuality so that they could quell any signs of "deviance." Although their concern about sexual activity among inmates did not reach the heights of that of staff members at the Training School for Girls at Geneva, staff members' surveillance was a reflection of homophobia in the larger society. Boys at St. Charles, unlike girls at Geneva, were rarely arrested, sent to juvenile court, and committed to an institution for engaging in sexual behavior with the opposite sex. Boys found engaging in sexual behavior with other boys, however, were processed in juvenile court and sent to institutions for delinquent children.

Like employees at homes for delinquent children across the country, staff members at St. Charles monitored homosexual activity and punished boys who engaged in it.[14] To prevent this type of behavior, staff members arranged cottage beds in a way that made surveillance of the boys easier, prohibited them from going to cottage basements without supervision, and subjected them to a rigorous recreational and physical education program. When boys were found engaging in "immoral" practices, staff members punished them by making them stand silently for up to three hours, whipping them, or putting them in a detention cottage.[15]

Social scientific studies of boys at St. Charles, staff memoirs, and institutional records, unlike those at Geneva, make no mention of sexual acts between boys as a source of major trouble in the institution. Although same-sex acts at St. Charles were considered "immoral" and staff members were expected to closely monitor and prevent it, institutional records gave scant attention to the issue. Reports and institutional records for the Illinois Training School for Girls at Geneva—where housing arrangements, class schedules, and daily activities were arranged in a way to prevent interracial sexual acts in particular—explicitly detailed the ways in which staff attempted to prevent sexual relationships. Former administrators of the girls' institution at Geneva described these efforts, as did visiting social scientists whose analyses attempted to make meaning of sexual acts among the girls there. This is likely linked to the reality that unlike for boys, society's perception of deviance and delinquency among girls was linked primarily to girls' sexual behavior, so institutional staff members had more of an incentive to monitor it.

St. Charles staff's comparatively lower concern over sexual acts among the boys differed markedly from the wider society, where hypervigilance over sexual acts between men predominated, and homosexuality was characterized as an unacceptable form of sexual perversion and condemned. In Chicago itself, boys who were found engaging in homosexual behavior were promptly brought before Cook County Juvenile Court, committed to an institution for delinquent children, or sent for psychological treatment at the Institute for Juvenile Research. In 1949, this divergence between St. Charles's relatively hands-off approach to same-sex activity among boys and the larger society's treatment came into conflict, as a result of a rape charge that sent shock waves all the way up to the state capital. The controversy surrounded an incident involving the alleged rape of a white boy by a black boy and a public statement by school staff that homosexual acts at St. Charles were "common." The community's reaction—as well as the state's intervention into the school—was fueled by an explosive intersection of notions of childhood, race, gender, sexuality, and white residents' belief that black males were prone to committing sexually violent crimes.

In May 1949, Gerald Klindinst, a fifteen-year-old, accused Albert Racliffe, a fourteen-year-old, of subjecting him to a "crime against nature." When Gerald told his father about the incident during visiting hours, his father promptly took him to a nearby hospital for an examination. When the doctor's report concluded that Gerald's injuries "might have been caused" by sexual acts, his father notified State's Attorney Preston Kimball and Hancock County judge J. A. Baird.[16] Mr. Klindinst demanded that St. Charles administrators release his son, and Gerald's case was taken before a grand jury. School administrators and staff members did not believe Gerald was "without fault," however, as he was older and heavier than Albert and labeled "emotionally unstable." Albert was nevertheless punished by being sent to Pierce Cottage—a disciplinary building—for twenty-one days. There he was "watched every minute—disciplined all the time."[17]

The case was publicized and widely reported on in area newspapers. The grand jury, which was composed mostly of women, refused to indict Albert based on its belief that the behavior was ubiquitous at the school. The jury ultimately decided to allow St. Charles administrators to resolve the case. One grand jury member told a reporter, "You couldn't send a boy to the pen in such a case. It goes on throughout the school—been going on for years." When Judge Baird of Hancock County heard about the grand jury's decision, he said he would hesitate to send more boys to St. Charles: "I've been sending boys there for nine years but in view of [this] admission that such immoralities are common at the school, I don't know. . . . They don't appear to be excited at all by the case."[18]

In response, Fred K. Hoehler, the Illinois director of public welfare, criticized St. Charles administrators and began an effort to "determine the extent of sex perversion practices" at St. Charles. Hoehler said he was shocked when the assistant superintendent and clinic director at St. Charles characterized "immoral acts between the boys as 'common.'" Hoehler decided to pay a personal visit to St. Charles so he could determine for himself how common "sex perversion practices" were and "whether there's any evidence of how often they occur and find some way to check them. . . . Perversions should not only be kept to a minimum at the school[,] it should be stopped."[19]

Hoehler sought the cooperation of members of the legislature's State Youthful Offenders Commission in eliminating these practices. He told the *Chicago Tribune*, "Now I am going out there myself. If these immoral acts between young boys are 'common' we've got to find some way to check them. I must find out how often they have been reported and whether there's any evidence of how often they occur." State senator Walker Butler, chair of the Youthful Offenders Commission, concurred: "The problem of erratic sex behavior in the training school should receive the first attention of the [school's] managing officer. . . . Perversion should not only be kept to a minimum at the school, it should be stopped. . . . Some professionals in the field of juvenile delinquency are too inclined to write off some problems as natural, therefore hopeless. That philosophy should not control at the training school."[20] Hoehler and Butler ordered Charles W. Leonard, the superintendent of St. Charles, to "have ready all records which may throw any light on acts, legally called crimes against nature." In spite of his strict stance against "immorality" and "perversion" at St. Charles, once he arrived at the institution, Hoehler concluded that the allegation that precipitated the scandal was untrue and that Albert "wasn't at fault."

It is not clear what—if any—"evidence" of immorality Hoehler and Butler found as a result of their investigation. Hoehler strongly urged Superintendent Leonard to keep careful records of "any infraction of rules that might have even a remote connection with sexual misbehavior, including

exposures that might be unintentional." Superintendent Leonard consequently made a public promise to take homosexual acts between the boys
more seriously. As one *Tribune* reporter noted, "Superintendent Leonard
now understands that anything in the character of an infraction must be
reported immediately. . . . In the future he will immediately make a report
to [state] General H. E. Thornton." This publicized scandal only fueled white
city residents' perceptions that black boys' mere presence in the institution
bred chaos and danger.[21]

Demographic Change and the Training School for Boys

The large and disproportionate increase in the number of African American boys committed to the Illinois Training School for Boys at St. Charles
marked the beginning of the institution's transition to a more punitive institution. The total average number of all of boys at St. Charles stayed around
four hundred through 1915, with about one-third of the boys being "foreign-
born." The total population of boys at St. Charles was almost double the
population of the Training School for Girls at Geneva. By the 1920s, the
daily population was regularly at a minimum of six hundred, and the
school often housed an average of between seven hundred and eight hundred boys. Half of all boys sent to St. Charles were committed there by the
juvenile court in Chicago through the 1930s. By 1940, over 60 percent of all
boys at St. Charles had been committed there by Cook County Juvenile
Court.[22]

The vast majority of boys at St. Charles were committed to the institution
after appearing before a judge in court. Unlike girls, whom judges committed
to institutions for delinquent children primarily for "sex offenses," boys
were committed to St. Charles for a variety of offenses, including larceny,
burglary, aggravated assault, disorderly conduct, vagrancy, and sometimes
even murder. Some publicly funded institutions for delinquent children,
such as the Chicago Home for Girls and Chicago Home for Boys, regularly
admitted children at the request of their parents, but this was not true for
St. Charles throughout the period. A 1940 statistical review of Illinois state
prisons shows, for example, that of 528 boys admitted to St. Charles,
355 boys were committed there from courts, 146 were returned because of
parole violations, twenty-six were returned escapees, and one was marked
as "other."[23]

Although most boys were committed to St. Charles by a juvenile court
judge, a few parents volunteered to have their boys sent there. One mother

Boys sitting in front of a log cabin they built at the Illinois Training School for Boys at St. Charles, 1925. Reproduction of photo appearing in *Abraham Lincoln Log Cabin,* published by the Illinois Training School for Boys, 1925.

wrote a letter to Eleanor Roosevelt in 1936, when the institution's reputation among black Chicagoans was relatively good, in the hopes that Mrs. Roosevelt would convince administrators to admit her son. As she explained in the letter, "I have gone to the State's Attorney and also the Superintendent of the Schools here, and they have given me no consideration whatsoever. I want to have him sent to the St. Charles School in or near Chicago. . . . I would so much rather send him myself than have him get into anything because he does nothing but idle his time away. . . . I have been told that at this school they teach the boys grades and they have tasks that they must perform each day. . . . He would be a much better citizen."[24] Whether administrators made the unusual decision to admit the fifteen-year-old because of First Lady Eleanor Roosevelt's intervention or because of the continued persistence of his mother is unclear, but the boy was eventually admitted to St. Charles.

The number of African American boys at St. Charles began to increase rapidly in the 1920s and continued to do so through the 1940s. Between 1915 and 1923, the percentage of African American boys at St. Charles rose from 8 to 12.5 percent—roughly half as rapidly as the black population in Chicago. In 1934, African Americans made up 22 percent of the institution, and by 1940, they comprised a solid 30 percent of all boys at St. Charles.[25]

The high number of African American boys being committed to St. Charles by the juvenile court had a significant impact on Chicago's black community. Since the school's opening, boys from Chicago made up approximately half of all commitments. Over time, however, a growing percentage of boys Cook County Juvenile Court sent to St. Charles were black. The Chicago Commission on Race Relations investigation found that between 1915 and 1921, the proportion of African American boys committed to St. Charles by Cook County Juvenile Court had increased twice as rapidly as Chicago's black population.[26] An Illinois Board of Welfare 1937 study revealed that seven times as many African American boys were committed to St. Charles by the juvenile court as should be expected based on their population. Black people made up 4.3 percent of Illinois's population, but 29 percent of all boys committed to the institution were black. Although the absolute number of black boys sent to St. Charles was higher than the number of black girls sent to Geneva, twenty-four of the twenty-seven girls—89 percent—the juvenile court sent to Geneva that same year were black. In 1940, almost 38 percent of all juvenile court commitments to St. Charles were black boys from Chicago. At both Geneva and St. Charles, African American children made up roughly one-third of the total population.[27] By 1950, the proportion of black boys the juvenile court sent to St. Charles had risen to almost 50 percent.[28]

This overrepresentation of black boys at St. Charles signaled not only population changes that accompanied the Great Migration but discriminatory surveillance by law enforcement and the juvenile justice system's inability to escape the racism in child welfare services and, more broadly, in society. The majority of African American boys came from the city's racially segregated neighborhoods. A 1946 Department of Public Welfare report noted that 36 percent of the boys committed to St. Charles were "Negroes from the South Side of Chicago." The Southside Committee, a branch of the Chicago Area Project, found that one out of five of all boys on the South Side had appeared in court between 1939 and 1940.[29]

Public and private child welfare institutions discriminated against black boys by excluding them because of their race. The increase in the number of African Americans in Chicago, as well as the relatively small number of private and public institutions that were willing or able to care for dependent African American children, made St. Charles the default option for poor or orphaned boys who were not able to find a suitable foster or institutional placement. Like the Training School for Girls at Geneva, a high proportion of the black boys admitted to St. Charles between 1910 and 1940 were actually dependent. Black sociologist Earl Moses found in his 1936 study of black delinquency in Chicago that "The difficulty of providing adequate care for the dependent and neglected colored children constitutes one of the greatest problems with which the Court has to deal. The situation is complicated by a lack of resources in the community comparable with those available for white children in the same circumstances. Practically no institutions are to be found in the community to which this group of colored children may be admitted."[30]

The experiences of Wayne Stevens and Chris Taylor, both of whom were committed to St. Charles in 1943, illustrate the way many orphaned African American boys ended up there. When Wayne's parents died, the juvenile court eventually sent him to St. Charles because child welfare agencies could not successfully place him. His school records described Wayne as a "very quiet boy" who was "lazy, stubborn, and unreliable." At first, Wayne was placed with a middle-class African American family in Chicago's Morgan Park neighborhood. Unfortunately, the family proved to be a poor match for Wayne, and he was ultimately committed to St. Charles.[31] Juvenile court and public welfare officers similarly had a difficult time finding an appropriate placement for fifteen-year-old Chris. After his mother and father passed away, Chris lived with his aunt until she, too, fell ill and died. First, the court sent him to Chicago Parental School—an institution for truants and children who had behavioral problems in school. There he was labeled "incorrigible" for reasons that were not made apparent in his school records and sent to St. Charles.[32]

In a few cases, African American boys who were victims of physical or sexual abuse also ended up at St. Charles. That same year, Edward Adams, a seventeen-year-old boy from Chicago who had spent most of his life under some sort of state supervision or care, was also committed to St. Charles. His parents had abandoned him when he was an infant, and he was temporarily placed in the Illinois Children's Home and Aid Society. Thereafter, Edward was placed with an older man who had other foster children. When Edward's foster father decided to move to Ohio, he sent Edward back to the Children's Home and Aid Society, which eventually transferred his case to the Catholic Home Society Bureau. The caseworkers there discovered that Edward and some of the other children in the home had been sexually abused by their foster father. Unfortunately, his social worker seemingly blamed him for his abuse when she discouraged a woman who was interested in caring for Edward from adopting him. She claimed he had been involved in "sex perversions" and was "prone to be a degenerate." Edward was subsequently committed to St. Charles.[33]

Black Hypervisibility and Segregation at St. Charles

Early institutional reports from the Training School for Boys at St. Charles made virtually no reference to the racial composition of boys in the institution. Unlike the Illinois Training School for Girls, which tracked the number of immigrants, native-born whites, and African Americans from the moment it opened, St. Charles administrators tracked nationality, European ethnicity, and religion but not race until the 1920s. In its 1908 institutional report, for example, St. Charles documented that 186 out of 388 boys were "foreign born." The majority of boys with foreign heritage were from Germany, Ireland, Russia, and Italy. Although juvenile court records indicate a very small number of African American boys were present at the institution, they were counted as "American" in St. Charles's records. In the next biennial report, Superintendent C. W. Hart noted that although there was "a large increase in the number of boys of foreign parentage, and a slight decrease in the boys of American parentage" in the institution, "the percentage of Afro-Americans in the school is small." Superintendent Hart did not deem it important to specify the number of black boys at the institution, and they were again included under the American count in 1909.[34] Between 1910 and 1928, institutional reports continued to refer only to the number of "American" and "foreign born" boys in the institution, indicating that administrators did not feel a need to internally track the specific number of African American boys in the school.

The school's 1928 annual report marked an important shift. For the first time, St. Charles specified the number of African American boys in its institution and continued to do so in subsequent years. The superintendent reported that 163 out of 800 boys were "colored." The number of "American" and "foreign born" boys were still documented in the 1928 report, but this, too, changed in 1929. The institution's annual report to the Department of Public Welfare marked a moment when the boys' nationality and ethnicity became less important in institutional records than their race. The report noted that of the 760 boys in the institution, 168 "colored" boys made up 22 percent of the institution, whereas 592 were simply "white."[35] This trend of collapsing European ethnicity into whiteness while highlighting blackness—as opposed to simple Americanness—marked a permanent shift.

The folding of European ethnicity into whiteness in institutional records mirrored the transitional shift in redefinitions of whiteness elsewhere in the city and the nation. Administrators', legislators', and community members' anxiety over the dramatic shift in the demographics at St. Charles— along with the growing belief that there was "a different sort of boy" in the institution—eventually led to changes in institutional polices. By the 1940s, administrators and state officials began to abandon the rehabilitative ideal and ignore the institution's original purpose—which was to "save" delinquent boys—by asserting that that St. Charles had always been intended as a home for dependent boys. Specific concerns—like attempted escapes and runaways—became more salient, and administrators and state legislatures began to advocate for racial segregation and more punitive treatment of boys in the institution.

Unlike at the Training School for Girls at Geneva, where by 1910 the practice of racial segregation had been formalized barely a decade after its founding, administrators at St. Charles did not racially segregate boys until 1935. Institutional reports echo the 1921 findings of the Chicago Commission on Race Relations, that boys at the school had not experienced any racial separation. The report noted, "Negro and white boys live in the same cottages, eat in the same dining room, and use the same playground." African American boys even had the opportunity to take on leadership roles in the institution, as the report found that "four out of the twelve cadet companies have Negro captains, and these have more white than Negro boys under them." St. Charles managing officer Colonel C. B. Adams told investigators, "I really think mentally, and I am sure physically, the colored boys such as come into the institution today are superior to the white boys. We make much of the athletics in the school and the best athletes we have are colored boys." Similarly, social scientist Evelyn Randall found during her 1925 visit to St. Charles that under the school's official admission plan, the rule was that boys should be separated based on age and the type of offense they had committed, and "colored boys are to be sent to all cottages and farms in accordance with the classification [system] outlined." No "racial difficulties in regard to employment or discipline" were reported, "and the general conduct of Negro and white boys was reported to be the same."[36]

In 1929, a reporter for the *Chicago Defender* praised St. Charles for not resorting to racial segregation when he became aware of the institution's integrationist ethos. As the reporter noted, "In many institutions where boys of the Race are confined we find them segregated into separate groups, but not so at this great training school. In every cottage throughout the entire institution, members of the Race are assigned and in many instances find them commanders of companies and leaders of details." Interestingly enough, the *Defender* indicated that school administrators had considered instituting racial segregation in 1922. Rumors that the cottages would become racially segregated led to negative comparisons to the Geneva girls school, where girls "of the Race are all thrown together in one cottage." This fear never came to pass, however, as in 1932, the *Defender* continued to praise St. Charles: "the outstanding feature of the school is the absolute absence of the race question."[37]

In 1935, on the heels of the *Lattimore* decision and when the first wave of black migration had nearly reached its end, administrators at St. Charles suddenly concluded that boys in the institution had severe—though unspecified—behavioral problems. Their sole solution to these purportedly new behavioral problems was racial segregation. Although institutional reports did not link any specific instances of bad behavior with racial integration, the school's managing officer, William T. Harmon, began developing a plan of racial segregation in the cottages during the summer of 1935 because he thought it would lead to "good behavior." Harmon "reported that by the gradual process of elimination of the white boys, one cottage had been turned over completely for colored occupancy with good results." Although she did not specify the specific benefits she observed, the school secretary similarly concluded in the report that "the largest colored boys were segregated with satisfactory results" and "the smaller boys had been segregated by color" as well.[38] Harmon's report indicated that the school was undergoing a general "readjustment of the populations" and that "the establishment of certain cottages exclusively for colored boys" was a part of the reorganization of cottages by age and size. This new policy of racial segregation led to the type of severe overcrowding in black cottages found in the institution for girls at Geneva—particularly in cottages belonging to the older African American boys.[39]

This new policy of racial segregation had an immediate impact on black boys by severely compromising their living conditions there and elsewhere in the juvenile justice system. Because each cottage at St. Charles had a maximum occupancy of forty boys, administrators' decision to restrict black boys to a set number of cottages created a backlog at the Cook County Juvenile Detention Center, which held children before they were transferred to a correctional institution. Boys sentenced to St. Charles could be held in juvenile detention for as many as three to six months before even beginning to serve their time. In 1938, a "Mr. Barry" of the Cook County Juvenile

Detention Center complained that the "necessity of holding the boys awaiting commitment" was causing disciplinary problems. The overflow at the Juvenile Detention Center meant that many of the older boys were forced to take up residence in the center's basement, which meant they had no immediate access to toilets and limited opportunities to get out. Barry reported that the increase in disciplinary problems "developed from [the boys'] resentment at being held for months without counting on time to be spent in St. Charles."[40]

A Different "Type of Boy": Escaped "Fugitives" and Hysteria

In spite of their growing hypervisibility and more explicit differential treatment, African American boys resisted their confinement in a variety of ways. In a few cases, they defended themselves from physical abuse and threats by staff. Seventeen-year-old Noah Betts, for example, was removed from St. Charles and sentenced to the Kane County jail in 1942 on a charge of "assault with a deadly weapon." He attacked two staff members with a mop handle as a result of an altercation. Other staff members eventually overpowered him.[41]

More often than not, African American boys used escape—usually for only a few days—as a method of resistance. In 1934, for example, the *Chicago Defender* featured a story on William F. Hawkins, a seventeen-year-old who ran away from St. Charles on February 23 in an effort to go back home. After a few days, "with his feet frost bitten so badly he was unable to walk ... he summoned the police" and gave himself up. Police officers took him to the Bridewell, Chicago's main jail house, for hospital treatment. After that, William was promptly returned to St. Charles.[42]

In the late 1920s, newspapers such as the *Chicago Tribune*, *St. Charles Tribune*, *Elgin Daily Courier*, and *Geneva Republican* increasingly featured stories about African American boys hiding in and running through their towns in an effort to escape the harsh nature of their confinement. These stories were written against a backdrop of negative media depictions of black boys more generally. These often sensational journalistic accounts fueled notions of black hypermasculinity, erased black boys' vulnerability, and reinforced notions that black men were menacing, innately dangerous criminals. A June 1938 *Chicago Tribune* article, which featured a full-length story about high school student Robert Nixon's attempt to escape city police by climbing a building, illustrates this. The article gave a lengthy account of Robert's life, emphasizing his southern roots and the color of his skin. The reporter stated that Robert came from a "pretty little town in the old South" called Tallulah, Louisiana, but possessed "none of the charm of speech of manner that is characteristic of so many southern darkies." For the reporter, Robert was in fact an apelike "savage," because "so far as manner and appearance go, civilization has left Nixon practically untouched. His hunched shoulders and long, sinewy arms that dangle almost to his knees . . . his out-thrust head and catlike tread all suggest an animal." Robert was also described as "very black—almost pure Negro," with "physical characteristics suggest[ing] an earlier link in the species . . . a jungle Negro."

For the reporter, Robert also represented a recognizable and dangerous archetype of young black masculinity that could be subdued only through brute strength. "This type is known to be ferocious and relentless in a fight. Though docile enough under ordinary circumstances, they are easily aroused . . . [and] the veneer of civilization disappears." The article also invoked the archetype of the insensate pickaninny, which cast black children as beings who could not feel pain. The writer portrayed boys like Robert as physically invulnerable beings with a high capacity for pain because they "didn't mind" being "whipped" as punishment for playing hooky from school. As policemen watched Robert, who was accused of rape and murder and allegedly climbed onto the fifth floor of a building, one of them apparently remarked, "Look at him go. Just like an ape." A crowd gathered below the building Robert climbed and yelled "Lynch him! Kill him!" Robert, who the reporter claimed "showed no fear, just as he showed no remorse," simply backed against a wall and "bared his teeth." Robert was ultimately sentenced to death by electrocution.[43]

When black boys from St. Charles appeared in local newspapers, they almost always did so as dangerous runaway burglars, rapists, and assailants. Newspaper descriptions of their escape attempts were often paired with demands for a more punitive form of treatment at St. Charles and demands from legislatures and community members that a fence be built around the school's grounds. A 1939 *Tribune* article, for example, quoted state senator Thomas Gunning, who represented residents at St. Charles: "The citizens of the Fox River valley are terribly concerned with frequent escapes and it is the duty of the legislature to help them." He described an escape attempt involving four boys, "in their late teens and all colored," who were arrested after they "clubbed the night watchman with a cleaning brush," then "stole the guard's keys" before attempting to flee back to Chicago with a stolen car. A 1941 article described eight "negro" inmates, "five of them robbers," who left surrounding communities in a state of panic after they fled the school and "disappeared into nearby cornfields."[44] Stories like this, which featured "negro youths" who "overcame guards" at St. Charles and stole cars and money in their attempts to escape and go back home, appeared regularly through the 1950s. The boys featured in these newspaper accounts—many of whom were trying to find their way back home to Chicago—utilized a variety of tactics in their escape attempts. They often formed groups—sometimes across racial lines—and concocted elaborate escape plans. They climbed fences, destroyed school property, physically overpowered staff members, and sometimes stole food and money from neighboring homes in their attempts to free themselves. The boys' resistance against their confinement, as well as newspaper accounts of the growing "menace" of St. Charles escapees, was one of the factors that led to a punitive shift in the institution and in the juvenile justice system more broadly.[45]

By 1939, these negative depictions had a tangible impact on the surrounding community, as neighboring residents called for harsh physical punishment and stricter discipline at St. Charles. The earliest example of this coincided with the beginning of black boys' hypervisibility in the institution. The spectacle of Nathaniel Moffet's 1928 attempt to escape from St. Charles led nearby residents to call not only for corporal punishment but for a harsher form of military training. Nathaniel Moffet was a sixteen-year-old African American boy who escaped from St. Charles and was sent to county jail after he was caught stealing a purse belonging to the wife of an advertising executive who lived nearby. She endured bruises and scratches from beating him off until he fled with her purse. Chief of police Ruben Anderson petitioned St. Charles administrators and asserted, "Women residents are afraid to venture out at night since the Moffet case." By 1932, municipal officers, civic leaders, and residents of Kane County also criticized St. Charles administrators and urged the "immediate return of strict military training and corporal punishment" because they believed it was the "only effective method of discipline for the inmates." Kane County residents called for a reinstatement of Major Butler, a former superintendent who had authorized the use of corporal punishment during his tenure and asserted that "Whipping is the only remedy for these young criminals."[46]

In one of the most notorious escape attempts, eight African American boys—one from Evanston and the rest from Chicago—caused quite a stir in 1941. They threw Kane County residents into a panic after they escaped from St. Charles and eluded capture for over twenty-four hours. According to the *Chicago Tribune*, "All available police and deputy sheriffs in the surrounding towns were sent and thrown into the hunt for the fugitives." The group of escapees included two fourteen-year-olds, two sixteen-year-olds, two seventeen-year-olds, and two eighteen-year-olds. The boys were all housed in Harding Cottage, which by now was a dorm for African American boys who had been in the institution for less than thirty days.

Their "carefully planned" escape began when the boys pretended to study on the first floor of the cottage. When the housemother's back was turned, one of the boys signaled and they all ran to a window. Another boy raised a chair and smashed it through a window before three others forced the heavy screen out. The boys, all of whom were barefoot, ran thirty yards to the corner of the thirteen-foot barbed-wire steel fence enclosing St. Charles and climbed over. The more agile members of the group helped the boys who needed assistance getting over the fence. One of the school's patrol guards almost caught the last boy by grabbing his heel as he scrambled over the fence, but he successfully pulled away and joined the other boys, who then "disappeared into the cornfields."[47]

Like the vast majority of runaways at St. Charles, their escape was short-lived as six of the boys were found in the fields the very next day. The last two were found "wet and hungry" on the west side of Chicago two days later. According to the *Chicago Tribune*, the residents near St. Charles began "breathing easier" after all of the escapees were found. Assistant managing officer Harold Johnson planned to send all eight boys to the disciplinary cottage for thirty days as punishment, but the Illinois director of public welfare Rodney Brandon had another idea. He urged Criminal Court judge Julius Miner to sentence five of the oldest boys to the state penitentiary at Pontiac because he felt it was a more "secure" place. Judge Miner made an unprecedented move and sentenced two of the boys to Pontiac for a term of one year to life in prison. Judge Miner stated that this harsh penalty, which essentially punished the boys' escape attempts with potential life in prison, was intended to protect both law enforcement and the public by sending a message to boys at St. Charles. "The public and the police must be protected," he asserted. "This will serve as a warning to all boys sent to the training school that the courts are not joking and will not hesitate to send them to the penitentiary if they violate the confidence judges place in them by sending them to the school."[48]

Despite the growing public hysteria over escapees, runaway St. Charles boys were not a new problem, and the actual number of runaways had declined. As Mr. and Mrs. Johnson, the first housefather and housemother to take charge of a cottage after the school's opening, told managing officer

William Harmon in 1939, "We had runaways right from the beginning.... There have always been runaways."[49] A 1915 institutional report showed that one out of six boys at St. Charles—over one hundred boys in total—were missing as a result of absconding from the institution. According to the superintendent, the chances that these boys would be returned to St. Charles were less than one in ten. In spite of this, Kane County residents did not demand more rigorous military discipline, corporal punishment, transfers to state prisons, or stricter rules of confinement during the institution's early years.[50] Local newspapers, such as the *St. Charles Chronicle*, which had followed happenings at the school since its 1901 founding and reported on minutiae like the school cattle getting inspected, and the *Chicago Tribune*, did not feature stories about runaways or sound a rallying cry of danger.[51]

The runaway boy issue became salient in the late 1920s and began to be viewed as a new crisis. This erroneous perception that boys escaping from St. Charles was a new problem led to community-wide calls for the containment and punishment of escapees. Kane County residents' sentiments were fueled by newspaper headlines like "Colored Boys Escape State School" and "Three Negro Youths Who Escaped School Held to Grand Jury" and by articles about high-profile incidents—such as the Nathaniel Moffet case and the escape of the eight black inmates. One *Chicago Tribune* reporter wrote that members of Chicago's "young 42 gang, Negroes, who have escaped from half a dozen jails; small bright eyed youngsters, and every variety of juvenile hoodlum and petty offender" occupied St. Charles.[52]

These news reports were more likely to include references to escapees' physical size or perceived strength if they were black. Newspaper reporters described escaped black boys with words like "husky," "strong," and "formidable" while often featuring information about their height and weight. These physical characteristics were mentioned not simply for informational purposes but to portray the boys as physically menacing and underline the danger they could have posed to the community. Moreover, most of articles on escapees were about boys who had already been caught. For example, a *Chicago Tribune* article about the group of eight black escapees highlighted that the youngest in the group—the fourteen-year-old—stood "over six feet tall" and obliterated the chance that his young age could mitigate the symbolic threat he and other group members could pose to the community. Similarly, former superintendent Major Butler used the image of a physically imposing black youth in particular to rationalize his use of corporal punishment during an interview with *Tribune* reporters. Butler relayed the story of a "Negro youth, standing over 6 feet in height and weighing more than 185 pounds," whom he beat with a whip as punishment for terrorizing a "small white boy."[53]

Whipping was an action that evoked the brutal disciplinary regime of racial slavery for white and black Americans alike. Major Butler's proud assertion that he "beat" a black boy with a whip as "punishment" for terrorizing a "small white boy" was intended to reassure surrounding residents through his evocation of this historical form of racialized terror and control. Kane County residents' new demands that St. Charles inmates be whipped in order to restore control at the school relied on a similar logic.

Within the context of popular conceptions surrounding black males' innate proclivity for rape and other violent crimes, and racial animosity against migrants, Kane County residents' hysteria is not surprising. The stories of escapees began to be paired with calls for a "stricter regime" of discipline and corporal punishment at the school. Headlines such as "Return of Strap Rule Demanded for St. Charles," "Five Towns Live in Fear of 'Boys' at State School," and "Whipping Urged to End Mass Escapes" appeared regularly between 1928 and 1950. As a result, St. Charles escapees developed an increasingly notorious reputation among Kane County residents.[54]

Kane County residents' accusations that runaway attempts and successful escapes occurred because school personnel "coddled or pampered" St. Charles inmates put administrators on the defensive. Their "constant fear of escaped hoodlums from the St. Charles school" who were "husky enough to be in the prize ring" coincided with residents' demands for stricter punishment at the school.[55] In addition to promoting whipping as a disciplinary tool at the school, the residents condemned the school's failure to reinstitute the "the harmless but effective practice of throwing cold water at unruly miscreants." By 1935, as a result of public pressure and staff members' own changing perceptions about the boys in their custody, school administrators introduced a new policy at St. Charles. Boys who stole a car as part of their effort to escape the institution would now be confined to a disciplinary cottage for six months.[56] In spite of this harsh new disciplinary rule, former superintendent Major Butler, who had become a spokesperson for Kane County residents, demanded stricter punishment. In 1939, Major Butler demanded that St. Charles administrators officially embrace whipping as a form of punishment and enforce stricter disciplinary policies across the board at the school.[57]

The negative sentiment surrounding community members' angst over the runaway boy issue caused A. L. Bowen, director of the Illinois Department of Public Welfare, to respond to Kane County residents' criticism that same year. A *Chicago Tribune* article reported that Bowen accused the state legislature of enabling the "miscreant" boys by not taking Kane County residents' concerns seriously. He asserted that the state legislature "lacked legislative sympathy and cooperation" and that as a result he could not effectively address problems at St. Charles.[58]

St. Charles superintendent William Harmon asserted that demographic changes and the type of boy courts sent to the institution were responsible for the "new" challenges in management and the prevention of escapes. Harmon blamed the residents' "constant fear of burglary, robbery, and rape" on Cook County Circuit Court judges for "sending unruly and tough criminals to the school."[59] The deeper issue for Harmon, however, was the "radical changes in the population of Illinois during the last half of the century" and the consequent introduction of "racial stocks which mature more quickly" into the institution. He explained, "today we are no longer dealing with petty criminals, but boys who have the ambition for becoming gangsters and elite criminals. . . . At the same calendar age of the delinquent of thirty-five years ago he is vastly older in experience, and he obviously requires much sterner treatment." Harmon alleged that the situation was so dire, "separate institutions may be necessary" to separate boys who had committed petty crimes from "elite criminals." His assertion that St. Charles was no longer equipped to handle the type of boys being committed to the institution and his claim that a separate institution where this new type of boy could be sent "may be necessary" foreshadowed the state's decision to build its first maximum-security prison for boys in 1941.[60]

Superintendent Harmon did not explicitly refer to African American boys in his discussion of new "racial stocks which mature more quickly" in the institution. In light of the increase in the number of black boys in the institution, their new hypervisibility in institutional reports and the community, the general anxiety surrounding the increasing number of black people in Chicago, popular conceptions about black males possessing menacing and animalistic brute strength, and newspaper articles about black escapees, it is likely that Harmon was using coded language to signal blackness in his discussion of "racial stocks" that matured "more quickly."

The historical practice of ignoring black children's age-based physical and emotional vulnerabilities undergirded St. Charles administrators' sense that they were dealing with a different "type of boy."[61] This is further illustrated by the case of a dependent black boy who was committed to St. Charles in 1941. Russell Ballard, who was superintendent of St. Charles at the time, singled out an African American boy, Jim Barnes, in an internal memo for unspecified reasons. He claimed, "it was doubtful" that Jim, who was committed to the school because his father was a drunkard and his mother deceased, "will benefit from further training." Although Jim had not committed any crimes and was sent to St. Charles because child welfare agents could not find an appropriate place for him, Superintendent Ballard concluded that he was akin to an adult criminal with no chance of rehabilitation.[62]

The 61st General Assembly: Debating Control, Containment, and Racial Segregation Policies at St. Charles

At the 61st General Assembly meeting in 1939, Kane County residents' fear of St. Charles escapees dominated the discussion. The mayor of St. Charles, Dr. Langu, spoke on behalf of residents in his city when he claimed that the "criminal type of boy" at the school had the seemingly new tendency "to run over [their] countryside wherever they [took] it into their head to do so." At that same meeting, Senator Gunning urged other state representatives to approve the building of a "new cell house at Pontiac Prison for the exclusive incarceration of criminally inclined boys." Senator Gunning went on to describe a recent group of four escapees—"all the boys in their late teens and all colored"—to illustrate the problem and convey a sense of urgency to the other legislators.[63]

In the context of the growing paranoia over escapes among the institution's neighboring residents and anxieties surrounding race both inside the institution and outside of it, Gunning's pairing of a call for more punitive policies at St. Charles and decision to cite as an example an escape attempt involving four black boys was not coincidental. It was intended to play upon whites' racial fears and buttress his claim that there was a new type of boy who was ill fitted for the institution's rehabilitative purpose and better suited for commitment among irredeemable adult criminals at Pontiac.[64]

Representatives of Illinois's public welfare agencies, St. Charles administrators, concerned black citizens, and interested persons from Cook and Kane Counties all journeyed to Springfield to weigh in on the proposed new policies at St. Charles. The main question was not whether policy changes should be implemented at St. Charles but what kind of changes needed to occur and how they should be implemented. The General Assembly meeting was intended to serve as a brainstorming session, which would result in a series of recommended changes and solutions for the perceived new problems at St. Charles. A Joint Commission, composed of five House members and five Senate members, was charged with studying "conditions existing at the St. Charles School for Boys to determine whether the present method of grouping inmates is satisfactory or whether a system of segregation should be maintained" for the purposes of the meeting. "Segregation" in this context referred to age and type of infraction rather than race.[65]

An objective discussion of the runaway issue would have acknowledged that the percentage of escape attempts at St. Charles had declined over the years. In 1933, 52 percent of St. Charles inmates reportedly made escape attempts. In 1937 and 1938, respectively, 17 percent and 20 percent of inmates made escape attempts.[66] The General Assembly debate nevertheless focused on whether changing the age range of boys admitted to the school, excluding boys who committed certain kinds of crimes, and changing criminal and juvenile court sentencing policies would effectively remedy the escapee problem.

The legislature also took up Senator Gunning's call for a separate institution for the new "criminally inclined" boys being sent to St. Charles. The assembly did not debate whether this step was actually necessary, particularly in light of the dramatic decrease in the number of boys running away. Rather, they debated whether boys who were considered too dangerous to be included in St. Charles's general population should be housed in a new facility or a separate branch at the men's reformatory at Pontiac. This debate over whether certain boys should be excluded from St. Charles and put in a new branch or facility marked the state's official first step toward building its first maximum-security prison for youths.

A. L. Bowen, director of the Department of Public Welfare, favored an age limit of fifteen or sixteen at St. Charles. He also advocated the implantation of a program that would specifically "save boys" whom they knew would "be benefitted by treatment" and working out a separate plan for boys "for whom the school can do nothing." For boys whom they decided could not benefit from treatment, Bowen recommended "special segregated quarters . . . at one of the prison branches, preferably Pontiac," far away from boys judged redeemable and admitted to St. Charles, as creating a separate branch would be cheaper than establishing a completely new building.[67]

St. Charles's superintendent, William Harmon, also suggested that courts place only boys under the age of sixteen—but older than ten—in St. Charles.[68] For him, regulating the age of boys in the institution was a critical part of solving the problems there. It was also intimately tied to the problem of race and the different "kind of boy" in the institution and who "at the same calendar age of the delinquent of thirty-five years ago . . . [was] vastly older in experience."[69] To Harmon, the solution to the problem of these new boys who were perceived as physically larger and more experientially mature was fixing the age at which boys could be admitted to St. Charles at sixteen. He was so convinced that this intersecting problem of age and the different "kind of boy" being sent to the institution was the root of the problem that he demanded that judges who committed boys to St. Charles "be required to verify ages through presentation to the school of certified copies of birth certificates"[70]

This fervent belief that a new and more dangerous type of boy was being admitted to St. Charles was also being implied through a curious debate about the original purpose of the institution. In 1901, the Illinois legislature had mandated the establishment of a "State Home for Delinquent Boys." The institution's earliest administrators were aware that St. Charles "was founded for the express purpose of caring for delinquent boys between the ages of 10 and 17" and explained this purpose in institutional reports.[71] Nevertheless, in spite of the school's original name and stated purpose, legislators debated whether St. Charles was meant to be a home for dependent boys alone or include delinquent boys. Director of public welfare A. L. Bowen answered this question by arguing that it was for dependent boys alone: "The purpose of this institution was to take care of dependent and neglected boys who were likely to become delinquent, because of their neglect and dependency." Judge Frank Bicek of Cook County's Juvenile Court found Director Bowen's conception of the school's original purpose too liberal. He asserted that the institution was not even intended as a preventative measure for dependent boys "who were likely to become delinquent" and accused Bowen of conflating dependency with delinquency. Although Senator Abraham Marovitz resolved the issue by reading the relevant portion of the statute, which showed that St. Charles was in fact intended for delinquent boys, the Assembly collectively advocated a punitive shift in policies toward St. Charles.[72]

Kane County residents, government officials, and school administrators were not the only constituencies that inserted their voices into the debate about policies at St. Charles, however. Black state legislators and representatives of the Urban League and YWCA interjected their concerns about the experiences of African American boys at St. Charles into the legislative debates. State senator William A. Wallace and Assemblyman Charles J. Jenkins's decision—as some of the few black state legislators at the time—to call upon the General Assembly to address the unique experiences of black inmates at St. Charles is significant. As political representatives of their community, they were speaking on behalf of Black Chicagoans and making sure city and state resources supported their community.

By the early 1930s, when African American boys began to make up a sizable portion of its population, black Chicagoans identified St. Charles as an institution where the "problem of wayward youth" in the community could be addressed. They hoped that it would function as the child-saving rehabilitative institution Progressive-era reformers envisioned. In 1932, community activists together with juvenile court and state agency officials traveled fifty miles to St. Charles to answer a question at the forefront of some activists' mind: "What shall we do with our delinquent boys?" The black community was clear on the institution's original purpose to educate delinquent and dependent boys alike.

Brainstorming about ways to prevent African American boys from being committed to the institution in the first place, and preventing their recommitment because of parole violations, was at the top of the agenda.[73] Among the attendees were Judge Albert George, a member of the state Board of Pardons; Howard Robinson of the Chicago Urban League; and "welfare workers and directors of the Race work" under the auspices of the Chicago Church Federation. After touring the school and meeting with five hundred boys in the gym, the group met with managing officer Robert Havlik to "formulate some feasible plan whereby the wayward youth of our Race may be reclaimed from the ranks of the potential criminal and made useful members of society."[74] State representative Jenkins echoed this same sentiment at the Assembly meeting when he declared that "the problem of [N]egro youth, to those of us who are serious minded, is of the greatest problem in our opinion in this country today."[75]

State senator Wallace and representative Jenkins made St. Charles's new racial segregation policies—in light of the perception that there was a dangerously new type of boy in the institution—their chief concern. Senator Wallace introduced a resolution at the 61st General Assembly of the Illinois legislature demanding that racial segregation and discrimination at the Training School for Boys at St. Charles cease. Representative Jenkins introduced it this way: "During the Revolutionary War when our country was established, some 1,200 negroes served as soldiers for the United States. . . . The first blood was shed by Crispus Attucks. . . . We didn't have Negro segregation then. We have since developed that segregation. . . . I say therein lies the fate of Democracy, because if we are to exist, this local problem of ours is just as urgent as the problem of racial prejudices today."[76]

Embedded in Representative Jenkins's words was the idea that racial seg-regation at St. Charles both marked black residents with a stain of inferi-ority and compromised the state and nation writ large in their move toward full democracy and freedom for all citizens. In light of the United States' impending intervention in World War II, these allegations of racism, un-Americanness, deprivations of citizenship rights, and anti-democratic behaviors had rhetorical power. By linking the race-based discrimina-tory treatment of black boys in the justice system with the discourse of democracy, Jenkins also tapped into the still raw emotion over nine young black men and boys who (excluding a thirteen-year-old) were sentenced to death in Scottsboro, Alabama, after two white women falsely accused them of rape. Black Chicagoans, twenty thousand of whom marched in protest in 1933 and celebrated the 1937 Supreme Court's overturning of the death sen-tences, were among the many activists around the world who highlighted the dangerous nexus of racial stereotypes, segregation, and the unconstitutional deprivation of Sixth and Fourteenth Amendment rights for young African Americans in the criminal justice system.[77]

Representative Jenkins, who served as the spokesperson for Senator Wallace's resolution, pointed out the illogical basis for racial segregation of the boys. First, he noted that four of the nineteen homes at St. Charles had recently been "set aside on a segregation rule for the Negro boys only," and that there were only two homes "in which the American Rule is ob-served." Jenkins then questioned the utility of this new racial segregation when institutional reports indicated that the "conduct of the boys who are in the mixed homes is just as good as the conduct of the boys who are in the other homes."[78] Jenkins, by calling the racially mixed cottages homes where the "American Rule" was observed, utilized a discursive strategy civil rights activists around the nation employed in their fight against racial segrega-tion. His intent was to highlight the philosophical and legal principles of constitutional equality.

Jenkins also portrayed racial segregation in a state institution for children as an inherently backward practice the rest of the nation was moving away from. "I care not whether it has existed for a half a century," Jenkins asserted. "We are living in a new era, an era when our country is the last bulwark of freedom ... we are living in an era where we must practice democracy." He pointed out that racial segregation violated a 1937 state law, which man-dated that "any person in charge of any State building who does not allow the facilities equally to all citizens should be discharged by the appointed authority." He added, "I have always felt that above all things, State institutions and things that belong to the State should be blind, like the image of Justice, when it comes to the question of race. . . . [State institutions] should set the example for citizens of the State, by rising above petty prejudices."[79] Representative Jenkins's argument amounted to an assertion that the state—vis-à-vis racial segregation policies at St. Charles—was subjecting children to differential treatment simply because of their race and denying them the equal treatment they were entitled to as citizens and state residents.

Mr. Bose of Chicago's Wabash Avenue Branch of the YMCA and Joseph Jefferson of the Urban League also attended the 61st General Assembly and criticized St. Charles for hiring only a small number of black employees. These representatives of the YMCA and Chicago Urban League framed their allegations of discriminatory hiring practices at St. Charles in a way that highlighted the negative impact the lack of black employees had on African American boys at St. Charles. "We do feel that the number of Negro boys in St. Charles," Jefferson stated, "warrants more Negro men of training and educational background to be out there to serve as an inspiration." Representative Jenkins expressed a similar concern that there was "not a single colored housefather" there even though "approximately one-third of the population at the St. Charles School for Boys is colored." Jefferson and Bose also called attention to the "very rapid turn-over in the employment of Negro men" and asserted "there must be something wrong when seven are seemingly dismissed within one year." They essentially argued that racially discriminatory hiring practices and the hostile work environment black employees faced was indicative of a larger problem that reflected a rapidly deteriorating and adverse racial climate for black boys at St. Charles.[80]

The attention black state legislators and community activists paid to African American boys' experiences at St. Charles, as well as the symbolic implications of the institution's racial policies, suggests that the institution and the juvenile justice system more generally was an important vehicle through which African Americans could highlight black children's vulnerability, attempt to protect them, and lay claims on democratic citizenship for all black people.[81] Chicago's African American community began to mount a cohesive grassroots struggle for access to public and private facilities and economic freedom in the 1930s and early 1940s.[82] Black residents' increasing agitation for social, economic, and political rights mirrored the development of early civil rights struggles that accelerated in urban areas across the North during World War II.[83] Black legislators' and community activists' decision to insert themselves into the legislative conversations surrounding St. Charles shows that they identified the institution as a site that had an important influence on black children in Chicago. It also shows they believed that the institutional policies that shaped African American boys' experiences directly affected Black Chicagoans' state civil rights.

The General Assembly had a set agenda, and other legislators did not anticipate black representatives' and community members' activism on behalf of African American boys at St. Charles. Their advocacy nevertheless resulted in important additions to the policy recommendations for the school. Even though Superintendent Harmon denied the allegations of racial bias at St. Charles and argued that black employees and inmates were all treated with the "utmost respect," the General Assembly mandated that a "a larger percentage of members of that race [be] presented in the institution's supervising activities." Within days of the General Assembly meeting, discharged black employee Fletcher Thompson of Chicago was reinstated to his position as recreation instructor at the school. He alleged he had been dismissed because of "race prejudice" and credited black representatives and activists at the 61st General Assembly for his reinstatement. Internal memos from St. Charles show administrators also took up the activists' and legislators' calls for increased diversity among its staff. Administrators began contacting "employment agencies on the Southside [of Chicago, and] some churches," because they believed these groups could be an important ally for "tapping resources" in Chicago's black community.

The bulk of the General Assembly's final policy recommendations for St. Charles was ultimately centered on instituting measures that would provide for the more efficient control and containment of boys. The Assembly asked for an amendment to the 1901 act, which for the first time would "exclude any one convicted of a felony from being committed" to St. Charles. The Assembly also instituted a new age limit for boys admitted to the institution and asked that a complete case history and age verification accompany boys who were committed there. Later, the new admits would be photographed and fingerprinted before being integrated into the institution. The state legislature also passed Senate Bill No. 399, emergency legislation with the express purpose of erecting a wire fence and properly lighting St. Charles at night.

The General Assembly's approval of the "acquisition of property" and construction of the first maximum-security facility for persons under the age of eighteen was considered the highlight of the new provisions. This decision was a seminal moment in the evolution of the juvenile justice system, as it represented an unequivocal shift away from the rehabilitative ideal that undergirded the very emergence of the system toward a punitive approach to delinquent children. The facility was to be located forty miles away from St. Charles and sixty miles away from Chicago. This prison, named the State Reformatory at Sheridan, operated under the same administrative control of the Training School at St. Charles.[84]

The Murder of James Williams and the Increasingly Punitive Turn

On Thursday, February 13, 1941, James Williams, a sixteen-year-old African American, became the first boy to die at the hands of staff members at St. Charles. He died as a result of a skull fracture and other injuries he sustained when two housefathers brutally beat him. The two employees, Robert Adams and William Laird, were formally charged with murder by the Kane County state attorney's office. Boys who witnessed the incident reported that the housefathers began beating James on a Wednesday afternoon while he and some other boys were shoveling coal near their cottage. James stopped shoveling and approached Adams, who may have been drunk and was supervising the boys, and told him he was not feeling well. Adams's response to James was to slap him and threaten him with more physical violence: "You wait till I get you in the cottage. I'll give you a hot reception." Adams then told James to "step back into line."[85]

When it was time to go back to the cottage that evening, James was so sick that he could barely walk or remove his clothing for a shower in the basement. Adams, completely unsympathetic to James's illness, yelled, "Get in with the others." Then he found a wooden paddle, returned to James, and began to strike him with it. Later, when James had finished showering but was dressing more slowly than the others because he was sick, Adams became more enraged and hit him with the paddle again. This time, Adams hit James with so much force that the paddle broke as it made contact with James's body.

James's cries of pain did not deter Adams. "Shut up!" he yelled, "I'll give you the hose, I'll turn the water on you." Adams then ordered another boy, Norman De Vore, to bring him a hose. Adams meanwhile took a brass nozzle and club off the shelf and proceeded to beat James with the back of the club. James eventually picked up a chair in an attempt to protect his body from Adams's blows. When that did not work, James tried to run back to the shower room, but Adams tackled him to the floor. When the other housefather, William Laird, entered the room, Adams screamed, "Hit him with the nozzle!" Laird obeyed and hit James with the brass nozzle so hard that he collapsed and became unconscious. James eventually died in Kane County Hospital.[86]

James Williams's murder at the hands of staff charged with protecting and caring for him caused a shake-up in black Chicago and the institution "of proportions unheard of." The controversy surrounding having a boy die at the hands of St. Charles employees for the first time in the school's history, alongside new race-based institutional policies and James Williams's identity as an African American, inevitably raised questions about racism and disciplinary practices at the institution. A *Tribune* writer reported a mood shift at St. Charles: "a hostile attitude on part of the youths followed closely on the heels of the slaying of James Williams." It manifested itself in a rebellion on March 12, 1941. Two boys at St. Charles said they feared for their own lives when they "told authorities" they wanted to leave the institution and be "transferred to the state prison" at Joliet for men.[87]

Governor Dwight Green ordered state welfare director Rodney Brandon to investigate the incident. Superintendent Frank Whipp opined to *Chicago Defender* reporters, "There is no doubt it is murder." Governor Green also received a telegram from state representative John Friedland of Elgin within a week of James's murder demanding the removal and suspension of William Harmon. Although Harmon was not fired, over twenty-four employees at St. Charles were forced to resign less than three weeks later, and Superintendent Whipp personally took charge of the school in order to quell criticism.[88]

Chicago's black community was incensed at James's murder and demanded that St. Charles institutionally redress the murder by eliminating racial segregation and reforming disciplinary practices. A group of black clergymen sent a telegram to the legislature calling James's death a "major blot in the penal history of Illinois and America." They insisted the governor launch a more extensive investigation of the tragedy. Reverend J. Branham of Olivet Baptist Church, Joseph M. Evans of Metropolitan Community Church, U. S. Robinson of Carey Temple African Methodist Episcopal Church, Bishop James A. Bray of the Christian Methodist Episcopal Church, and Dean H. M. Smith of the Chicago Baptist Institute also cosigned the telegram. Attorney Georgia Jones-Ellis, one of the most prominent women lawyers, began to procure a group of "militant women" that would "go to St. Charles, look into the death of the young inmate there," to put pressure on authorities. Despite the evidence from the injuries James sustained and his attempts to run away from his assailant, a jury in Geneva, Illinois, voted to acquit Robert Adams of murder. The jury was convinced of Adams's claim that he was acting out of self-defense and feared for his life when he beat James to death. The jury decision foreshadowed what would become a common state practice of refusing to hold law enforcement officials accountable when they unjustly tortured and killed the black children and adults they were charged to protect.[89]

In December 1941, black state representative Ernest A. Green introduced a resolution that called for a more extensive investigation of James's death. The proposed investigatory committee would examine not only the circumstances surrounding his death but the disciplinary methods at St. Charles and the qualifications of employees working at the institution, while also subpoenaing witnesses.[90] Rather than initiate an investigation, however, the Board of Public Welfare and St. Charles's administrators embraced Representative Jenkins's calls to end segregation in the institution and hire a new black administrator. On March 24, state representatives Jenkins and Greene met with the Board of Public Welfare and argued that James Williams's murder was a natural outgrowth of the racial bias inherent in the school's segregation policies. They demanded that "the un-American custom of segregation cease and desist . . . and to treat all alike." As a result, the State Welfare Commission—with the support of director Rodney Brandon—publicly prohibited all discrimination at St. Charles. Five months later, St. Charles also hired Walter J. Payne as a counselor. He was the first African American administrator at St. Charles.[91]

At an internal meeting later that year, however, St. Charles administrators and staff reneged on their promise to end racial segregation. At the meeting, all attendees were in "agreement that the statute which provides that there shall be no segregation in State institutions is democratically sound and should be adhered to." Nevertheless, they did not believe an immediate end to racial segregation in the institution was wise and violated the State Welfare Commission's prohibition. Rather, they recommended that "no racial change should be made at once but that within a reasonable length of time." They argued that segregation should be abolished slowly, "through a process based upon a scientific classification of all boys."[92]

Race and the Insatiable Thirst for Punishment

The culture of physical brutality and the vulnerability of inmates at St. Charles that was revealed as a result of James Williams's death did not thwart the growing thirst for harsher discipline and containment of juvenile inmates at St. Charles or Sheridan. Even though escapes from Sheridan were virtually nonexistent, fear and a desire to control and contain inmates at the new maximum-security prison developed among residents surrounding the new reformatory. Boys at Sheridan were housed on a campus enclosed by two steel fences—one twelve feet high, the other eight feet high. Barbed wire was placed on top of and inside the fences. Armed guards who were stationed at four different towers on the campus were prepared to shoot any would be escapees.[93] Neighbors opposed state senator Thomas Gunning's attempt to make the reformatory more "comfortable and pleasant for inmates." Speaking on behalf of the town's residents, R. W. Dvorak of the Chicago Crime Commission articulated this fear and animosity when he stated, "Inmates in such an institution shouldn't be coddled. They should be taught obedience and should understand they are being punished. Sentimentality and the maudlin sympathy for criminals are poor substitutes for material safeguards."[94]

When staff members at Sheridan held an open house to ease the surrounding community's fear of the boys, they were shocked to find that "the people came with many distorted ideas about the School and the boys." It seemed as if "all the visitors were anxious to see the boys, expecting to see something strange and unusual." One of the visitors stated with surprise, "Why they look like any other boy on the street, there really is nothing different about them." Another visitor commented, "Why they even smile." Such statements were evidence of the public perception of delinquent boys and the many years of negative media publicity surrounding St. Charles and (later) Sheridan. Employees' notes revealed their sense that people generally came with "a hostile attitude" about the school. Visitors reportedly left with a "sympathetic attitude," however, after they were reassured by staff members' statements and the physical setup of the school, which made "the impossibility of escapes from the School" clear. One visitor noted with relief, "Gee, nobody will ever get out of there."[95]

Only a few years after its opening, African American boys were even more disproportionately represented at Sheridan than they were at St. Charles. In 1943, African American boys made up 36 percent of the population at Sheridan and 29 percent of the population at St. Charles. That same year, staff members at Sheridan toyed with the idea of placing well-behaved boys on the first floor and leaving the doors unlocked. This idea was vetoed, however, on suspicion that "such a setup may segregate the white boys from the colored and lead to race distinction."[96] This suggests that staff members believed that African American boys were so inherently dangerous that even among boys who needed a maximum-security prison, special measures needed to be taken to secure their containment.

Conditions at St. Charles and Sheridan continued to be a source of controversy among legislators and Chicago-area residents through the 1940s. Rather than quell or mitigate any concerns surrounding delinquent boys in state institutions, the legislature's creation of a new maximum-security facility at Sheridan and increasingly strict punishment and containment policies at St. Charles only seemed to fuel hysteria and misperceptions about children committed to state institutions for delinquent children. It was as if the public desire for the control, discipline, and punishment of delinquent boys was insatiable. Despite rampant evidence of the abuse inmates at both institutions suffered at the hands of staff members, a number of residents in Kane and Cook counties continued to accuse legislators and administrators of failing to "discipline misbehaving inmates."

The construction of a new fence around St. Charles in 1939 and transfers of the most "problematic" boys at St. Charles to Sheridan did not stem surrounding residents' fear of the possibility of boys escaping from the school. There was widespread support in the city of St. Charles of Russell Ballard, who became the new head of the institution in 1941 as a result of his promise to "weed out the thugs and incorrigibles" and send them to the new branch at Sheridan. By 1942, Governor Dwight H. Green had ordered police squads to patrol the fence surrounding St. Charles and install floodlights that would illuminate the fence.[97] An administrator at the Juvenile Detention Home wrote to Governor Green imploring him to prohibit boys at Sheridan from using tools because he feared the boys "would use them as weapons and a means of escape, perhaps attacking the guards with fatal results." Meanwhile, the *St. Charles Chronicle*, along with the *Chicago Tribune* and *Chicago Sun*, continued to monitor the physical containment of boys in the school very closely.[98]

Black Boyhood and the Impact of Racialized Delinquency on Juvenile Justice

This has been a story of institutional change and the rearticulation of the original rehabilitative purpose of the Training School for Boys at St. Charles. James Williams was murdered against a backdrop of notions of black children's invulnerability and black masculinity that increasingly symbolized superhuman brute strength and violent sexuality. St. Charles's commitment to doing the redemptive work of "training" delinquent boys for "manhood and citizenship" faltered at the intersection of race and sex as the number of African Americans in the institution began to increase and blackness became hypervisible. In light of this demographic change and fear surrounding the image of a young criminal black rapist captured so poignantly in Richard Wright's 1940 Chicago-based novel *Native Son*, administrators decided to institute racial segregation to ostensibly help manage behavioral problems and argued that there were new irredeemable and adult-like inmates who came from "racial stocks which mature more quickly" and were intrinsically expert at committing heinous crimes. This decision was a seminal moment in the evolution of the juvenile justice system, as it represented an unequivocal shift away from the rehabilitative ideal toward a more retributive approach.

The implementation of new racial segregation polices that separated and excluded black boys at St. Charles was but an early step toward a system-wide revolution in juvenile justice. The laws governing the commitment of delinquent children to state correctional facilities grew more and more punitive over time. A 1941 state law further divested the juvenile court and public institutions for delinquent children of their jurisdiction over children when it mandated that "every person, male or female, over ten years of age" found guilty of a felony or any other crime "punishable by imprisonment in a penitentiary," would, in fact, be sentenced to prison. Although the law gave criminal courts discretion over where to send children convicted of crimes, this change marked a dramatic shift in the treatment of delinquent children, as children who committed felonies were by default ineligible for admission to facilities that were built for children and intended to fall under the cloak of rehabilitation.[99] This meant that any child over the age of ten who was convicted of a felony could be sentenced to an adult prison.

The legal codification of the more punitive approach to children expanded again in 1949, when an amendment made the maximum-security State Reformatory at Sheridan the default institution for any boy under the age of seventeen who was convicted of a crime punishable by imprisonment in a penitentiary. That same year, state legislators and administrators at St. Charles conducted several investigations and held thirty-two meetings to give "careful study of the many complex problems" and implement more severe containment and disciplinary policies.[100] In 1951, the State Reformatory at Sheridan severed all of its ties to St. Charles and became an independent maximum-security prison for boys with its own independent staff and administration.[101] The fear and resentment Chicago-area residents and state officials had toward delinquent boys continued to run high despite these marked punitive shifts.

St. Charles's transition to a more punitive institution and the emergence of the maximum-security prison for youths at Sheridan reveals the contingent nature of conceptions of childhood rehabilitation and delinquency, as well as the impact intersecting notions of race, gender, sexuality, and age had on the evolution of a juvenile justice. School administrators, state legislators, and the public at large essentially constructed a dividing line between "salvageable" and "unsalvageable" children even as race motivated, rearticulated, and erased the original rehabilitative purpose of the institution. This story of contested transitions at the Training School at St. Charles, and the ways in which these contestations reshaped the legal and institutional landscape of juvenile justice, elucidates the ways in which race shaped constructions of delinquency and the evolution of the justice system for all children in the state.

Epilogue

Irene McCoy Gaines, a prominent clubwoman who had advocated on behalf of black children in Chicago since the 1920s, stood before the Senate in 1954 as a representative of the National Association of Colored Women's Clubs. She urged the federal government to encourage her home state of Illinois and other states to "modernize" juvenile justice laws. She began her speech by contrasting the rehabilitative "children's court" Progressive reformers envisioned with the punitive juvenile justice system that had arisen in its place:

> In the year 1899, in Cook County, Illinois, there was established the first Juvenile Court not only in the US but the first to be established in the world. . . . It heralded an era of personalized justice in contrast to punishment. . . . Now we are tempted to abandon fundamental principles heretofore held. We appear to be entertaining notions that regardless of age . . . juvenile delinquency should warrant a return to criminal procedures and punishment for criminal acts. . . . Therefore, the NACW will deplore and oppose any movement in this country to ascribe adult status to juveniles by replacing protective procedures with criminal procedures in meeting the present juvenile justice system.[1]

Irene McCoy Gaines's reference to the "movement" to "ascribe adult status to juveniles" flagged not only the Illinois Supreme Court's 1935 decision to give the adult criminal court primary jurisdiction over children being prosecuted for a felony but also the retributive—as opposed to rehabilitative—turn in the state's juvenile justice system writ large. By the time Gaines stood before the Senate in 1954, the flagship institutions for delinquent children in Illinois had become even more punitive. The state legislature's 1939 decision to build the State Reformatory at Sheridan, the first maximum-security prison for boys under seventeen who had been convicted of felonies, had become a catchall institution for "unruly inmates" at St. Charles by 1950. Although the State Reformatory at Sheridan was originally conceived of as a small institution of last resort for boys deemed incapable of rehabilitation, by 1946 it had become an expansive campus with twenty-one cottages, each housing ten to forty boys.[2]

In spite of the existence of the State Reformatory at Sheridan, an institution meant to cleanse St. Charles of "irredeemable" boys, St. Charles itself had introduced harsher disciplinary policies. By 1955, there was a long-standing practice of staff members at St. Charles using a security cottage, which the boys at St. Charles referred to as "the box," for the purpose of solitary confinement. Staff members placed the boys in "isolation" for a variety of infractions, including running away, homosexuality, hitting an employee, and "general incorrigibility."[3] By 1945, almost every single boy—98 percent—Cook County Juvenile Court committed to the Training School for Boys at St. Charles was black. A social scientist who conducted a study of the boys at the school, after noticing the disproportionately high numbers of African American boys there, noted that the "culture of the Cook County Negro" dominated the institution.[4]

Administrators at the Training School for Girls at Geneva had also embraced a more explicitly punitive disciplinary policy at the school. In January 1956, the *Aurora Beacon* interviewed an employee of the school, Mrs. Moore, who envied St. Charles for its ability to exclude "troublesome" children from its institution. Mrs. Moore explained, "Unlike St. Charles which can send the boys to Sheridan . . . we have no place to send them but must still harbour them here. In other words, we cannot segregate the troublesome ones from those responding to our rehabilitation program other than via our discipline cottage." In lieu of a separate institution, Geneva relied on solitary confinement and a disciplinary cottage to house girls staff members deemed incapable of rehabilitation. Staff members regularly locked girls in either Willow Cottage or Oak Cottage by 1959. Like the Training School for Boys at St. Charles, at least 85 percent of the girls Cook County Juvenile Court sent to Geneva were black.

Girls housed at the Training School for Girls did not passively accept the institution's punitive turn. They individually and collectively defied the terms of their new disciplinary regime in myriad ways but especially through riots. In the 1950s, Geneva mirrored St. Charles in the 1930s as local newspapers like the *Aurora Beacon*, *Geneva Republican*, and *Chicago Daily News* regular featured stories about the Training School for Girls. As opposed to escapees, the papers focused on the frequency of "riots" and "protests" at the school. An article appearing in a June 1956 issue of the *Chicago Daily News* described a "massive riot" of "twenty-one girls who had been locked in individual rooms" in Willow Cottage. Miss Donoghue, the cottage matron, reported that seven girls expressed their outrage at being locked in their rooms by forcing open the locks, racing to the second floor, and help-

Oak Cottage, a maximum-security residence built at the Illinois Training School for Girls at Geneva in 1959. Courtesy of the Geneva Historical Society.

ing the girls quartered free themselves as well. The girls then collectively "hooked up a fire hose and began flooding the cottage" with water and tossing debris down the stairs. The three matrons present at the time "locked themselves in a second floor room" and called the police for help. The police themselves had a hard time subduing the girls as some of "the rioters turned the hose on them and [others] threw furniture at the policemen as they tried to climb the stairs to the second floor." They were "finally subdued after the police wrestled the fire hose from them." That same month, another *Chicago Daily News* article featured the story of a girl whom policemen "forcibly returned to her room" on a Thursday afternoon because she refused "to obey the orders of matrons" who wanted to lock her in her room. Once she was forced into the room and the doors were locked, she demonstrated her continuing protest when she "dismantled her bed and smashed two window panes and also pounded the door."[5]

Intersecting notions of childhood, race, gender, and sexuality always undergirded juvenile justice practice in Illinois. However, the confluence between the number of black children entering the juvenile justice system, racist constructions of black children, and a punitive turn in juvenile justice institutions was not coincidental. It reinforced, clarified, and rearticulated notions of race, delinquency, and ultimately humanity. This criminalization of black children was both symbolic and real, as it shaped the public image of the type of child entering the juvenile justice system and, for black children and their families, shaped the very meaning of what it meant to be black and living in Chicago.

This story about African American children and an early juvenile justice system underscores the race-based criminalization and confinement of a significant number of black people long before the modern era of hyper-incarceration. Race-based criminalization was not confined to the Jim Crow South or the post–War on Drugs era. It was alive and well in the "promised land" of the urban North long before the modern Civil Rights movement. This account also introduces another branch in the genealogic map of late twentieth-century discourses about "super-predator" children. This notion of "super-predator" children—black children—who were so vicious and irredeemable in spite of their youth was used by both liberal and conservative politicians in the late twentieth century to argue that only the most punitive measures a criminal justice system has to offer, like life imprisonment and even death, were rational and just responses to childhood delinquency.[6]

Irene McCoy Gaines highlighted this retributive turn in her speech before the Senate. The confluence of the juvenile justice system's retributive turn, its abandonment of the rehabilitative deal, and the racist construction of black children was not lost on this long-time Chicago-based clubwoman and advocate for black children. She ended her speech by underscoring the necessity of "nurture" and "protection" as opposed to "punishment" and "hostility" for all children, but particularly those whose vulnerabilities led them to the doorsteps of juvenile and criminal courts: "In the United States we are agreed upon basic rights of children in our Democracy . . . that every child has a right to authority—not hostility as a frame of reference for his growth. . . . Authority in this sense is nurture . . . but until we recognize authority, stripped of all elements of hate, power, abuse and punishment, is basic to nurture of the young, we deny children of one of their basic rights; that every child has a right to protection."[7] On the surface, Gaines's admonition to "modernize" juvenile justice laws by stripping the system of "all elements of hate, power, abuse and punishment" is simply a call to treat all children in the justice system the same. Her argument that there are agreed-upon "basic rights of children" and that "every child has a right to protection" also emphasizes the reality that juvenile and criminal justice systems have never existed as islands unto themselves. Therefore, an exhortation for true justice and equality must necessarily look beyond the walls of juvenile justice institutions.

The very construction of behavior deemed "criminal" or "delinquent," and the construction of "criminal" and "delinquent" people, is intimately tied to exercises of power and the way in which a society values particular groups above others, invests in its children, and distributes resources. This account of the criminalization of black children in Chicago historicizes the dynamic and necessarily adaptable nature of black life in the urban North and the evolution of a juvenile justice. It also reveals the ways in which notions of race can become constructed, reinvented, and ultimately embedded in institutions. Black children's experiences in Chicago's juvenile justice system underscore the importance of being cognizant of the pliable nature of racial domination, the ways in which it can be propagated, and the importance of truly investing in and protecting the most vulnerable members of society.

Notes

Introduction

1. Case no. 85983, Cook County Circuit Court Archive, Juvenile Court Records. The actual names of children—with an exception of those whose stories may have wound up in newspapers or other published works—have been replaced with a pseudonym to protect their privacy. The author has kept the initial letters of their first and last names of the pseudonyms the same in the interest of scholars and investigators who may want to access the children's files. This is in accordance with Illinois state laws intended to protect the privacy of children who have been charged with crimes in juvenile court.

2. Ibid.

3. Ibid.

4. McGerr, *Fierce Discontent*; Southern, *Progressive Era and Race*; Willrich, *City of Courts*; Platt, *Child Savers*, 45; Mintz, *Huck's Raft*, 176–78.

5. Grossberg, "Changing Conceptions of Child Welfare," 3–42, 17; Tanenhaus, "Evolution of Juvenile Courts," 38–39, 42–74; Tanenhaus, "Degrees of Discretion," 42–43.

6. Gittens, *Poor Relations*; Platt, *Child Savers*; Sutton, *Stubborn Children*; Steven L. Schlossman, *Love and the American Delinquent: The Theory and Practice of "Progressive" Juvenile Justice, 1825–1920* (Chicago: University of Chicago Press, 1977); Elizabeth J. Clapp, *Mothers of All Children: Women Reformers and the Rise of Juvenile Courts in Progressive Era America* (University Park: Pennsylvania State University Press, 1998); David J. Rotham, *Conscience and Convenience: The Asylum and Its Alternatives in Progressive America* (Boston: Little, Brown, 1980); Ellen Ryerson, *The Best-Laid Plans: America's Juvenile Court Experiment* (New York: Hill and Wang, 1978); Feld, *Bad Kids*; Barry C. Feld, "Race and the Jurisprudence of Juvenile Justice: A Tale in Two Parts 1950–2000," in Hawkins and Kempf-Leonard, *Our Children, Their Children*, 3–15; Lee Teitelbaum, "Status Offenses and Status Offenders," in Rosenheim, *A Century of Juvenile Justice*, 158–77, here 162; Michael A. Rembis, *Defining Deviance: Sex, Science, and Delinquent Girls, 1890–1960* (Chicago: University of Illinois Press, 2011), 79; Grossberg, *A Study of Negro Girls*, 1–75.

7. Cahn, *Sexual Reckonings*; Meda Chesney-Lind and John M. Hagedorn, *Female Gangs in America: Essays on Girls, Gangs, and Gender* (Chicago: Lake View Press, 1999); Anne Meis Knupfer, *Reform and Resistance: Gender, Delinquency, and America's First Juvenile Court* (New York: Routledge, 2001); Mary Odem, *Delinquent Daughters*.

8. See, for example, Schlossman, *Love and the American Delinquent*; Feld, *Bad Kids*; Hawkins and Kempf-Leonard, *Our Children, Their Children*.

Chapter One

1. See Case no. 185, Cook County Circuit Court Archive, Juvenile Court Records (JCR), for Mary Tripplet's case, which was filed on a form labeled "Delinquent Girl Petition."

2. Feld, *Bad Kids*, 20; Mintz, *Huck's Raft*, 176–78; Platt, *Child Savers*, 45; Willrich, *City of Courts*, 14, 79–80, 209.

3. Lasch-Quinn, *Black Neighbors*, 15–17.

4. Tanenhaus, *Juvenile Justice in the Making*, 4–12, 23; Platt, *Child Savers*, 9–10, 77–78, 92–93; Willrich, *City of Courts*, 80.

5. McGerr, *Fierce Discontent*; Southern, *Progressive Era and Race*; Willrich, *City of Courts*.

6. Mintz, *Huck's Raft*, 176–78; Platt, *Child Savers*, 134–35; Tanenhaus, *Juvenile Justice in the Making*, 5.

7. Mintz, *Huck's Raft*, 172–78; Platt, *Child Savers*, 10, 55.

8. Grossman, *Land of Hope*, 4.

9. For information on black incentives for migration in Chicago, see Grossman, *Land of Hope*. For statistical information about population change in Chicago, see "Negroes in the United States 1920–32 Census Supplement," series 3, box 211, folder 267, University of Illinois at Chicago (hereafter referred to as UIC), Special Collections Research Center; Gregory, *Southern Diaspora*, 120; Chicago Commission on Race Relations, *Negro in Chicago*, 331.

10. See U.S. Census and document discussing the growth of Chicago's black population, series 1, box 1, folder 12, UIC, Special Collections Research Center, Chicago Urban League (hereafter referred to as CUL) Papers, for information on population growth between 1910 and 1920. For information on 1890 statistics, see Grossman, *Land of Hope*. More on the demographics of black Chicago during the 1930s can be found in Drake and Cayton, *Black Metropolis*, 9.

11. Gregory, *Southern Diaspora*, 120.

12. Cayton, *Black Metropolis*, 176–77.

13. Grossman, *Land of Hope*, 162–69. See also Chicago Commission on Race Relations, *Negro in Chicago*, 29–30, 524.

14. Dray, *At the Hands of Persons Unknown*; Grossman, *Land of Hope*, 164; Chicago Commission on Race Relations, *Negro in Chicago*, 328; Gugliemo, *White on Arrival*, 9.

15. Willrich, *City of Courts*, xxii, 78–80, 159; Altgeld, *Live Questions*.

16. St. Charles School for Boys, *3rd Biennial Report*, Municipal Reference Collection, Harold Washington Library, Chicago Public Libraries, 6–7.

17. Platt, *Child Savers*, 45; Mintz, *Huck's Raft*, 176–78; Young, "Race and Gender in the Establishment of Juvenile Prisons," 246; Feld, *Bad Kids*, 20.

18. Tanenhaus, "Degrees of Discretion."

19. Mintz, *Huck's Raft*, 17–19.

20. Ibid., 3, 17–19, 23–24; Hoofert, "'A Very Peculiar Sorrow,'" 605–8.

21. Mintz, *Huck's Raft*, 76–79.

22. Ibid., 93; Ward, *Black Child Savers*, 22–23.

23. Bernstein, *Racial Innocence*, 63.

24. Ibid., 34; Goings, *Mammy and Uncle Mose*; Turner, *Ceramic Uncles and Celluloid Mammies*.

25. Turner, *Ceramic Uncles and Celluloid Mammies*, 15; Bernstein, *Racial Innocence*, 33–35.

26. Bernstein, *Racial Innocence*, 33–35, 63.

27. Bryan, "Variations in the Responses of Infants"; Gatewood and Weiss, "Race and Sex Differences in Newborn Infants"; Holmes, "Low Sex Ratio in Negro Births"; Schultz, "Relation of the External Nose to the Bony Nose," 329–38.

28. MacDonald, *Colored Children*, 1140, 1143.

29. Pyle, "Mentality of the Negro Compared with Whites"; Pyle, "Mind of the Negro Child," 357–60; Pyle, "Learning of Negro Children," 82–83.

30. Phillips, "Binet Tests," 3; Peterson, "Comparative Abilities of White and Negro Children"; Stetson, "Some Memory Tests of Whites and Blacks," 285–89.

31. Muhammad, *Condemnation of Blackness*, 4.

32. Lasch-Quinn, *Black Neighbors*, 6.

33. Ovington, *Half a Man*.

34. Holloway, "Introduction," 14–15. Black sociologist E. Franklin Frazier, a student of Robert Park, reiterated this argument in his 1932 text when he argued that "The widespread disorganization of Negro family life must be regarded as an aspect of the civilizational process in the Negro group." Frazier, *Negro Family in Chicago*, 252. See also Bannister, "Sociology," 342.

35. Ovington, *Half a Man*, 190–91, as cited in Muhammad, *Condemnation of Blackness*, 4, 122–24.

36. Addams, " 'Social Control' Crisis"; Muhammad, *Condemnation of Blackness*, 124.

37. Gugliemo, *White on Arrival*, 6.

38. Lasch-Quinn, *Black Neighbors*, 24–26.

39. Bowen, *Colored People of Chicago*, 117–20.

40. Lasch-Quinn, *Black Neighbors*, 24.

41. Muhammad, *Condemnation of Blackness*, 4.

42. Du Bois, "Negro and American Democracy," 229; Grossman, *Land of Hope*; Muhammad, *Condemnation of Blackness*.

43. Chicago Vice Commission, *Social Evil in Chicago*, 38–39; Bowen, *Colored People of Chicago*. For more on the concentration of vice districts in black neighborhoods in Chicago, see Mumford, *Interzones*, 123–49; Blair, *I've Got to Make My Livin'*.

44. Grossman, *Land of Hope*, 170–71.

45. Telegram to Mr. L. Hollingsworth Wood by T. Arnold, box 6, folder 3, Julius Rosenwald Papers, Special Collections Research Center, University of Chicago.

46. Davarian L. Baldwin, *Chicago's New Negroes*, 15.

47. Colored People of Chicago Pamphlet, box 1, folder 128, Juvenile Protection Agency (JPA) Papers, Special Collections Research Center, University of Chicago; Cmiel, *Home of Another Kind*, 126–27.

48. "A Study of the Need of Facilities for Negro Children under the Supervision of the Juvenile Court of Cook County: Report to the Citizens' Committee on

Juvenile Court by F. T. Lane," 1–5, box 234, folder 2294, UIC, Special Collections Research Center, CUL Papers; Fitz-Simons et al., "Foster Home Care for Negro Children in Atlanta," 1–2.

49. The population of Catholic children also decreased; however, this was due to the presence of an increasing number of Catholic institutions that provided care for dependent children of the same faith. Stehno, "Foster Care for Dependent Black Children in Chicago," 5.

50. "Illinois Technical School for Colored Girls," box 14, folder 20, Illinois Workers Project, Vivian Harsh Collection, Carter G. Woodson Library, Chicago Public Libraries; Crawley, "Dependent Negro Children in Chicago," 37; Stehno, "Foster Care for Dependent Black Children in Chicago," 24–25.

51. Chicago Urban League, *10th Annual Report*, 1926, series 1, box 1, folder 8, UIC, Special Collections Research Center, CUL Papers.

52. "Report on Juvenile Court," 2–7, box 234, folder 2294, UIC, Special Collections Research Center, CUL Papers.

53. The black community had a long-standing tradition of taking in orphaned and neglected children who were in need of proper parental care. More often than not, family members and local community residents stepped in. At the turn of the century, black-founded and -controlled institutions began to play an increasingly vital role in this practice. See for example Du Bois, *Efforts of Social Betterment*, 77.

54. Ward, *Black Child Savers*, 127–29.

55. Jenkins, "Do We Need Reformatories?," 70–72; Ward, *Black Child Savers*; Young, "Race and Gender in the Establishment of Juvenile Prisons," 255.

56. Jimenez, "History of Child Protection in the African American Community," 897.

57. Cahn, *Sexual Reckonings*, 69, 74; Anne M. Knupfer and Leonard Silk (eds.), *Toward a Tenderer Humanity*, 25–27; Hicks, *Talk with You Like a Woman*; Dorothy C. Salem, *To Better Our World*; Ward, *Black Child Savers*.

58. Knupfer, "African-American Facilities for Dependent and Delinquent Children in Chicago"; Blair, *I've Got to Make My Livin'*, 203–4.

59. Blair, *I've Got to Make My Livin'*, 202–3.

60. "President's Annual Report," dated January 1, 1925, box 1, folder 9, Chicago Historical Society, Irene McCoy Gaines Papers; Annual Session of Federation of Colored Women's Clubs Pamphlet, dated 1926, Chicago Historical Society, Irene McCoy Gaines Papers.

61. "Inaugural Address of Irene Mccoy Gaines"; Chatfield, "Study of the Federated Home," 4.

62. Blair, *I've Got to Make My Livin'*, 200.

63. "Mator M'ferrin's Assailant Found Guilty and Sent to Jail."

64. "Splendid Work of Probation Officers."

65. "Roots out Nests of Iniquity"; for another example of an article praising Jessie Thomas's work, see "In the Grip of the Law."

66. "Woman's Children's Aid Society."

67. "Miss Gertrude Smith Laid to Rest: Mourn West Side Probation Officer."

68. Bowen, *Colored People of Chicago*, 128; Crawley, "Dependent Negro Children in Chicago," 2.

69. Du Bois, *Efforts of Social Betterment among Negro Americans* (Atlanta: Atlanta University Press, 1909), 76–79.

70. "Amanda Smith School for Girls Formed in Court Room."

71. Crawley, "Dependent Negro Children in Chicago," 27–31.

72. Juvenile Protective Association Papers Supplement, UIC, Special Collections Research Center, Richard Daley Library; Stehno, "Foster Care for Dependent Black Children in Chicago," 29–31.

73. "Colored Boys to Get School," *Chicago Inter-Ocean*, July 18, 1913, box 14, folder 2, Illinois Workers Project Papers, Vivian Harsh Collection, Carter G. Woodson Library, Chicago Public Libraries; Stehno, "Foster Care for Dependent Black Children," 27–28.

74. Untitled memo dated July 9, 1919, box 11, folder 12, Julius Rosenwald Papers, Special Collections Research Center, University of Chicago; Correspondence from Edith Wyatt on behalf of ICHA to Dr. Shephardson, March 3, 1922, Julius Rosenwald Papers, Special Chicago Research Center, University of Chicago.

75. Untitled memo dated July 9, 1919, box 11, folder 12, Julius Rosenwald Papers, Special Collections Research Center, University of Chicago; Memo by W. C. G. on July 14, 1919, box 11, folder 12, Special Collections Research Center, University of Chicago; Correspondence from Amanda Sears to Mr. Phillips, March 13, 1919, box 11, folder 12, Special Collections Research Center, University of Chicago.

76. For information about the Illinois Technical School for Colored Girls being the only institution for dependent children left, see Stehno, "Foster Care for Dependent Black Children in Chicago," 89–91.

77. Baldwin, *Chicago's New Negroes*, 33–34.

78. Crawley, "Dependent Negro Children in Chicago," 86.

79. Stehno, "Foster Care for Dependent Black Children in Chicago," 53–60; Crawley, "Dependent Negro Children in Chicago," 88.

80. "Brief Summary of the Work of the Chicago Urban League," series 1, box 1, folder 1, UIC, Special Collections Research Center, CUL Papers.

81. 4th Annual Report of the Chicago Urban League, 1920, 10, series 1, box 1, folder 3, UIC, Special Collections Research Center, CUL Papers.

82. 19th Annual Report of the Chicago Urban League, 3, series 1, box 1, folder 1, UIC, Special Collections Research Center, CUL Papers.

83. "A Study of the Need of Facilities for Negro Children under the Supervision of the Juvenile Court of Cook County," 1–5.

84. Double-shift schools educated one group of children in the morning and another in the afternoon. Students typically had less instruction time in these schools. A disproportionate number of double-shift schools were located in the city's black communities. "Step by Step Planning for Community Action and Causes of Juvenile Delinquency," series 2, box 234, folder 2294, UIC, Special Collections Research Center, CUL Papers.

85. Chicago Urban League 1938 Report, 7–10, series 1, box 1, folder 13, UIC, Special Collections Research Center, CUL Papers.

86. Chicago Board of Education, *Annual Report of the Superintendent of Schools, 1936–1937* (Chicago: Board of Education, 1937); Chicago Board of Education, *Annual Report of the Superintendent of Schools, 1937–38* (Chicago: Board of Education, 1938).

87. Fourth Annual Report, 1919–1920, 12, box 1, folder 12, UIC, Special Collections Research Center, CUL Papers.

88. Ibid.; Strickland, *History of the Chicago Urban League*; Muhammad, *Condemnation of Blackness*, 42.

89. Chicago Urban League Social Problem Case 3/19/48–3/20/48, series 3, box 6, folder 64, UIC, Special Collections Research Center, CUL Papers.

90. Chicago Urban League Social Problem Case 5/5/48, series 3, box 6, folder 64, UIC, Special Collections Research Center, CUL Papers.

91. Chicago Urban League Social Problem Case 9/7/48, series 3, box 6, folder 64, UIC, Special Collections Research Center, CUL Papers.

92. Chicago Urban League Social Problem Case 9/2/48, series 3, box 6, folder 64, UIC, Special Collections Research Center, CUL Papers.

93. "Brief Summary of the Work of the Chicago Urban League," series 1, box 1, folder 1, UIC, Special Collections Research Center, CUL Papers.

94. Chicago Urban League, *18th Annual Report, 1931–1932*.

95. "Minutes 7/6/44," supplement 1, folder 11, Chicago Historical Society, JPA Papers; McGuinn, "Recreation," 311–12.

96. Chicago Urban League, *18th Annual Report, 1931–1932*.

97. Board of Administration of the State of Illinois, *Sixth Annual Report*, 28, 120; Board of Administration of the State of Illinois, *Seventh Annual Report*, 51–57.

98. Board of Administration of the State of Illinois, *First Annual Report*, 322; Board of Administration of the State of Illinois, *Second Annual Report*, 223.

99. Correspondence from E. C. Wentworth to Reynolds, October 17, 1913, box 75, Illinois Children's Home and Aid Society Papers, Special Collections Research Center, University of Chicago.

100. Elmer P. Martin and Joanne Mitchell Martin, The Black Extended Family (Chicago, 1978), as cited in O'Donnell, "Care of Dependent African-American Children in Chicago," 765.

101. Ibid., 764–66.

102. Correspondence from Amelia Dears to William C. Graves, April 10, 1919, folder 12, box 11, Julius Rosenwald Papers, Special Collections Research Center, University of Chicago.

103. Correspondence from Edith Wyatt to Francis Shephardson, March 3, 1922, folder 13, box 11, Julius Rosenwald Papers, Special Collections Research Center, University of Chicago.

104. Summary of Year's Work and Estimated Budget for Colored Children: January 1 to December 31, 1920, box 11, Julius Rosenwald Papers, Special Collections Research Center, University of Chicago; Correspondence from Edith Wyatt to Francis Shephardson, March 3, 1922, folder 13, box 11, Julius Rosenwald Papers, Special Collections Research Center, University of Chicago; O'Donnell, "Care of Dependent African-American Children in Chicago," 767.

105. "Dependent Children's Aid Object for Big Meeting." See also, for example, "Illinois Home Aid Society Issues Plea for Homeless Children during Christmas; Organization Needs More Money: Seem to Really Appreciate"; "Citizens Given Chance to Help Poor Kiddies"; "Children's Aid Society Helps Homeless Waifs."

106. Correspondence from Edith Wyatt to Francis Shephardson, March 3, 1922, folder 13, box 11, Julius Rosenwald Papers, Special Collections Research Center, University of Chicago; Correspondence to Julius Rosenwald with Wyatt's budget report, February 6, 1926, folder 6, box 20, Julius Rosenwald Papers, Special Collections Research Center, University of Chicago; Correspondence from Edith Wyatt to Mr. Stern, September 1926, folder 6, box 20, Julius Rosenwald Papers, Special Collections Research Center, University of Chicago.

107. Brochure for the Colored Children's Auxiliary of the ICHA, folder 6, box 20, Julius Rosenwald Papers, Special Collections Research Center, University of Chicago; Stehno, "Foster Care for Dependent Black Children in Chicago," 490.

108. "In Regard to Facilities for the Care of Colored Dependent Children," memorandum, February 1928, box 38, Illinois Children's Home and Aid Society Papers, Special Collections Research Center, University of Chicago; Gilmartin, "Use of the Psychiatric Clinic in the Treatment of Dependent Negro Children," 3.

109. Crawley, "Dependent Negro Children in Chicago," 78–80; O'Donnell, "Care of Dependent African-American Children in Chicago," 769.

110. Davis, "Study of the Disposition," 18, 60; Crawley, "Dependent Negro Children in Chicago," 5.

111. Statistics calculated from *Cook County Juvenile Court Annual Reports*, 1921–1926, Municipal Reference Collection, Harold Washington Library, Chicago Public Libraries. The annual report also includes causes of dependency in African American children.

112. Knupfer, "'If You Can't Push, Pull,'" 221–31.

113. Moses, *Negro Delinquent in Chicago*, 16–18; Minutes of the Third Meeting between Representatives of the Social Service, series 1, box 0, folder 76, UIC, Special Collections Research Center, Russell Ballard Papers.

114. Moses, *Negro Delinquent in Chicago*, 16–18; Minutes of the Third Meeting between Representatives of the Social Service, series 1, box 0, folder 76, UIC, Special Collections Research Center, Russell Ballard Papers.

115. Moses, *Negro Delinquent in Chicago*, 16–18; Minutes of the Third Meeting between Representatives of the Social Service, series 1, box 0, folder 76, UIC, Special Collections Research Center, Russell Ballard Papers.

116. Moses, *Negro Delinquent in Chicago*, 18.

Chapter Two

1. Juvenile Court transcript in regard to case numbers 87093 and 804204, series 2, box 6, folder 73, Mary Bartelme Papers, University of Illinois at Chicago (UIC), Special Collections Research Center.

2. Ibid.

3. Cook County Juvenile Court Annual Report 1906, 7.

4. Juvenile Court and Juvenile Detention Home Annual Report of 1924, Municipal Reference Collection, Harold Washington Library, Chicago Public Libraries.

5. The Industrial and Training Schools Act originally provided for the subsidy of public and private institutions for dependent and delinquent children in 1878. Generally, institutions chartered under the act were for specific religious and ethnic groups.

6. Tanenhaus, *Juvenile Justice in the Making*, 6, 9; Cook County Juvenile Court Annual Report 1906, 6.

7. Bowen, *Growing up with a City*, 300–305; Knupfer, "Chicago Detention Home," 52; Osborn, "Study of the Detention of Two Hundred Six Children," 8; Cook County Juvenile Court Annual Report 1906, 7–8; Link, "Analysis of Thirty-Five Negro Problem Children," 16.

8. Initially called the Juvenile Psychopathic Institute, the Institute for Juvenile Research was renamed by the state in 1917.

9. Auer, "Study of the Services of the Institute for Juvenile Research," 1; Cook County Juvenile Court Annual Report 1906, 16.

10. Cook County Juvenile Court Annual Report 1906, 4–6.

11. 1925 Chicago Parental School Annual Report, 3. The only city in Illinois with a large enough population to satisfy the law at the time it was passed was Chicago.

12. Cook County Juvenile Court Annual Reports, 1913–1920, 30–31; Juvenile Court and Juvenile Detention Home of Cook County Annual Report of 1921, 8, Municipal Reference Collection, Harold Washington Library, Chicago Public Libraries.

13. Statistics calculated from Juvenile Court and Juvenile Detention Home Annual Report of 1912 (Municipal Reference Collection, Harold Washington Library, Chicago Public Libraries), which indicate that 1,899 children came before the juvenile court. Of this number, 265 were black.

14. Chicago Commission on Race Relations, *Negro in Chicago*, 333; Moses, *Negro Delinquent in Chicago*, 15.

15. 1924 and 1925 Juvenile Court and Juvenile Detention Annual Report; Frazier, *Negro Family in Chicago*, 206.

16. Moses, *Negro Delinquent in Chicago*, 1–2.

17. Ibid., 10.

18. Ibid., 10–11.

19. Ibid., 12.

20. Smith, "Selected Case Studies of Dependent Negro Children," 9–16.

21. Chatelain, *South Side Girls*, 5–6.

22. The Morals Court was a branch of the city's Municipal Court. The Municipal Court of Chicago was established by a 1906 act of the Illinois General Assembly. The Municipal Court operated separately from the juvenile court. The Municipal Court was made up of a system of thirty-seven civil and criminal courts. Criminal defendants were channeled into special socialized branches, including a Domestic Relations Court for desertion and nonsupport proceedings, a Morals Court for prostitution and other sex offenses, and a Boys' Court to try young men over Juvenile Court age. Willrich, *City of Courts*, xxxiii–xxxv.

23. Moses, *Negro Delinquent in Chicago*, 1–2.

24. For information about court officials amending black children's petitions, see Holland, "Analysis of the Case Histories," 2, 17; Knupfer, "'If You Can't Push, Pull,'" 197. For more information about Frances's case, see Carey, "Survey of the Girls Released," 26.

25. Smith, "Selected Case Studies of Dependent Negro Children," 78–80, 190–91.

26. Frazier, *Negro Family in the United States*, 372.

27. Chicago Commission on Race Relations, *Negro in Chicago*, 328–30.

28. Work, "Crime among the Negroes of Chicago," 210.

29. Report of the Committee on *Negro Housing: Housing Conditions and Delinquency in Chicago* (1932), box 37, folder 16, Illinois Workers Project, Vivian Harsh Collection, Chicago Public Libraries; Bowen, *Safeguards for City Youth*, 174.

30. Blair, *I've Got to Make My Livin'*, 2; See also Canaan, "Economic and Class Dimensions," 46.

31. Chicago Vice Commission, *Social Evil in Chicago*, 38–39; Bowen, *Colored People of Chicago*; Blair, *I've Got to Make My Livin'*.

32. "Cornering the Corner Gang."

33. Department of Public Welfare, *11th Annual Report*.

34. Bowen, *Safeguards for City Youth*, 173–74.

35. Moses, *Negro Delinquent in Chicago*, 20.

36. Case no. 198, Cook County Circuit Court Archive, Juvenile Court Records (JCR).

37. Case nos. 1680 and 21690, Cook County Circuit Court Archive, JCR.

38. Grossman, *Land of Hope*, 170–71.

39. Irene McCoy Gaines, "Plea for the Colored Girl," *Chicago Daily News*, May 28, 1920; Department of Public Welfare, 10th Annual Report: 1925–1926.

40. "Report from the Executive Secretary of the Wabash Ave YMCA, January 22, 1926," box 7, folder 1, UIC, Special Collections Research Center, Wabash Avenue YMCA Papers.

41. Hoyt and Scherer, "Female Juvenile Delinquency."

42. Case no. 83381, Cook County Circuit Court Archive, JCR.

43. Statistics calculated from *Cook County Juvenile Court Annual Reports*, 1921–1926, Municipal Reference Collection, Harold Washington Library, Chicago Public Libraries. For more on migration and dependency, see Crawley, "Dependent Negro Children in Chicago," 115; Cmiel, *Home of Another Kind*, 126; Stehno, "Foster Care for Dependent Black Children in Chicago," 93.

44. Lasch-Quinn, *Black Neighbors*, 15–17.

45. Dolinar, *Negro in Illinois*, 128.

46. Holland, "Analysis of the Case Histories," 2, 8.

47. Case no. 103942, Cook County Circuit Court Archive, JCR.

48. The majority of "delinquent" girls were incarcerated for violating Victorian norms of gendered behavior and engaging in behaviors as widely variant as flirting, staying out late at night, or engaging in premarital sex. In some cases, victims of incest were labeled "sex delinquents" when judges believed they willingly participated in or provoked their sexual abuse. Tanenhaus, *Juvenile Justice in the Making*, 68.

49. Under the Juvenile Court Act of 1899, dependent children were poor, neglected, or abused children who lacked proper parental care. The majority of girls who were labeled delinquent in juvenile court were incarcerated for widely variant behaviors like flirting, staying out late at night, or engaging in premarital sex. In some cases, victims of incest were labeled "sex delinquents" when judges believed they willingly participated in or provoked their sexual abuse.

50. Moses, *Negro Delinquent in Chicago*, 12–13, 18.

51. Ibid., 18.

52. Statement of Committee on Care of Colored Child to the Board of Directors of the ICHA, April 17, 1928, folder 14, box 11, Julius Rosenwald Papers, Special Collections Research Center, University of Chicago.

53. Memo on Joint Service Bureau's Division of Child Placing of Negro Children, folder 13, box 11, Julius Rosenwald Papers, Special Collections Research Center, University of Chicago; Report of the Subcommittee on the Care of Negro Children, Chicago Council of Social Agencies, April 1921, folder 14, box 11, Julius Rosenwald Papers, Special Collections Research Center, University of Chicago; Minutes of Luncheon Meeting of the Special Committee on Child Placing Department, April 28, 1931, folder 14, box 11, Julius Rosenwald Papers, Special Collections Research Center, University of Chicago. Cited in Gilmartin, "Use of the Psychiatric Clinic," 3.

54. Moses, *Negro Delinquent in Chicago*, 16–18.

55. U.S. Bureau of the Census, Children under Institutional Care, 1923 (Washington, DC: Government Printing Office, 1927), 301–2, quoted in Thornsten Sellin, "The Negro Criminal: A Statistical Note," 140 (1928).

56. Department of Public Welfare, *21st Annual Report*, 9; Chicago Commission on Race Relations, *Negro in Chicago*, 339; Bertha Corman, "A Study of Delinquent Girls," 10; "Report on Juvenile Court," 2–7, box 234, folder 2294, University of Illinois at Chicago (UIC), Special Collections Research Center, Chicago Urban League (CUL) Papers.

57. E. Franklin Frazier tabulated these data in his 1933 study of delinquency among African Americans. Sixty-seven courts furnished data on race. See Frazier, *Negro Family in the United States*, 358.

58. Mintz, *Huck's Raft*, 179–80; Tanenhaus, *Juvenile Justice in the Making*, 55; Crawley, "Dependent Negro Children in Chicago," 71.

59. See, for example, Board of Commissioners of Cook County, *Charity Service Reports*; Tanenhaus, *Juvenile Justice in the Making*, 55, 74–75.

60. See statistical tables in 1923 Cook County Juvenile Court Annual Report.

61. For this year, 199 families received pensions, and only fourteen of these families were African American. Calculated from "Chief Probation Officer's Report," table 45, p. 53, in Juvenile Court and Juvenile Detention Home Annual Reports 1925, Municipal Reference Collection, Harold Washington Library, Chicago Public Libraries.

62. For examples of notions of African Americans' cultural backwardness and inability to properly care for their children, see Jane Addams, "'Social Control' Crisis"; Dollard, *Caste and Class*, 150–53.

63. Case no. 44897, Cook County Circuit Court Archive, JCR.

64. Frazier, *Negro Family in the United States*, 359.

65. Lawrence, "Some Problems Arising," 3, 14–20.

66. Juvenile Court and Juvenile Detention Home of Cook County Annual Report of 1921, 88–91.

67. Juvenile Court and Juvenile Detention Home of Cook County Annual Report of 1921, 82–88.

68. See Juvenile Court and Juvenile Detention Home of Cook County Annual Report of 1921, 82–83, 88, for information on the physical separation of delinquent girls from other children in the institution; and quotation about the majority of girls being processed in juvenile court for "immorality."

69. Cook County Juvenile Court Annual Report 1906, 6–8; Juvenile Court and Juvenile Detention Home of Cook County Annual Report of 1921, 34, 82; Tanenhaus, *Juvenile Justice in the Making*, 6, 9; Bowen, *Growing up with a City*, 300–305; Knupfer, "Chicago Detention Home," 52; Osborn, "Study of the Detention of Two Hundred Six Children," 8; Link, "Analysis of Thirty-Five Negro Problem Children," 16.

70. Chicago Board of Education, Annual Report of the Superintendent of Schools, 1925–1926, 153.

71. Juvenile Court and Juvenile Detention Home of Cook County Annual Report of 1921, 54, 88.

72. Ibid., 80.

73. Moses, *Negro Delinquent in Chicago*, 18; Juvenile Court and Juvenile Detention Home of Cook County Annual Report of 1921, 80; see also Board of Education Annual Report, 153, for average length of stay.

74. Gittens, *Poor Relations*; Hirsch, *Doing Justice*, 11–12; Holland, "Analysis of the Case Histories," 7; Tanenhaus, *Juvenile Justice in the Making*, 32–26.

75. Link, "Analysis of Thirty-Five Negro Problem Children," 24.

76. Danzig, "Thirty-One Adolescent Boys," 65–66.

77. Link, "An Analysis of Thirty-Five Negro Problem Children," 21.

78. Ibid., 21–23; Giddings, "Some Factors Affecting the Outcome," 2.

79. Auer, "Study of the Services of the Institute for Juvenile Research," 43.

80. Danzig, "Thirty-One Adolescent Boys," 65–66.

81. Giddings, "Some Factors Affecting the Outcome," 3.

82. Phillips, "Binet Tests Applied to Colored Children," 193; Peterson, "Comparative Abilities of White and Negro Children,"; Stetson, "Some Memory Tests of Whites and Blacks."

83. Giddings, "Some Factors Affecting the Outcome," 4; Danzig, "Thirty-One Adolescent Boys," 65–66.

84. Juvenile Court and Juvenile Detention Home of Cook County Annual Report of 1921, 1.

85. Juvenile Court and Juvenile Detention Home of Cook County Annual Report, 1913–1920, 30; Holland, "Analysis of the Case Histories," 9; Gault, "Parental Schools and Juvenile Crime," 163.

86. Juvenile Court and Juvenile Detention Home of Cook County Annual Report of 1921, 30–31; Chicago Board of Education, Annual Report of the Superintendent of Schools, 1925–1926, 31.

87. Chicago Board of Education, Annual Report of the Superintendent of Schools, 1925–1926, 51; Juvenile Court and Juvenile Detention Home of Cook County Annual Report of 1921, 17.

88. Case no. 103989, Cook County Circuit Court Archive, JCR.

89. Chicago Board of Education, Annual Report of the Superintendent of Schools, 1925–1926, 5–6, 21–24.

90. Chicago Board of Education, Annual Report of the Superintendent of Schools, 1925–1926, 51; Report, 51; Juvenile Court and Juvenile Detention Home of Cook County Annual Report of 1921, 15–16.

91. Holland, "Analysis of the Case Histories," 1, 17, 22.

92. "Orders Arrests in School Flogging Cases."

93. Long, "Children Referred to the Schools by a Child Guidance Clinic," 22.

94. Lawrence, "Some Problems Arising," 34–38.

95. Case no. 103881, Cook County Circuit Court Archive, JCR.

96. Drake and Cayton, *Black Metropolis*, 684.

97. "Social Workers Defend Coddling of Young Toughs." See also "Escapes at St. Charles"; "Rules Juvenile Court No Haven for Criminals"; "Oppose Juvenile Court Trials of Youths up to 21"; "Five Towns Lie in Fear of 'Boys' at State School"; "Charges Boys Learn Crime at St. Charles."

98. Illinois Revised Statutes, 1911, ch. 23, secs. 169–190, "An act relating to children who are now or may hereafter become dependent, neglected or delinquent" (1905); Dodge, "Reform Struggles and Legal Challenges," 85; Willrich, *City of Courts*, 209.

99. "Rules Juvenile Court No Haven for Criminals."

100. Dodge, *Whores and Thieves*, 85.

101. "Schoolgirl Slays Rival in Beer Tavern"; Transcript for *People of the State of Illinois v. Susie Lattimore*, Vault no. 48092, Illinois State Archives at Springfield.

102. Brief for Defendant in Error, *People of the State of Illinois v. Susie Lattimore*, case no. 23103 362 Ill. 206, Illinois State Archives, Supreme Court of Illinois Records.

103. Case Summary for Board of Correction, November 25, 1944; Prison and Parole Docket, Illinois State Archives at Springfield.

104. "Social Workers Defend Coddling of Young Toughs." See also "Escapes at St. Charles"; "Rules Juvenile Court No Haven for Criminals"; "Oppose Juvenile Court Trials of Youths up to 21"; "Five Towns Lie in Fear of 'Boys' at State School"; "Charges Boys Learn Crime at St. Charles."

105. *People of the State of Illinois v. Susie Lattimore*, case no. 23103, 362 Ill. 206, Illinois State Archives; Superior Court of Cook County Records Transcript and Judgment, Illinois State Archives. See also Tanenhaus, *Juvenile Justice in the Making*, 150–53; Gittens, *Poor Relations*, 132–33; Dodge, *Whores and Thieves of the Worst Kind*, 85.

106. Untitled document, supplement 1, folder 10, UIC, Special Collections Research Center, JPA Papers.

107. "Oppose Juvenile Court Trials of Youths up to 21."

108. Dodge, *Whores and Thieves of the Worst Kind*, 86.

Chapter Three

1. Mary Ellen's story is based on 1928 reports in the *Chicago Defender*. "Daniels Gets 9 Months," *Chicago Defender*, October 27, 1928; Evangeline Roberts, "Governor to Investigate State School," *Chicago Defender*, April 7, 1928. For common reasons girls were sent to training schools and reformatories, see Mary Odem, *Delinquent Daughters*.

2. See, for example, Regina Kunzel, *Fallen Women, Problem Girls: Unmarried Mothers and the Professionalization of Social Work, 1890–1945* (New Haven, CT: Yale University, 1995); Odem, *Delinquent Daughters*; Ruth Alexander, *The Girl Problem: Female Sexual Delinquency in New York, 1900–1930* (Ithaca, NY: Cornell University, 1995); Kathy Lee Peiss, *Cheap Amusements: Working Women and Leisure in Turn-of-the-Century New York* (Philadelphia: Temple University Press, 1986).

3. Kunzel, *Fallen Women*, 1–2; Alexander, *Girl Problem*, 38–40; Odem, *Delinquent Daughters*, 3–4.

4. Mann Act of 1910, chapter 395, section 2.

5. Ibid., section 6 and 8.

6. Blair, *I've Got to Make My Livin'*, 190; Mumford, *Interzones*, 4–5.

7. Michael Grossberg, "A Protected Childhood: The Emergence of Child Protection in America," in *American Public Life and the Historical Imagination*, ed. Wendy Gamberg, Michael Grossberg, and Henrik Hartog (Notre Dame: University of Notre Dame Press, 2003); Odem, *Delinquent Daughters*; Sutton, *Stubborn Children*; Illinois State Training School for Girls, *Biennial Report*, 9; Department of Public Welfare, *9th Annual Report of the Department of Public Welfare* (Springfield: Illinois State Journal Company, 1926), 263–66.

8. Anne Meis Knupfer, "'To Become Good, Self-Supporting Women': The State Industrial School for Delinquent Girls at Geneva, Illinois, 1900–1935," *Journal of the History of Sexuality* 9 (2000): 420–446, 422.

9. Ibid., 422.

10. Sophonisba Breckinridge and Edith Abbott, *The Delinquent Child and the Home* (New York: Russell Sage Foundation, 1912), 314; Corman, "A Study of Delinquent Girls," 15. See also Department of Public Welfare, *Welfare Bulletin* 37:14; Illinois Youth Council, *Illinois Youth Council Biennial Report*, 53.

11. Charlotte Ruth Klein, "Success and Failure on Parole," 9; Tanenhaus, "Degrees of Discretion," 108.

12. Illinois State Training School for Girls, *Biennial Report*; "Department of Public Welfare," *Welfare Bulletin* 22; Illinois Youth Council, "Illinois Association for Criminal Justice," box 10, folder 1, Ernest Burgess Papers, Special Collections, University of Chicago.

13. Department of Public Welfare, *8th Annual Report of the Department of Public Welfare*; Cahn, *Sexual Reckonings*; Department of Public Welfare, *12th Annual Report of the Department of Public Welfare* (Springfield: Illinois State Journal Company, 1929), 201; Department of Public Welfare, *21st Annual Report*; Illinois Board of Administration, *The Institution Quarterly*, vol. 11 (Springfield: Department of Public Welfare, 1920); Illinois State Training School for Girls, *Seventh Biennial Report of the Trustees, 1904–1906* (Springfield, IL: Hartman State Printer, 1906), 27–29; Chicago Commission on Race

Relations, *Negro in Chicago*, 339; Corman, "Study of Delinquent Girls," 10; "5 Girls Escape Geneva; 90 Boys Flee St. Charles."

14. "Mildred Davis" is used as a pseudonym to protect the inmate's identity in light of the 1989 Illinois statute on juvenile case record confidentiality. The initial letters in the first and last names are the same. Geneva Historical Society, Illinois Training School for Girls, box 122.1, Discharge and Correspondence.

15. Department of Public Welfare, *8th Annual Report*; Cahn, *Sexual Reckonings*; Department of Public Welfare, *12th Annual Report*, 201; Department of Public Welfare, *21st Annual Report*; Illinois Board of Administration, *Institution Quarterly*, vol. 11; Illinois State Training School for Girls, *Seventh Biennial Report*, 27–29; Corman, "Study of Delinquent Girls," 10.

16. Illinois Board of Administration, *Institution Quarterly*, vol. 13 (Springfield: Department of Public Welfare, 1922), 264; Department of Public Welfare, *9th Annual Report*, 202; Illinois State Training School for Girls, *Biennial Report*, 8; Geneva Illinois State Training School for Girls, *Third Biennial Report of the Trustees, Superintendent and Treasurer of the State Home for Juvenile Female Offenders at Geneva*, 7.

17. Illinois Board of Administration, *Institution Quarterly* 13:264; Department of Public Welfare, *9th Annual Report*, 202; Illinois State Training School for Girls, *Biennial Report*, 8.

18. Department of Public Welfare, *Welfare Bulletin* 37; Department of Public Welfare, *8th Annual Report*.

19. Klein, "Success and Failure on Parole," 10; Grossberg, "Study of Negro Girls"; Michael A. Rembis, *Defining Deviance: Sex, Science, and Delinquent Girls, 1890–1960* (Chicago: University of Illinois Press, 2011), 79.

20. Grossberg, "Study of Negro Girls," 23, 25.

21. Department of Public Welfare, *Welfare Bulletin* 37; Walker, "Geneva School Has Discipline and It Works."

22. Geneva Historical Society, Illinois Training School for Girls, box 122.14, case no. 6526 (1933), Correspondence and Deportment.

23. Geneva Historical Society, Illinois Training School for Girls, box 122.1, D.L. (1935), Discharge and Correspondence.

24. David. J. Rotham, *Conscience and Convenience: The Asylum and Its Alternatives in Progressive America* (Boston: Little, Brown, 1980), 272–73.

25. Illinois State Charities Commission, Illinois Board of Administration, State Psychopathic Institute, *The Institution Quarterly*, vol. 12 (Springfield: Department of Public Welfare, 1921), 503.

26. Anne Meis Knupfer, *Reform and Resistance: Gender, Delinquency, and America's First Juvenile Court* (New York: Routledge, 2001), 453.

27. Geneva Illinois State Training School for Girls, *Seventh Biennial Report of the Trustees, Superintendent and Treasurer of the State Home for Juvenile Offenders, at Geneva* (Springfield: Phillips Bros State Printing, 1906), 10; Knupfer, *Reform and Resistance*, 453; Ward G. Walker, "Geneva School Has Discipline and It Works," *Chicago Tribune*, March 7, 1941; "Illinois Association for Criminal Justice."

28. "Girl Hurt in Flight," *Chicago Defender*, April 27, 1912, 7.

29. Geneva Historical Society, Illinois Training School for Girls, box 121, Illinois Statewide Death Index (1916–1950); "Geneva Home Inmate Electrocuted on 3d Rail," *Batavia Herald*, July 31, 1924; "State School Inmate Killed by Third Rail," *Geneva Republican*, August 1, 1924; "Illinois Deaths and Stillbirths, 1916–1947," database, *FamilySearch*, Elizabeth Marie Cooksey, February 11, 1924, Public Board of Health, Archives, Springfield, FHL microfilm, 1,452,344; Illinois Deaths and Stillbirths, 1916–1947," database, *FamilySearch*, Sadie Cooksey, in entry for Elizabeth Marie Cooksey, February 11, 1924, Public Board of Health, Archives, Springfield, FHL microfilm, 1,452,344; "United States Census, 1920," database with images, *Family Search*, Sadie Cook, Geneva, Kane, Illinois, United States, citing sheet 4, National Archives and Records Administration (NARA) microfilm publication T625 (Washington, DC: National Archives and Records Administration, n.d.), FHL microfilm, 1,820,374; "United States Census, 1920," database with images, *FamilySearch*, Martin Hopper, Chicago Ward 3, Cook (Chicago), Illinois, United States, citing sheet 3A, NARA microfilm publication T625 (Washington, DC: National Archives and Records Administration, n.d.), FHL microfilm, 1,820,313.

30. Geneva Historical Society, Illinois Training School for Girls, box 122, "State School Girls Sentenced for Prison Riot," *Geneva Republican*, August 1, 1941.

31. "Illinois Association for Criminal Justice"; see also Illinois State Training School for Girls, *4th Biennial Report*; Illinois State Training School for Girls, *6th Biennial Report*; Department of Public Welfare, *8th Annual Report*; Department of Public Welfare, *11th Annual Report*.

32. Michael W. Sedlak, *Youth Policy and Young Women, 1870–1972*, [1982] 45–57.

33. Chicago Commission on Race Relations, *Negro in Chicago*, 348.

34. Department of Public Welfare, *21st Annual Report*, 529; see also the *Institutional Quarterly* publications, 1912–1913, 1921–1922, and annual reports of the Department of Public Welfare, 1928–1931 and 1936–1939.

35. Department of Public Welfare, *21st Annual Report*.

36. "Illinois Association for Criminal Justice." See also Walker, "Geneva School Has Discipline and It Works," for reference to segregated disciplinary cottages.

37. Illinois Board of Administration, *Institution Quarterly*, vol. 3 (Springfield: Department of Public Welfare, 1912), 49; Illinois Board of Administration, *The Institution Quarterly*, vol. 4 (Springfield: Department of Public Welfare, 1913), 118–19; Illinois Board of Administration, *Institution Quarterly*, vol. 9 (Springfield: Department of Public Welfare, 1918); Illinois Board of Administration, *Institution Quarterly*, vol. 12 (Springfield: Department of Public Welfare, 1921).

38. Illinois Board of Administration, *Institutional Quarterly*, 4:119.

39. Chicago Commission on Race Relations, *Negro in Chicago*, 334.

40. Illinois Board of Administration, *Institutional Quarterly*, 3:49; Chicago Commission on Race Relations, *Negro in Chicago*, 348.

41. Madeleine Z. Doty, *Society's Misfits* (New York: Century Co., 1916), quoted in Cheryl D. Hicks, *Talk with You Like a Woman: African American Women, Justice, and Reform in New York, 1890–1935* (Chapel Hill: University of North Carolina Press, 2010), 125–26.

42. Dodge, *Whores and Thieves*, 123.

43. Eugenia C. Lekkerkerker, *Reformatories for Women in the United States* (Groningen, Netherlands: J. B. Wolters' Uitgevers-Maatschappij, 1931), 199–203.

44. Ibid.

45. Hicks, *Talk with You Like a Woman*, 126; Hazel V. Carby, *Reconstructing Womanhood: The Emergence of the Afro-American Woman Novelist* (New York: Oxford University Press, 1987), 25; Evelyn Brooks Higginbotham, *Righteous Discontent: The Women's Movement in the Black Baptist Church, 1880–1920* (Cambridge: Harvard University Press, 1993), 189–90. See also Gross, *Colored Amazons*, 134.

46. Hicks, *Talk with You Like a Woman*, 126.

47. Gross, *Colored Amazons*, 134.

48. "Illinois Association for Criminal Justice."

49. Margaret Otis, "A Perversion Not Commonly Noted," *Journal of Abnormal Psychology* 8 (1913): 113–16; "Illinois Association for Criminal Justice."

50. Monahan and Lawes, *Women in Crime*, 223.

51. Otis, "A Perversion Not Commonly Noted," 113–16; Lekkerkerker, *Reformatories for Women*, 234.

52. Freedman, "Prison Lesbian," 397–423; Lekkerkerker, *Reformatories for Women*.

53. Klein, "Success and Failure on Parole"; Esther H. Stone, "A Plea for Early Commitment to Correctional Institutions of Delinquent Children, and an Endorsement of Training and Vocational Training in These Institutions," *Institutional Quarterly* 9 (1918): 9, 65.

54. Otis, "A Perversion Not Commonly Noted," 113.

55. Ibid., 114.

56. Klein, "Success and Failure on Parole," 66–67.

57. Stone, "A Plea for Early Commitment," 65–66.

58. Otis, "A Perversion Not Commonly Noted," 115–16.

59. Paula J. Giddings, *Ida: A Sword Among Lions* (New York: Amistad, 2008), 221–29.

60. Stone, "A Plea for Early Commitment," 66.

61. Otis, "A Perversion Not Commonly Noted," 114.

62. Klein, "Success and Failure on Parole," 66.

63. Otis, "A Perversion Not Commonly Noted," 114.

64. Ibid.

65. Theodora M. Abel, "Dominant Behavior of Institutionalized Subnormal Negro Girls: An Experimental Study," *American Journal of Mental Deficiency* 67 (1943): 429–36.

66. Edith R. Spaulding, "Emotional Episodes among Psychopathic Delinquent Women," *Journal of Nervous and Mental Disease* 54 (1921): 299–306.

67. Klein, "Success and Failure on Parole," 68.

68. Otis, "A Perversion Not Commonly Noted," 113.

69. Regina Kunzel, "Situating Sex: Prison Sexual Culture in the Mid-Twentieth-Century United States," *GLQ: A Journal of Lesbian and Gay Studies* 8 (2002): 262.

70. Freedman, "Prison Lesbian," 400; Regina Kunzel, *Criminal Intimacy Prison and the Uneven History of Modern American Sexuality* (Chicago: University of Chicago Press,

2008), 130–31; Catherine I. Nelson, "A Study of Homosexuality among Women Inmates at Two State Prisons" (PhD diss., Temple University, 1974), 156; Tamsin Fitzgerald, *A Study of Homosexuality* (New York: Dial Press, 1973), 188.

71. Fitzgerald, *Study of Homosexuality*, 188.

72. Rupe Simms, "Controlling Images and the Gender Construction of Enslaved African Women," *Gender and Society* 15 (2001): 879–97.

73. Cahn, *Sexual Reckonings*, 69.

74. Cahn, *Sexual Reckonings*, 46, citing *Charlotte Observer*, February 19, 1939, box 163, folder "North Carolina Training School for Negro Girls, 1919–1934," Records of the State Board of Public Welfare, North Carolina State Archives Raleigh and Old Records Center; and Cahn, *Sexual Reckonings*, 69, citing "Moral Advancement in North Carolina," *Danville Register*, February 20, 1931, in Harriet L. Herring clipping file, North Carolina Collection, University of North Carolina Library, Chapel Hill.

75. Cahn, *Sexual Reckonings*, 46; Trost, *Gateway to Justice*, 122–24.

76. "Police Start War on Vice: Social Evil on South Side Is Appalling."

77. "Place Matrons in Home at Geneva"; Monahan and Lawes, *Women in Crime*, 120–22; "Move to Segregate Boys at School Bitterly Fought"; "Senate Probers Hear of Jim Crow at St. Charles"; Roberts, "Governor to Investigate State School."

78. "Move to Segregate Boys at School Bitterly Fought."

79. Roberts, "Governor to Investigate State School."

80. "Move to Segregate Boys at School Bitterly Fought"; "Ignorance Predominates at Girls' School," *Chicago Defender*, November 29, 1930.

81. "Seek Ouster of Head of Girls' School," *Chicago Defender*, November 2, 1940; "Order Color Line Dropped at St. Charles."

82. "Friend of Juvenile Delinquents Dies"; "Place Matrons in Home at Geneva."

83. Department of Public Welfare, *Welfare Bulletin* 37.

84. Ernest Gifford, "399 Girls on Parole from Geneva School: Where Are They? Ask Civic Leaders"; Jane Logan, "How Vice Ring Traps Girls into Slavery"; "Raid South Side Vice Den, Find Missing Girls: 40 Inmates Lured from Geneva Home"; "Delay Trial in Vice Cases." All preceding articles were published in the *Chicago Daily News* (1934) and can be found in the Juvenile Protective Association Records, Special Collections Library, Richard Daley Library, University of Illinois.

85. "Sift Charges against Police in Vice Syndicate."

Chapter Four

1. Monthly report of Managing Officer Robert F. Havlik, November 8, 1933, series 2, box 8, folder 112, Mary Bartelme Papers, University of Illinois at Chicago (UIC), Special Collections Library.

2. Gregory, *Southern Diaspora*, 20.

3. Under the Juvenile Court Act of 1899, a "dependent child" referred to any male child, while under the age of seventeen years, or any female child, while under the age of eighteen years, who was for any reason destitute, homeless, or abandoned. A "delinquent child" was any male child under seventeen and female child under eighteen who committed a criminal act.

4. In St. Charles Home for Boys, *1st Biennial Report* (Springfield, IL: Abraham Lincoln State Library, 1904); *2nd Biennial Report* (Springfield, IL, 1906); *5th Biennial Report* (Springfield, IL, 1912); *3rd Biennial Report* (Springfield, IL, 1907). In 1905, the institution's name was changed to "St. Charles School for Boys." In 1939, it was renamed the Illinois State Training School for Boys. St. Charles Home for Boys, *2nd Biennial Report*, 6; Feld, *Bad Kids*, 48–54.

5. "A Famous Institution," *St. Charles Chronicle*, December 16, 1904, cited in St. Charles Home for Boys, *1st Biennial Report*.

6. "A Famous Institution"; Department of Public Welfare, *10th Annual Report of the Department of Public Welfare* (Springfield: Illinois State Journal Company, 1927), 240; St. Charles Home for Boys, *1st Biennial Report*, 7; *2nd Biennial Report*, 6–8; *5th Biennial Report*, 14–16; *3rd Biennial Report*, 388.

7. St. Charles School for Boys, *5th Biennial Report*, 14–16; *3rd Biennial Report*, 388.

8. St. Charles School for Boys, *3rd Biennial Report*, 6–7; Department of Public Welfare, *10th Annual Report*, 241; *14th Annual Report of the Department of Public Welfare* (Springfield: Illinois State Journal Company, 1931).

9. Department of Public Welfare, *9th Annual Report of the Department of Public Welfare* (Springfield: Illinois State Journal Company, 1926), 254–55; St. Charles Home for Boys, *1st Biennial Report*, 8; *2nd Biennial Report* 7; *5th Biennial Report*, 6–8; *3rd Biennial Report*, 5–6; Illinois Board of Administration, *Institution Quarterly* 3 (Springfield, IL: Department of Public Welfare, 1912), 264.

10. St. Charles Home for Boys, *1st Biennial Report*, 5–6; Department of Public Welfare, *14th Annual Report*, 306; Illinois Board of Administration, *Institution Quarterly* 3:94.

11. Illinois Board of Administration, *Institution Quarterly* 3; St. Charles Home for Boys, *1st Biennial Report*, 5–6; Tamara Myers, "Embodying Delinquency: Boys' Bodies, Sexuality, and Juvenile Justice History in Early-Twentieth-Century Quebec," *Journal of the History of Sexuality* 14, no. 4 (2005): 384.

12. "Letter to Dr. Herman Adler, Director, Bureau of Juvenile Research," box 18, folder 10, Ernest Burgess Papers, University of Chicago, Special Collections Research Center.

13. "St. Charles Boys Say They Prefer Cells in Pontiac."

14. George Ordahl, "Study of 341 Delinquent Boys," *Journal of Delinquency* 1 (1916): 83; Myers, "Embodying Delinquency," 387.

15. Department of Public Welfare, *12th Annual Report of the Department of Public Welfare*, 197; *19th Annual Report of the Department of Public Welfare* (Springfield: Illinois State Journal Company, 1936), 323, 33; *23rd Annual Report of the Department of Public Welfare, December 31, 1937* (Chicago: Illinois Board of Public Welfare Commissioners, 1939), 3.

16. "Immoral Acts Called Common at Boys School."

17. Ibid.; "Hoehler Acts on Immorality in Boys School."

18. Ibid.; "Hoehler Acts on Immorality in Boys School"; "Quick Reports on Sex Cases in School."

19. "Hoehler Acts on Immorality in Boys School."

20. Ibid.

21. "Commission Aid in Boys School Cleanup Sought," *Chicago Tribune*, May 19, 1949; "Quick Reports on Sex Cases in School."

22. "A Famous Institution"; Department of Public Welfare, *10th Annual Report of the Department of Public Welfare* (Springfield: Illinois State Journal Company, 1927), 240; St. Charles Home for Boys, *1st Biennial Report*, 7; *2nd Biennial Report*, 6–8; *5th Biennial Report*, 14–16; *3rd Biennial Report*, 388; Department of Public Welfare, *Statistical Review of State Prisons and Correctional Schools* (Springfield: State of Illinois, 1940).

23. Department of Public Welfare, *Statistical Review of State Prisons and Correctional Schools* (Springfield: State of Illinois, 1940).

24. Kahlert, *Study of Commitments*, 15.

25. Training School for Boys and Youthful Offenders Commission, *A Report and Recommendations Submitted to the 61st General Assembly of the Illinois Legislature* (Springfield: Illinois, 1939), 56; "Age of Boys," 1941, series 1, box 0, folder 87, Russell Ward Ballard Papers, UIC, Special Collections Library.

26. Chicago Commission on Race Relations, *Negro in Chicago*, 339.

27. Kahlert, *Study of Commitments*, 3; Letty Joyce Grossberg, "A Study of Negro Girls Committed to the Geneva State Reformatory in 1937–1938" (Chicago: University of Chicago, 1940), 4.

28. Faris, "Study of Boys," 13–14; Department of Public Welfare, *32nd Annual Report of the Department of Public Welfare* (Springfield: Illinois State Journal Company, 1949), 191.

29. Marn, "Psychiatry in the Illinois State Training School for Boys"; Grant, *Boy Problem*, 169.

30. Moses, *Negro Delinquent in Chicago*, 16–18.

31. Monthly report of Managing Officer Robert F. Havlik, November 8, 1933.

32. Memo to Ballard from Lake County Department of Public Welfare Court House, March 27, 1943, series 1, box 0, folder 76, Russell Ward Ballard Papers, UIC, Special Collections Library.

33. Ibid.

34. St. Charles Home for Boys, *3rd Biennial Report*, 388; *4th Biennial Report*, 3; "Age of Boys at Institution."

35. Department of Public Welfare, *11th Annual Report*, 85; *12th Annual Report*, 198; Illinois Board of Administration, *Institution Quarterly*, vols. 3–13. See also Department of Public Welfare, *8th Annual Report*, *9th Annual Report*, and *10th Annual Report*.

36. Chicago Commission on Race Relations, *Negro in Chicago*, 339; Evelyn Harriet Randall, *The St. Charles School for Delinquent Boys* (Chicago: University of Chicago, 1927), 32; "Move to Segregate Boys at School Bitterly Fought."

37. "St. Charles School Trains Wayward Boys," *Chicago Defender*, September 14, 1929; "Pledge Aid to Boys at St. Charles School," *Chicago Defender*, May 7, 1932.

38. Minutes of St. Charles Advisory Committee, July 31, 1935, St. Charles Advisory Committee Minutes of Meetings, 1933–1937 (IJR), Record Group 266.00, Illinois State Archives at Springfield; Minutes of the St. Charles Advisory Committee Meeting Chicago Bar Association, Friday, March 13, 1936, St. Charles Advisory Committee Minutes of Meetings, 1933–1937 (IJR), Record Group 266.00, Illinois State Archives at Springfield.

39. Department of Public Welfare, *19th Annual Report*, 322; Minutes of the St. Charles Advisory Committee called at the request of Mr. Brown at the Medical and Dental Arts Building, July 19, 1938, St. Charles, IL, School for Boys, 1937–1939, Record Group 266.00, Illinois State Archives at Springfield. See also Department of Public Welfare, *22nd Annual Report*, 449; *Annual Report*, 675–76.

40. Minutes of the St. Charles Advisory Committee Meeting, June 17, 1938, July 19, 1938, St. Charles, IL, School for Boys, 1937–1939; Record Group 266.00, Illinois State Archives at Springfield; Minutes of the St. Charles Advisory Committee called at the request of Mr. Brown at the Medical and Dental Arts Building, July 19, 1938, St. Charles, IL, School for Boys, 1937–1939, Record Group 266.00, Illinois State Archives at Springfield.

41. "Sentence Seven Ex-Inmates of Training School," *Chicago Tribune*, February 24, 1942.

42. "Return Escaped Boy to St. Charles Home."

43. Leavelle, "Brick Slayer Is Likened to Jungle Beast."

44. "Call Committee to Halt Escapes at St. Charles." See also "Five Towns Lie in Fear of 'Boys' at State School."

45. See, for example, "Three Negro Youths Who Escaped School Held to Grand Jury," *Geneva Republican*, December 18, 1942; "42 Boys Escape St. Charles in 15 Days"; "Escapes at St. Charles"; "Boys' Escapes at St. Charles Stir up Public"; "Return of Strap Rule Demanded for St. Charles"; "Find St. Charles Fails to Reform Inmates"; "Steel, Concrete to Hem Toughs of St. Charles"; "Nine Recaptured after Training School Escape"; "Admits Rape Attempt after School Parole," August 25, 1948.

46. "42 Boys Escape St. Charles in 15 Days"; "Escapes at St. Charles"; "Boys' Escapes at St. Charles Stir up Public"; "Return of Strap Rule Demanded for St. Charles"; "Find St. Charles Fails to Reform Inmates"; "Steel, Concrete to Hem Toughs of St. Charles."

47. "8 Smash Way out of State Boys' School," *Chicago Tribune*, October 12, 1941; "Capture 8 Who Broke out of Boys School," *Chicago Tribune*, October 13, 1941; "5 Boys Who Fled Training School Called to Court," *Chicago Tribune*, October 13, 1941; "Sent to Prison," *Chicago Tribune*, November 6, 1941.

48. "8 Smash Way out of State Boys' School"; "Capture 8 Who Broke out of Boys School"; "5 Boys Who Fled Training School Called to Court"; "Sent to Prison."

49. *Report and Recommendations Submitted to the 61st General Assembly of the Illinois Legislature*, 42.

50. Henry M. Hyde, "Worst Boys at St. Charles Flee under Lax Rule," *Chicago Tribune*, October 30, 1915.

51. For references to newspaper coverage of everyday happenings at the school, see *St. Charles Chronicle*, January 31, 1909, and May 21, 1909.

52. "Charges 'Sob Sister Policies' Would Wreck St. Charles School Boys," *Chicago Tribune*, July 25, 1928.

53. Ibid.; "Tough 16, Hurls Fists in Court and Races Out," *Chicago Tribune*, August 2, 1950; "2 Boys School Inmates Flee," *Chicago Tribune*, July 17, 1950; "Escape State School," series 1, box 0, folder 67, Russell Ward Ballard Papers, UIC, Special Collections Library; "8 Smash Way out of State Boys' School"; "Three Negro Youths Who

Escaped School Held to Grand Jury," *Geneva Republican*, December 18, 1942. Conclusion based on examinations of articles on St. Charles escapees written between 1910 and 1950 in the *Chicago Tribune* and *Geneva Republican*.

54. See, for example, "Five Towns Lie in Fear of 'Boys' at State School"; George Tagge, "Whipping Urged to End Escapes at St. Charles," *Chicago Tribune*, April 11, 1939; "Return of Strap Rule Demanded for St. Charles"; Hyde, "Worst Boys at St. Charles Flee under Lax Rule," Chicago Tribune, October 30, 1915; "Boys' Escapes at St. Charles Stir up Public"; "Escapes at St. Charles"; "St. Charles Again"; "Seeks to Clear St. Charles of Its Bad Boys."

55. Tagge, "Whipping Urged to End Escapes at St. Charles"; "Steel, Concrete to Hem Toughs of St. Charles"; George Wright, "Pamper Toughs or Get Out! It's St. Charles Rule," *Chicago Tribune*, May 29, 1939.

56. *Report and Recommendations Submitted to the 61st General Assembly of the Illinois Legislature*, 21.

57. Department of Public Welfare, *19th Annual Report*, 333.

58. "Prisons' Chief Fears Scandal at St. Charles."

59. Ibid.

60. Department of Public Welfare, *19th Annual Report*, 333.

61. "Cases Illustrating the Problem," case D, p. 1, supplement 1, box 0, folder 44, Russell Ward Ballard Papers, UIC, Special Collections Library.

62. Barnes Case Study, box 0, folder 44, Russell Ballard Papers, UIC, Special Collections Library.

63. "Story of 76 Escapes in 1939 at St. Charles."

64. *Report and Recommendations Submitted to the 61st General Assembly of the Illinois Legislature*, 21.

65. Ibid., 1, 21.

66. Ibid, 48.

67. Ibid., 5–6.

68. Ibid., 7.

69. Department of Public Welfare, *19th Annual Report*, 333.

70. *Report and Recommendations Submitted to the 61st General Assembly of the Illinois Legislature*, 7.

71. St. Charles Home for Boys, *2nd Biennial Report*; MacQueary, "Schools for Delinquent Children," 1–23, 12.

72. *Report and Recommendations Submitted to the 61st General Assembly of the Illinois Legislature*, 21, 30–33.

73. "Pledge Aid to Boys at St. Charles School."

74. "What Shall We Do with Our Delinquent Boys?"

75. "Senate Probers Hear of Jim Crow at St. Charles," *Chicago Defender*, March 25, 1939; "Probers Favor Racial Equality at St Charles," *Chicago Defender*, June 17, 1939.

76. "Report of the Board of Public Welfare: Commissioners on Re-organization of SC," November 1941, supplement 1, box 0, folder 44, Russell Ward Ballard Papers, UIC, Special Collections Library; "Order Color Line Dropped at St. Charles."

77. Thomas, "20,000 March in Chicago"; "City Rallies to Help in Scottsboro Midnight Show"; "Scottsboro's Mass Meeting Date Changed."

78. *Report and Recommendations Submitted to the 61st General Assembly of the Illinois Legislature*, 53.

79. Ibid., 53–54.

80. Ibid., 53–55.

81. Grossman, *Land of Hope*; Christopher Robert Reed, *The Chicago NAACP and the Rise of Black Professional Leadership*; Drake and Cayton, *Black Metropolis*.

82. Alan B. Anderson and George W. Pickering, *Confronting the Color Line*, 29; James R. Ralph, *Northern Protest*, 10–12, 67.

83. Martha Biondi, *To Stand and Fight*, 1–3, 38.

84. Ibid., 64; George Tagge, "Senate Votes Wide Reforms at St. Charles," *Chicago Tribune*, June 9, 1939; George Tagge, "Agree on Plans to Cure Evils at St. Charles," *Chicago Tribune*, May 17, 1939; "Separate Prison for St. Charles Toughs Is Asked," *Chicago Tribune*, June 7, 1939.

85. *Report and Recommendations Submitted to the 61st General Assembly of the Illinois Legislature*, 64; "Dismissed St. Charles Instructor Reinstated"; Letter to Mr. Ballard and Eddy from M. Philbrick, series 1, box 0, folder 81, April 19, 1941, Russell Ward Ballard Papers, UIC, Special Collections Library; "12 Face Ouster in Death of Reform School Boy."

86. "Boy Auto Thief Killed: Guards Admit Slugging," *Chicago Tribune*, February 14, 1941.

87. "2 St. Charles Boys 'Change Their Minds.' "

88. "Report of the Board of Public Welfare: Commissioners on Re-organization of SC"; "12 Face Ouster in Death of Reform School Boy."

89. "Guard Freed in Death of Boy Prisoner," *Chicago Defender*, June 7, 1941; "24 Resign Posts after School Slaying," *Chicago Defender*, March 1, 1941.

90. "Guard Freed in Death of Boy Prisoner"; "24 Resign Posts after School Slaying."

91. "Order Color Line Dropped at St. Charles"; George Faris, "A Study of Boys under Fifteen Committed to the Illinois State Training School for Boys" (Chicago: University of Chicago, 1941).

92. Study and Reorganization of Illinois State Training School for Boys, p. 19, supplement 1, box 0, folder 44, 1941, Russell Ward Ballard Papers, UIC, Special Collections Library.

93. Department of Public Welfare, *Annual Report*, 103.

94. "Crime Fighters Oppose Coddling Sheridan Toughs," *Chicago Sunday Tribune*, January 25, 1942, series 1, box 0, folder 67, Russell Ward Ballard Papers, UIC, Special Collections Library.

95. Memo: Open House, series 1, box 0, folder 86, Russell Ward Ballard Papers, UIC, Special Collections Library.

96. Sheridan Branch Monthly Statistics, May 1943, series 1, box 0, folder 87, Russell Ward Ballard Papers, UIC, Special Collections Library; "Ages of Boys in SC School," June 30, 1943, series 1, box 0, folder 87, Russell Ward Ballard Papers, UIC, Special Collections Library; Minutes of Sheridan Staff Meeting, July 14, 1943, series 1, box 0, folder 86, Russell Ward Ballard Papers, UIC, Special Collections Library.

97. "Highway Police Posted at State Training School," *Chicago Tribune*, January 28, 1942; "St. Charles Floodlight Order," *Chicago Herald-American*, January 29, 1942. Series 1, box 0, folder 67, Russell Ward Ballard Papers, UIC, Special Collections Library.

98. "The St. Charles Chronicle New Sheridan Institution Badly Needed," *St. Charles Chronicle*, November 27, 1941; "Director Maps Wide Reforms at Boys School," *Chicago Sun*, December 6, 1941, series 1, box 0, folder 66, Russell Ward Ballard Papers, UIC, Special Collections Library; Letter from the Juvenile Detention Home to Governor Green, November 6, 1941, series 1, box 0, folder 86, Russell Ward Ballard Papers, UIC, Special Collections Library; "Steel, Concrete to Hem Toughs of St. Charles"; "Harmon Blamed for St. Charles' Useless Fencing," *Chicago Tribune*, September 26, 1940; "Age Differences Problem at Training School," *Chicago Sun Times*, September 25, 1940; "Dangerous hoodlums, in their late teens and as old as 21, Sit in the Same Halls with Impressionable Youngsters of 10," series 1, box 0, folder 66, Russell Ward Ballard Papers, UIC, Special Collections Library.

99. *62nd General Assembly of the Illinois Legislature*, Illinois State Archives at Springfield: Record Group 266, St. Charles School for Boys, 1943–1949 (Springfield, IL, 1941), Illinois State Archives at Springfield, Record Group 266: Folder-St. Charles School for Boys 1943–1949.

100. "3 Legislators to Pen Inquiry at Boys School," *Chicago Tribune*, May 18, 1948.

101. *66th General Assembly of the Illinois Legislature* (Springfield, IL, 1949); Department of Public Welfare, *Annual Report*, 103.

Epilogue

1. Testimony of the NACWC before the Senate Subcommittee to Investigate Juvenile Delinquency, January 21, 1954, NACWC Papers, Reel 2: 0001, University of Chicago Library.

2. Robert Howard, "Seek to Clear St. Charles of Its 'Bad Boys': Transfer to Sheridan by Welfare Department," *Chicago Tribune*, May 11, 1950; *Department of Public Welfare*, vol. 37, series 1.

3. Carlson, *Aspects of Student Culture*, 34; Department of Public Welfare, *Welfare Bulletin*, vol. 37, series 1.

4. Department of Public Welfare, *Welfare Bulletin*, vol. 37, series 1, 38.

5. "Girls Fight Cops at State School"; "Try to Restore Order at Geneva School for Girls."

6. Diulio, "Coming of the Super-Predators"; Diulio, "How to Stop the Coming Crime Wave"; Gearan and Phillip, "Clinton Regrets 1996 Remark."

7. Testimony of the NACWC before the Senate Subcommittee to Investigate Juvenile Delinquency, January 21, 1954.

Bibliography

Archives

Abraham Lincoln Library
Chicago Historical Society
Circuit Court of Cook County-Juvenile Court Records
Hull House Museum
Illinois State Archives at Springfield
Municipal Reference Collection at the Harold Washington Library
Northwestern University Government Data Library
Special Collections Research Center at the University of Chicago
University of Illinois at Chicago Special Collections Library
Vivian Harsh Collection at the Carter G. Woodson Library

Newspapers

Chicago Defender
Chicago Sun Times
Chicago Tribune
Geneva Republican
St. Charles Chronicle

Published Sources

Addams, Jane. "'Social Control' Crisis 1 (1911) Jan 22–23." In *Jane Addams Papers*. Chicago: Jane Addams Hull House Museum, 1911.

"Admits Rape Attempt after School Parole." *Chicago Tribune*, August 25, 1948.

Altgeld, John P. *Live Questions, Including Our Penal Machinery and Its Victims.* Ann Arbor: University of Michigan, 1884.

"Amanda Smith School for Girls Formed in Court Room." *Chicago Defender*, August 6, 1913.

Auer, Katharine. "A Study of the Services of the Institute for Juvenile Research to the Child Placing Agencies of Chicago." Amherst, MA: Smith College, 1936.

Baldwin, Davarian L. *Chicago's New Negroes: Modernity, the Great Migration, and Black Urban Life.* Chapel Hill: University of North Carolina Press, 2007.

Bannister, Robert. "Sociology." In *The Modern Social Sciences*, edited by Theodore M. Porter and Dorothy Ross, 329–53. Cambridge: Cambridge University Press, 2003.

Bernstein, Robin. *Racial Innocence: Performing American Childhood from Slavery to Civil Rights.* New York: New York University Press, 2011.

Biondi, Martha. *To Stand and Fight: The Struggle for Civil Rights in Postwar New York City*. Cambridge, MA: Harvard University Press, 2006.

Blair, Cynthia M. *I've Got to Make My Livin': Black Women's Sex Work in Turn-of-the-Century Chicago*. Chicago: University of Chicago Press, 2010.

Board of Administration of the State of Illinois. "First Annual Report of the Department of Visitation of Children Placed in Family Homes." In *Report of the Board of Public Charities*, 1906.

———. "Second Annual Report of the Department of Visitation of Children Placed in Family Homes." In *Report of the Board of Public Charities*, 1907.

———. "Seventh Annual Report of the Department of Visitation of Children Placed in Family Homes." In *Report of the Board of Public Charities*, 1913.

———. Sixth Annual Report of the Department of Visitation of Children Placed in Family Homes. In *Report of the Board of Public Charities*, 1912.

Board of Commissioners of Cook County. *Charity Service Reports*. Chicago, 1913.

Bowen, Louise de Koven. *The Colored People of Chicago*. Chicago: Juvenile Protective Association, 1913.

———. *Growing up with a City*. New York: Macmillan, 1926.

———. *Safeguards for City Youth at Work and at Play*. Chicago: Juvenile Protective Association, 1914.

"Boy Auto Thief Killed: Guards Admit Slugging." *Chicago Tribune*, February 14, 1941.

"Boys' Escapes at St. Charles Stir up Public." *Chicago Tribune*, August 15, 1928.

Bryan, Edith S. "Variations in the Responses of Infants during First Ten Days of Post-Natal Life." *Child Development* 1, no. 1 (1930): 56–77.

Cahn, Susan K. *Sexual Reckonings: Southern Girls in a Troubling Age*. Cambridge, MA: Harvard University Press, 2007.

"Call Committee to Halt Escapes at St. Charles." *Chicago Tribune*, April 9, 1939.

Canaan, Gareth. "The Economic and Class Dimensions of Juvenile Delinquency in Black Chicago During the 1920s." In *A Noble Experiment? The First 100 Years of the Cook County Juvenile Court, 1899–1999*, edited by Gwen Hoerr McNamee. Chicago: Chicago Bar Association, 1999.

Carey, Cecilia. *A Survey of the Girls Released from the Chicago Home for Girls during 1932*. Chicago: University of Chicago, 1936.

Carlson, David E. *Aspects of Student Culture: A Study of Male Juvenile Offenders in the Illinois State Training School for Boys*. St. Charles: Northern Illinois University, 1962.

"Charges Boys Learn Crime at St. Charles." *Chicago Tribune*, February 3, 1939.

Chatelain, Marcia. *South Side Girls: Growing up in the Great Migration*. Durham, NC: Duke University Press, 2015.

Chatfield, Suzanne Ruth. *A Study of the Federated Home for Dependent Negro Children*. Chicago: University of Chicago, 1941.

Chicago Commission on Race Relations. *The Negro in Chicago: A Study of Race Relations and a Race Riot*. Chicago: University of Chicago Press, 1923.

Chicago Vice Commission. *A Social Evil in Chicago: A Study of Existing Conditions*. Chicago: Gunthorp-Warren Printing Company, 1911.

"Children's Aid Society Helps Homeless Waifs." *Chicago Defender*, November 6, 1943.

"Citizens Given Chance to Help Poor Kiddies." *Chicago Defender*, September 19, 1925.

"City Rallies to Help in Scottsboro Midnight Show." *Chicago Defender*, April 29, 1933.

Cmiel, Kenneth. *A Home of Another Kind: One Chicago Orphanage and the Tangle of Child Welfare*. Chicago: University of Chicago Press, 1995.

Commission, Training School for Boys and Youthful Offenders. *A Report and Recommendations Submitted to the 61st General Assembly of the Illinois Legislature*. Springfield, IL, 1939.

———. *A Report and Recommendations Submitted to the 63rd Illinois General Assembly*. Springfield, IL, 1943.

"Commission Aid in Boys School Cleanup Sought." *Chicago Tribune*, May 19, 1949.

Corman, Bertha. "A Study of Delinquent Girls with Institutional Experience." A Dissertation Submitted to the Faculty of the Graduate School of Social Service Administration in Candidacy for the Degree of Master of Arts. University of Chicago, 1923.

"Cornering the Corner Gang." *Chicago Defender*, June 11, 1921.

Crawley, Charlotte Ashby. "Dependent Negro Children in Chicago." Chicago: University of Chicago, 1927.

Danzig, Robert. "Thirty-One Adolescent Boys Treated by Male Psychiatric Social Workers at the Institute for Juvenile Research." Chicago: Northwestern University, 1941.

Davis, Edna Ruth. "A Study of the Disposition of the Cases of 388 Polish, Italian, Negro, and American Delinquent Girls by the Juvenile Court of Cook County." Chicago: University of Chicago, 1932.

Department of Public Welfare. *Annual Report of the Department of Public Welfare*. Vol. 5. Springfield: Illinois State Journal Company, 1937.

———. *8th Annual Report of the Department of Public Welfare*. July 1, 1924–June 30, 1925, Springfield: Illinois State Journal Company, 1925.

———. *11th Annual Report of the Department of Public Welfare*. Springfield: Illinois State Journal Company, 1928.

———. *12th Annual Report of the Department of Public Welfare*. Springfield: Illinois State Journal Company, 1929.

———. *19th Annual Report of the Department of Public Welfare*. Springfield: Illinois State Journal Company, 1936.

———. *21st Annual Report of the Department of Public Welfare*. Springfield: Illinois State Journal Company, 1938.

———. *23rd Annual Report of the Department of Public Welfare*. Springfield: Illinois State Journal Company, 1940.

———. *32nd Annual Report of the Department of Public Welfare*. Springfield: Illinois State Journal Company, 1949.

———. *Statistical Review of State Prisons and Correctional Schools*. Springfield: State of Illinois, 1940.

"Department of Public Welfare." *Welfare Bulletin* 22, no. 1 (1931).

"Department of Public Welfare." *Welfare Bulletin* 37, ser. 1 (1946).

"Dependent Children's Aid Object for Big Meeting." *Chicago Defender*, April 21, 1921.

Dilulio, John J., Jr. "The Coming of the Super-Predators." *Weekly Standard*, November 27, 1995.

———. "How to Stop the Coming Crime Wave." New York: Manhattan Institute, 1996.

Dodge, L. Mara. "Reform Struggles and Legal Challenges: The Cook County Juvenile Court, 1924–1999. A Historical Overview." In *A Noble Experiment? The First 100 Years of the Cook County Juvenile Court, 1899–1999*, edited by Gwen Hoerr McNamee. Chicago: Chicago Bar Association, 1999.

———. *Whores and Thieves of the Worst Kind: A Study of Women, Crime, and Prisons, 1835–2000.* DeKalb: Northern Illinois University Press, 2002.

Dolinar, Brian. *The Negro in Illinois: The WPA Papers.* Urbana: University of Illinois Press, 2013.

Dollard, John. *Caste and Class in a Southern Town.* Madison: University of Wisconsin Press, 1936.

Drake, St. Clair, and Horace R. Clayton. *Black Metropolis: A Study of Negro Life in a Northern City.* New York: Harcourt, Brace, 1945.

Dray, Philip. *At the Hands of Persons Unknown: The Lynching of Black America.* New York: Random House, 2002.

Du Bois, W. E. B. *Efforts of Social Betterment among Negro Americans.* Atlanta: Atlanta University Press, 1909.

———. "The Negro and American Democracy." *City Club Bulletin* 5, no. 3 (May 28, 1912).

"Escapes at St. Charles." *Chicago Tribune*, September 2, 1935.

Faris, George. "A Study of Boys under Fifteen Committed to the Illinois State Training School for Boys." Dissertation, University of Chicago, 1941.

Feld, Barry C. *Bad Kids: Race and the Transformation of the Juvenile Court.* New York: Oxford University Press, 1999.

"Find St. Charles Fails to Reform Inmates." *Chicago Tribune*, June 6, 1932.

Fitz-Simons, Louise, Wayne Hopkins, Forrester Washington, Louis Evans, Leon Frost, Jacob Kepecs, and Ira Reid. "Foster Home Care for Negro Children in Atlanta, Chicago, Detroit, New York and Philadelphia." Publisher not identified, 1930.

"5 Girls Escape Geneva; 90 Boys Flee St. Charles." *Chicago Defender*, December 1, 1949.

"Five Towns Lie in Fear of 'Boys' at State School." *Chicago Tribune*, February 1, 1939.

"42 Boys Escape St. Charles in 15 Days." *Chicago Tribune*, August 16, 1928.

Frazier, E. Franklin. *The Negro Family in Chicago.* Chicago: University of Chicago Press, 1932.

———. *The Negro Family in the United States.* Notre Dame: University of Indiana Press, 2001.

Freedman, Estelle B. "The Prison Lesbian: Race, Class, and the Construction of the Aggressive Female Homosexual, 1915–1965." *Feminist Studies* 22, no. 2 (1996): 397–423.

"Friend of Juvenile Delinquents Dies." *Chicago Defender*, September 6, 1947.

Gatewood, Mary C., and Albert P. Weiss. "Race and Sex Differences in Newborn Infants." *Pedagogical Seminary and Journal on Genetic Psychology* 38 (1930): 20–30.

Gault, Robert H. "Parental Schools and Juvenile Crime." *Journal of the American Institute of Criminal Law and Criminology* 4, no. 2 (1913): 163–65.

Gearan, Anne, and Abby Phillip. "Clinton Regrets 1996 Remark on 'Super-Predators' after Encounter with Activist." *Washington Post*, February 25, 2016.

Giddings, Elizabeth. "Some Factors Affecting the Outcome of Treatment of Negro Cases in a Child Guidance Clinic." Master's thesis, Smith College, 1940.

Gilmartin, Helen L. "The Use of the Psychiatric Clinic in the Treatment of Dependent Negro Children." Master's thesis, University of Chicago, 1940.

"Girls Fight Cops at State School." *Chicago Daily News*, June 13, 1956.

Gittens, Joan. *Poor Relations: The Children of the State in Illinois, 1818–1990*. Urbana: University of Illinois Press, 1994.

Goings, Kenneth. *Mammy and Uncle Mose: Black Collectibles and American Stereotyping*. Bloomington: University of Indiana Press, 1994.

Grant, Julia. *The Boy Problem: Educating Boys in Urban America, 1870–1970*. Baltimore: Johns Hopkins University Press, 2014.

Gregory, James N. *The Southern Diaspora: How the Great Migrations of Black and White Southerners Transformed America*. Chapel Hill: University of North Carolina Press, 2007.

Gross, Kali N. *Colored Amazons: Crime, Violence, and Black Women in the City of Brotherly Love, 1880–1910*. Durham, NC: Duke University Press, 2006.

Grossberg, Letty Joyce. "A Study of Negro Girls Committed to the Geneva State Reformatory in 1937–1938." Master's thesis, University of Chicago, 1940.

Grossberg, Michael. "Changing Conceptions of Child Welfare in the United States, 1820–1935." In *A Century of Juvenile Justice*, edited by Margaret K. Rosenheim. Chicago: University of Chicago Press, 2002.

Grossman, James R. *Land of Hope: Chicago, Black Southerners, and the Great Migration*. Chicago: University of Chicago Press, 1991.

Gugliemo, Thomas A. *White on Arrival: Italians, Race, Color, and Power in Chicago, 1890–1945*. New York: Oxford University Press, 2003.

Hicks, Cheryl D. *Talk with You Like a Woman: African American Women, Justice, and Reform in New York, 1890–1935*. Chapel Hill: University of North Carolina Press, 2010.

Hirsch, Andrew Von. *Doing Justice: The Choice of Punishments, Report of the Committee for the Study of Incarceration*. New York: Hill and Wang, 1976.

"Hoehler Acts on Immorality in Boys School." *Chicago Tribune*, May 18, 1949.

Holland, Rosetta Pyles. "An Analysis of the Case Histories of a Group of Dependent and Delinquent Negro Children Committed by the Juvenile Court of Cook County to the Chicago Parental School from January to June, 1945." Master's thesis, Loyola University, 1947.

Holloway, Jonathan Scott. "Introduction." In *Black Scholars on the Line: Race, Social Science, and American Thought in the Twentieth Century*, edited by Jonathan Scott

Holloway and Ben Keppel, 40–45. Notre Dame, IN: University of Notre Dame Press, 2007.

Holmes, Samuel J. "The Low Sex Ratio in Negro Births and Its Probable Explanation." *Biological Bulletin* (1927): 325–29.

Hoofert, Sylvia D. "'A Very Peculiar Sorrow': Attitudes toward Infant Death in the Urban Northeast, 1800–1860." *American Quarterly* 39, no. 4 (1987): 601–16.

Hoyt, Stephanie, and David G. Scherer. "Female Juvenile Delinquency: Misunderstood by the "Juvenile Justice System, Neglected by Social Science." *Law and Human Behavior* 22, no. 1 (1998): 81–107.

Hyde, Henry M. "Worst Boys at St. Charles Flee under Lax Rule." *Chicago Tribune*, October 30, 1915.

"Illinois Home Aid Society Issues Plea for Homeless Children during Christmas." *Chicago Defender*, December 1922.

Illinois State Training School for Girls. *Biennial Report of the Illinois State Home for Juvenile Female Offenders at Geneva: 1894–1896*. Springfield, IL: Hartman State Printer, 1896.

———. *4th Biennial Report of the Trustees*. Springfield, IL: Philips Bros. State Printing, 1900.

———. *6th Biennial Report of the Trustees*. Springfield, IL: Philipps Bros. State Printing, 1904.

Illinois Youth Council. *Illinois Youth Council Biennial Report*. 1953.

"Immoral Acts Called Common at Boys School." *Chicago Tribune*, May 17, 1949.

"In the Grip of the Law." *Chicago Defender*, May 3, 1919.

"Inaugural Address of Irene Mccoy Gaines." *Chicago Defender*, July 3, 1937.

Jenkins, M. Louise. "Do We Need Reformatories?" *National Notes* 3, no. 8 (1900).

Jimenez, Jillian. "The History of Child Protection in the African American Community: Implications for Current Child Welfare Policies." *Children and Youth Services Review* 28, no. 8 (2006): 888–905.

Kahlert, John. *A Study of Commitments to the St. Charles School for Boys July 1 through December 31, 1937*. Chicago: Illinois Board of Public Welfare Commissioners, 1939.

Klein, Charlotte Ruth. "Success and Failure on Parole: A Study of 160 Girls Paroled from the State Training School at Geneva, Illinois." Master's thesis, University of Chicago, 1935.

Knupfer, Anne Meis. "African-American Facilities for Dependent and Delinquent Children in Chicago, 1900 to 1920: The Louise Juvenile School and the Amanda Smith School." *Journal of Sociology & Social Welfare* 24, no. 3 (1997): 193–209.

———. "The Chicago Detention Home." In *A Noble Experiment? The First 100 Years of the Cook County Juvenile Court, 1899–1999*, edited by Gwen Hoerr McNamee. Chicago: Chicago Bar Association, 1999.

———. "'If You Can't Push, Pull, If You Can't Pull, Please Get out of the Way': The Phyllis Wheatley Club and Home in Chicago, 1896 to 1920." *Journal of Negro History* 82, no. 2 (1997): 221–31.

Knupfer, Anne Meis, and Leonard Silk, eds. *Toward a Tenderer Humanity and a Nobler Womanhood: African American Women's Clubs in Turn-of-the-Century Chicago*. New York: NYU Press, 1997.

Lasch-Quinn, Elizabeth. *Black Neighbors: Race and the Limits of Reform in the American Settlement House Movement, 1890–1945.* Chapel Hill: University of North Carolina Press, 1993.

Lawrence, Dorothy. "Some Problems Arising in the Treatment of Adolescent Negro Girls Appearing in the Los Angeles Juvenile Court." Master's thesis, University of Southern California, 1941.

Leavelle, Charles. "Brick Slayer Is Likened to Jungle Beast: Ferocity Is Reflected in Nixon's Features." *Chicago Tribune*, June 5, 1938.

Link, Winifred Ann. "An Analysis of Thirty-Five Negro Problem Children Referred to the Institute for Juvenile Research." Master's thesis, University of Chicago, 1935.

Long, Rose A. "Children Referred to the Schools by a Child Guidance Clinic: A Study of 46 Cases." Master's thesis, Smith College, 1938.

MacDonald, Arthur. *Colored Children: A Psycho-Physical Study.* Chicago: American Medical Association, 1899.

MacQueary, T. H. "Schools for Delinquent Children in Illinois." *American Journal of Sociology* 9, no. 1 (July 1903): 1–23.

Marn, Johann. "Psychiatry in the Illinois State Training School for Boys." *Illinois Medical Journal* 90, no. 5 (1946): 290–95.

"Mator M'ferrin's Assailant Found Guilty and Sent to Jail." *Chicago Defender*, November 30, 1912.

McGerr, Michael. *A Fierce Discontent: The Rise and Fall of the Progressive Movement in America, 1870–1920.* New York: Oxford University Press, 2005.

McGuinn, Henry J. "Recreation." *Journal of Negro Education* 9, no. 3 (1940): 311–12.

Mintz, Steven. *Huck's Raft: A History of American Childhood.* Cambridge, MA: Harvard University Press, 2004.

"Miss Gertrude Smith Laid to Rest: Mourn West Side Probation Officer." *Chicago Defender*, May 16, 1914.

Monahan, Florence, and Lewis E. Lawes. *Women in Crime.* New York: Ives Washburn, 1941.

Moses, Earl. *The Negro Delinquent in Chicago.* Washington, DC: Social Science Research Council, 1936.

"Move to Segregate Boys at School Bitterly Fought." *Chicago Defender*, September 30, 1922.

Muhammad, Khalil Gibran. *The Condemnation of Blackness: Race, Crime, and the Making of Modern Urban America.* Cambridge, MA: Harvard University Press, 2010.

Mumford, Kevin. *Interzones: Black/White Sex Districts in Chicago and New York in the Early Twentieth Century.* New York: Columbia University Press, 1997.

Myers, Tamara. "Embodying Delinquency: Boys' Bodies, Sexuality, and Juvenile Justice History in Early-Twentieth-Century Quebec." *Journal of the History of Sexuality* 14, no. 4 (2005).

"Nine Recaptured after Training School Escape." *Chicago Daily Tribune*, December 7, 1944.

Odem, Mary. *Delinquent Daughters: Protecting and Policing Adolescent Female Sexuality in the United States, 1885–1920.* Chapel Hill: University of North Carolina Press, 1995.

O'Donnell, Sandra M. "The Care of Dependent African-American Children in Chicago: The Struggle between Black Self-Help and Professionalism." *Social History* 27 (Summer 1994): 763–76.

"Oppose Juvenile Court Trials of Youths up to 21." *Chicago Tribune*, March 13, 1938.

Ordahl, George. "Study of 341 Delinquent Boys." *Journal of Delinquency* 1 (1916): 72–86.

"Order Color Line Dropped at St. Charles." *Chicago Defender*, April 5, 1941.

"Orders Arrests in School Flogging Cases." *Chicago Defender*, September 1, 1923.

Osborn, Phyllis Rae. "A Study of the Detention of Two Hundred Six Children." Chicago: University of Chicago, 1931.

Ovington, Mary White. *Half a Man: The Status of the Negro in New York.* New York: Longmans, Green, 1911.

Peterson, Joseph. "Comparative Abilities of White and Negro Children." *Comparative Psychology Monograph* 1, no. 5 (1923).

Phillips, Byron A. "The Binet Tests Applied to Colored Children." *Psychological Clinic* 8 (1915): 190–96.

Pickering, Alan B., and George W. Anderson. *Confronting the Color Line: The Broken Promise of the Civil Rights Movement in Chicago.* Athens: University of Georgia, 1987.

"Place Matrons in Home at Geneva." *Chicago Defender*, October 2, 1920.

Platt, Anthony. *The Child Savers: The Invention of Delinquency.* Chicago: University of Chicago Press, 1977.

"Pledge Aid to Boys at St. Charles School." *Chicago Defender*, May 7, 1932.

"Police Start War on Vice: Social Evil on South Side Is Appalling." *Chicago Defender*, May 12, 1917.

Pyle, W. H. "The Learning of Negro Children." *Psychological Bulletin* 13 (1916): 82–83.

———. "Mentality of the Negro Compared with Whites." *Psychological Bulletin* 12 (1915): 79–80.

———. "The Mind of the Negro Child." *School and Society* (1915): 357–60.

"Quick Reports on Sex Cases in School." *Chicago Tribune*, May 24, 1949.

Ralph, James R. *Northern Protest: Martin Luther King, Jr., Chicago, and the Civil Rights Movement.* Cambridge, MA: Harvard University Press, 1993.

Randall, Evelyn Harriet. *The St. Charles School for Delinquent Boys.* Chicago: University of Chicago, 1927.

Reed, Christopher Robert. *The Chicago NAACP and the Rise of Black Professional Leadership, 1910–1966.* Bloomington: Indiana University Press, 1997.

"Return Escaped Boy to St. Charles Home." *Chicago Defender*, March 17, 1934.

"Return of Strap Rule Demanded for St. Charles." *Chicago Tribune*, November 16, 1928.

"Roots out Nests of Iniquity." *Chicago Defender*, October 19, 1918.

"Rules Juvenile Court No Haven for Criminals." *Chicago Tribune*, December 21, 1935.

Salem, Dorothy C. *To Better Our World: Black Women in Organized Reform, 1890–1920*. Brooklyn, NY: Carlson Pub, 1990.

"Schoolgirl Slays Rival in Beer Tavern." *Chicago Defender*, March 9, 1935.

Schultz, Adolph H. "Relation of the External Nose to the Bony Nose and Nasal Cartilages in Whites and Negroes." *American Journal of Physical Anthropology* 1 (1918): 329–38.

"Scottsboro's Mass Meeting Date Changed: Boys Here on December 8 at Metropolitan Community Church." *Chicago Defender*, December 4, 1937.

"Seek to Clear St. Charles of Its 'Bad Boys' Transfer to Sheridan by Welfare Department Howard, Robert." *Chicago Tribune*, May 11, 1950.

"Seeks to Clear St. Charles of Its Bad Boys." *Chicago Tribune*, May 10, 1950.

"Senate Probers Hear of Jim Crow at St. Charles." *Chicago Defender*, March 25, 1939.

"Sentence Seven Ex-Inmates of Training School." *Chicago Tribune*, February 24, 1942.

"Sift Charges against Police in Vice Syndicate: Thrilling Exposé Seen Girls Lured from Geneva Home." *Chicago Defender*, February 17, 1934.

Smith, Iva Evelyn. "Selected Case Studies of Dependent Negro Children in Their Relationships to the Public School: A Study of the Records of a Child Placing Agency." Master's thesis, University of Chicago, 1932.

"Social Workers Defend Coddling of Young Toughs." *Chicago Tribune*, April 29, 1939.

Southern, David W. *The Progressive Era and Race: Reaction and Reform, 1900–1917*. Wheeling, IL: Harlan Davidson, 2005.

"Splendid Work of Probation Officers." *Chicago Defender*, March 20, 1915.

"St. Charles Again." *Chicago Tribune*, September 2, 1948.

"St. Charles Boys Say They Prefer Cells in Pontiac: Captured Fugitives Talk." *Chicago Daily Tribune*, November 7, 1939.

"St Charles School Trains Wayward Boys." *Chicago Defender*, September 14, 1929.

St. Charles School for Boys. *3rd Biennial Report*. St. Charles, IL, 1908.

State of Illinois. *66th General Assembly of the Illinois Legislature*. Springfield, IL, 1949.

"Steel, Concrete to Hem Toughs of St. Charles." *Chicago Tribune*, March 20, 1941.

Stehno, Sandra M. "Foster Care for Dependent Black Children in Chicago, 1899–1934." PhD diss., University of Chicago, 1985.

Stetson, G. R. "Some Memory Tests of Whites and Blacks." *Psychology Review* 4 (1897): 285–89.

"The Story of 76 Escapes in 1939 at St. Charles." *Chicago Daily Tribune*, November 3, 1939.

Strickland, Arvarh E. *History of the Chicago Urban League*. Columbia: University of Missouri, 2001.

Sutton, John R. *Stubborn Children: Controlling Delinquency in the United States, 1640–1981*. Berkeley: University of California Press, 1988.

Tagge, George. "Whipping Urged to End Escapes at St. Charles." *Chicago Tribune*, April 11, 1939.

Tanenhaus, David S. "Degrees of Discretion: The First Juvenile Court and the Problem of Difference in the Early Twentieth Century." In *Our Children, Their Children: Confronting Racial and Ethnic Differences in American Juvenile Justice*, edited by Darnell F. Hawkins and Kimberly Kempf-Leonard. Chicago: University of Chicago Press, 2005.

———. "The Evolution of Juvenile Courts in the Early Twentieth Century: Beyond the Myth of Immaculate Construction." In *A Century of Juvenile Justice*, edited by Margaret K. Rosenheim. Chicago: University of Chicago Press, 2002.

———. *Juvenile Justice in the Making*. New York: Oxford University Press, 2004.

Thomas, John. "20,000 March in Chicago Scottsboro Parade." *Chicago Defender*, April 22, 1933.

"3 Legislators to Pen Inquiry at Boys School." *Chicago Tribune*, May 18, 1948.

Trost, Jennifer. *Gateway to Justice: The Juvenile Court and Progressive Child Welfare in a Southern City*. Athens: University of Georgia Press, 2005.

"Try to Restore Order at Geneva School for Girls." *Chicago Daily News*, June 15, 1956.

Turner, Patricia. *Ceramic Uncles and Celluloid Mammies: Black Images and Their Influence on Culture*. Charlottesville: University of Virginia Press, 2002.

"12 Face Ouster in Death of Reform School Boy." *Chicago Defender*, February 22, 1941.

"2 St. Charles Boys 'Change Their Minds.'" *Chicago Defender*, April 19, 1941.

Walker, Ward G. "Geneva School Has Discipline and It Works." *Chicago Tribune*, March 7, 1941.

Ward, Geoff K. *The Black Child Savers: Racial Democracy and American Juvenile Justice*. Chicago: University of Chicago Press, 2012.

"What Shall We Do with Our Delinquent Boys?" *Chicago Defender*, May 7, 1932.

Willrich, Michael. *City of Courts: Socializing Justice in Progressive Era Chicago*. Cambridge: Cambridge University Press, 2003.

"Woman's Children's Aid Society." *Chicago Defender*, January 6, 1912.

Work, Monroe N. "Crime among the Negroes of Chicago: A Social Study." *American Journal of Sociology* 6, no. 2 (1900): 204–23.

Wright, George. "Pamper Toughs or Get Out! It's St. Charles Rule." *Chicago Tribune*, May 29, 1939.

Young, Vernetta. "Race and Gender in the Establishment of Juvenile Prisons: The Case of the South." *Prison Journal* 73, no. 2 (1995): 244–65.

Index

Note: Illustrations and tables are indicated by page numbers in *italics*.